Anonymous

Timely Topics

Political, Biblical, Ethical, Practical

Anonymous

Timely Topics
Political, Biblical, Ethical, Practical

ISBN/EAN: 9783337146344

Printed in Europe, USA, Canada, Australia, Japan

Cover: Foto ©ninafisch / pixelio.de

More available books at **www.hansebooks.com**

TIMELY TOPICS.

POLITICAL, BIBLICAL, ETHICAL, PRACTICAL.

DISCUSSED

By College Presidents, Professors and Eminent Writers of our Time.

A series of specially contributed and copyrighted papers.

NEW YORK:
E. B. TREAT, 5 Cooper Union,
1892.

PUBLISHER'S NOTE.

The publication in this handy volume of these special copyrighted contributions that have appeared in recent issues of

THE TREASURY MAGAZINE,

is in harmony with a proposed plan,—in the belief that it will aid in the accomplishment of the end sought,—the discussion and better understanding of vital questions and issues of the day.

CONTENTS.

THE PAPACY IN POLITICS.
By Chancellor JOHN HALL, D.D., LL.D., of the University of the City of New York.................................... 11

THE PROTESTANT CHURCH AND THE APOCRYPHA.
By JOHN HALL, D.D , LL.D.. 19

THE CHARACTER AND AIM OF THE SOCIETY OF JESUS.
By Rev. W. R. GORDON, S.T.D., Reformed Ch. of N. A... 25

HOW CAN JESUITISM BE SUCCESSFULLY MET?
By Principal D. H. MACVICAR, D.D., Presb. College, Montreal... 39

THE OPPONENTS OF CHRISTIANITY.
By Sir WM. DAWSON, LL.D., Principal of M'Gill University, Montreal... 55

RISE OF PRELACY AND ITS GRADUAL DEVELOPMENT.
By President W. D. KILLEN, D.D., Assembly College, Belfast, Ireland.. 59

PROOFS OF A THREEFOLD ORDER OF THE CHRISTIAN MINISTRY.
By J. F. SPALDING, Bishop of Colorado......................... 73

PROOFS OF AN HISTORIC EPISCOPATE.
By WM. STEVENS PERRY, D.D., Bishop of Iowa, and President of Griswold College... 91

CLAIMS OF THE HISTORIC EPISCOPATE EXAMINED.
By Pres. J. HARPER, D.D., U. P. Theo. Sem., Xenia, Ohio. 107

THE ONE HOLY CATHOLIC APOSTOLIC CHURCH.
By Prof. JAMES HERON, D D., Presb. College, Belfast, Ireland.. 123

CHRISTIANITY VERSUS FORMALISM.
By Pres. S. A. ORT, D.D., Wittenberg College, Springfield, Ohio.. 141

CONTENTS.

THE ENGLISH BIBLE AS A TEXT-BOOK IN THEOLOGICAL SEMINARIES.
   By Pres. ROBERT GRAHAM, D.D., Lexington, Ky.......... 153

THE MINISTER AND HIS BIBLE.
   By Prof. H. W. WARRINER, B.D., Congregational College of Canada, Montreal................................. 159

THE TEACHER REPRODUCED IN THE PUPIL.
   By Principal D. H. MACVICAR, D.D., LL.D., Presb. College, Montreal................................. 175

THE PULPIT AND ETHICS.
   By President B. P. RAYMOND, D.D., Wesleyan University, Middletown, Conn................................. 189

THE SOURCES OF MORALS.
   By President W. M. BLACKBURN, D.D., Pierre University, E. Pierre, S. Dakota................................. 201

LAW AND PERSUASION.
   By President W. M. BLACKBURN, D.D., Pierre University, E. Pierre, S. Dakota................................. 205

THE INDIAN QUESTION: THE FRIENDLIES.
   By Pres. W. M. BLACKBURN................................. 215

TEMPERANCE IN ALL THINGS: BIBLICAL TEACHINGS AND MODERN METHODS.
   By Prof. E. J. WOLFF, D.D., Gettysburgh, Pa............ 221

WHAT IS TRUTH?
   By Pres. F. L. PATTON, D.D., LL.D., Princeton College, N. J................................. 229

THE HIGHER CRITICISM.
   By Prof. M. S. TERRY, D.D., Garrett Biblical Institute, Evanston, Illinois................................. 235

INSPIRED FICTION.
   By Prof. M. S. TERRY, D.D., Evanston, Ill.............. 241

LIBERTY OF THOUGHT AND ITS LIMITATIONS.
   By Professor THEODORE W. HUNT, Princeton College, N. J. 249

SHEOL.
   By Prof. THOS. HILL RICH, Cobb Divinity School, Lewiston, Me................................. 257

CONTENTS.

NOTES ON THE NEGATIVE CRITICISM.
    By Professor W. H. ROBERTS, D D , LL.D., Lane Theological Seminary, Cincinnati, Ohio.................... 263

BIBLICAL ARCHÆOLOGY AND THE HIGHER CRITICISM.
    By Professor A. H. SAYCE, LL.D., Oxford, England...... 269

THE UNITY OF GENESIS: I. AND II. CHAPTERS.
    By Prof. W. H. GREEN, D.D., Princeton Theo. Sem., N. J. 275

MODERN CRITICISM OF THE PENTATEUCH.
    By Prof. M. LEITCH, D.D., Presb. College, Belfast, Ireland. 283

THE ORIGIN AND RELIGIOUS CONTENTS OF THE PSALTER.
    By Rev. J. S. STEELE, Ph.D., Lecturer on Hebrew.......... 307

THE BIBLICAL CRITICISM OF OUR DAY.
    By Rev. Professor GEO. H. SCHODDE, Ph.D., Columbus University, Ohio.. 315

UNITY OF THE SCRIPTURES.
    By Rev. Professor GEO. H. SCHODDE, Ph.D., Columbus University, Columbus, Ohio............................... 323

DOES THE CHRISTIAN MINISTRY MEET THE EDUCATIONAL REQUIREMENTS OF THE AGE?
    By Pres. E. B. ANDREWS, LL.D., Brown University, R. I. 329

OPPORTUNITIES AND OBLIGATIONS OF A COLLEGE EDUCATION.
    By Prof. G. P. FISHER, D.D., Yale University, New Haven, Conn... 337

BROTHERHOOD IN HIGHEST SERVICE.
    By Pres. M. E. GATES, LL.D., Amherst College, Mass.... 341

ESSENTIALS OF THE CURRICULUM.
    By Pres. B. P. RAYMOND, D.D., Wesleyan University..... 349

THE MORAL AND RELIGIOUS VALUE OF HIGHER EDUCATION.
    By Pres. E. B. ANDREWS, LL.D., Brown University, R. I. 355

THE PAPACY IN POLITICS.

BY CHANCELLOR JOHN HALL, D.D., LL.D., OF THE
UNIVERSITY OF THE CITY OF NEW YORK.

THERE are many excellent people who deprecate any severe strictures upon that system of religion the representatives of which in Rome, and in our own country, are making public and effusive declarations of their love for us and for our American institutions. It is natural that in a nation like ours, where all men are free and equal, anything savoring of narrowness and prejudice should be discouraged. But it is possible to make a discrimination that is often ignored in these criticisms upon the "narrow and bigoted" Protestants who stand with the Reformers, the Puritans, and the historians. I think there have been upright, humane and kind-hearted members of the imperial family of Russia; but I do not, as an American citizen, feel kindly to the Russian system of government. I have met extremely amiable members of the Russian aristocracy, but I do not like the system they represent. Or, to put it more directly, there were some excellent people in Great Britain in the close of the last century, but British sway was set aside notwithstanding. Now, is there not room for a candid discrimination on corresponding lines in regard to pronounced Protestants? Can they not be credited with the recognition of devoutness and piety in Roman Catholics, while pronounced against the system known as the Papacy? Are not the very critics who think us wanting in charity slightly defective themselves in that virtue which is so attractive when it is intelligent and genuine?

Again, it is common enough to say in relation to strictures on the Papacy that the past is not to be taken into account, for it had its bad features all around, and the evil has been discarded in the more enlightened times in which we live. Is this plea well founded? Protestant bodies might properly set it up. They make no claim to infallibility in their leaders and consequent unchangeableness. But it is different with the Papacy. We do not linger over the question whether the infallibility is personal as well as official. The claim is that the Popes fill an office divinely appointed, at the head of a Church that can make no mistakes. Its principles, therefore, admit of no change. What it was since the day, as it alleges, when the Apostle Peter ordained Clement I. as Pope, according to the "Decretals" which for centuries gave supremacy to the Pontiffs, it is now; an unerring infallible wisdom has shaped the policy and determined the character of the Papacy. What it has been, according to the nature it claims, it will be. Pope Gregory VII. counted it justification of his claims that former Popes had pursued the same policy. And in 1864 Pius IX. points to his illustrious predecessors for the defence of his Encyclical and Syllabus. "We will demonstrate," says that eminent Pontiff, "that Christ, in giving to the Apostle power to bind and loose men, excepted no one. The Holy See has absolute power over all spiritual things; why should we not also rule temporal affairs? God reigns in the heavens; His Vicar should reign over all the earth. These senseless wretches, however, maintain that the royal is above the Episcopal dignity. Are they, then, ignorant that the name of king was invented by human pride, and that the title of Bishop was instituted by Christ? St. Ambrose affirms that the Episcopate is superior to royalty as gold is superior to a viler metal." Has this principle ever been renounced? Was Gregory VII. infallible? If so, then the Church, where it is politic and safe, may be expected to teach the same doctrines and to pursue the same policy.

If any reader wishes to verify and follow further the statements here made, he has only to give a little attention to "Milman's Latin Christianity." "Ah! but," says some one, "that is a great, learned, many-volumed book, and life is full of work with me. I have no time for going through it." Well, there is another and easier way. Write to Harper & Brothers for a copy of "The Papacy and the Civil Power," and give it—there is but one volume—a careful study, and you will be better able to form a judgment as to your duty as an American citizen.

"But," it may be alleged, "ambitious Popes are one thing; we do not judge of the Papacy by them. There is a great body of intelligent people, refined, accomplished —look at their continental cities, picture galleries, and so forth; they can be depended upon to keep things right." Now let us see. Did you ever give any study to the agencies that built up the papal power for centuries? If not, please to consider the point of the following sentences. The Roman Bishop Siricius ruled from A.D. 384 to 398. Editors of ecclesiastical laws usually began their list with him; but the editor of the "Pseudo-Isidorean Decretals" went back to Clement, whom he made the immediate, or the second, successor to Peter. He gave letters, canons and decrees, assigning to the first Popes all that was claimed in pomp, power, control of nations and kings in the ninth century; and the Church, the great community under the Popes, accepted the whole. Nicholas I. (858–867) paraded these "Decretals" as his warrant for action. And they continued in authority for many centuries, and while no high-class authors now stand up for their genuineness, mild apologies are made for their "well-meant" errors and mistakes. They represent the clergy as including patriarchs, princes, archbishops, and so forth in the first century. They guard ecclesiastics against charges, trials and condemnations, requiring seventy-two trustworthy witnesses, sound in the faith, against a bishop, and, in fact, protect the clergy against all criticism, no matter what their lives might be. They assign, as their second great object, the power over civil rulers to the Popes, who are made judges in all contests ecclesiastical, and they call for "appeals to Rome" in all matters. The number, the audacity, the clumsiness of these forgeries would be incredible if they had not been examined and exposed. Think, for example, of some of the alleged thirty-three Popes, from Peter down to Siricius (A.D. 385), being credited with letters to men who did not live till two centuries after the alleged writers, with decisions and decrees of councils centuries after their time, with quotations from Popes in Encyclicals to Churches that did not then exist, and with passages from Popes who ruled in the fifth, sixth, seventh and eighth centuries, while they were all prior to A.D. 385 ! If the reader has any doubt about the accuracy of these statements, he has only to consult Dupin or Dorner ; and if these seem to him remote and too learned, he can take up Professor Fisher's "History of the Christian Church" (p. 169). Here are the words of this dispassionate historian : "The most advanced pretensions ever propounded or hinted at by the most ambitious Pontiffs were here explicitly and systematically set forth in spurious letters and decrees to which the names of venerated bishops of the early Church were attached."

Now, if it be thought that the community under the Papacy can be trusted to defend itself against personal ambition in the Popes, we reply that the history of these "Decretals," accepted for more than six hundred years, and only recognized as forgeries in the fifteenth century, shows how little reliance can be placed on the ruled as against papal rulers. As corroborating this view, we may add that while the forger of the "Decretals" wished, apparently, to protect the bishops and other dignitaries against the Popes, they were so adroitly used as to put in the hands of the Pontiff almost supreme power over them. Any reader desirous of verifying these statements can turn (in addition to others quoted) to the Schaff-Herzog Encyclopedia, where they come in their natural place, as "Pseudo-Isidorean." The extent to which the Papacy has been engaged in plans, schemes and conflicts outside the religious sphere and more or less in the political, can be verified by any fairly full Church history. Read the history of the "Holy Roman Empire," with its emperors making Popes and Popes making emperors. Read Pope Gregory's bull with its appeal to Peter and Paul as able to " take away, or to give to each, according to his merits, empires, kingdoms, duchies, marquisates, counties, and the possessions of all men." Study Innocent III., proclaiming that "the crowns of kings and the destinies of nations were lodged by a divine decree in" the hands of Peter's successors. But there is no room for a detailed reference to these chapters in history with their ample evidence that the Papacy, ever since its development, has been a political force in the degree in which it was possible, under the influence of aims and motives, good, bad, and indifferent. And nowhere has the Church renounced, deprecated or disclaimed the powers thus put forth and vindicated as conveyed by Christ through Peter to his "successors" to the end of time.

If to any reader the area of history on the subject in hand seem too wide, then let attention be given to the organization so intimately linked, in these later times, with the Papacy, namely the Jesuits. It is fair to say that while this "order" has been the child of the Church, it has often been a rebellious child, pushing its own interests irrespective of its mother's. It has never shrunk from political action in its own interests, and has often evaded, and disregarded Papal injunctions The Jesuits were put down by Portugal for their political trade. and commercial operations. Again and again put down and restored—as by papal bull in 1814—it is well known that they are now in papal favor, with infallible recognition, although they had been broken up in France, in Switzerland, Prussia, and Bavaria. An infallible Pope suppressed the order in 1773, and all Europe appeared to approve the decision reluctantly reached. It is a significant fact that the order is restored in our time.

Now the question may naturally arise in the reader's mind: "What is the use of discussing a matter of this nature? We are nineteenth century people, free, intelligent, and able to take care of ourselves. What is it to us how the Papacy has stood, or now stands, in politics?" Well, let us reflect. Our country is new, and in many respects prosperous. The Papacy has, as every one acquainted with history knows, repeatedly tried to get a hold on such regions. Would it be strange if a like effort were put forth in regard to the United States? Would it surprise one if His Holiness should profess the warmest admiration for our institutions and affection for our people, and if our resident prelates should loudly and ostentatiously announce their sympathy with our people and our policy?

Suppose we had two great opposing parties so nearly balanced in numbers that a body of six or seven millions in the care, and under the guidance of the Papacy, could decide the vote for one or the other as it was directed, would it be strange, or against history if the power should be used in this way: You promise to do such and such things for us, when in power, and we shall see that you get the power? The point might not be specifically stated; but there are other ways of conveying ideas than by set and articulate speech.

Would it be extraordinary and unprecedented, if the Papacy should say: "By common consent the State is not to be obeyed when it rules that which is contrary to the will of the Creator. So Paul an Peter taught and acted. Now the Holy See is the judge—the infallible judge of what is right and according to the divine will." Would it be strange if vexatious annoyances came up in this way, touching for example, charities, education, and forms of taxation? Suppose an element of discontented population among us making trouble for civil rulers, would it be a surprise to the student of the history of the past to find some such hints as this coming from the Vatican: "We have the consciences of these people under our control. There are certain claims of ours not recognized by your government. Let them be recognized, and we shall bring this discontented element into quiet and submission"?

But it is not needful to follow further this line of speculation. We do not fear the placing of this nation where other nations have often been to their real injury. But, a long way on this side of absolute victory over a nation, there may be inconveniences, losses, and hardships which foresight and firmness might have averted. A ship may not indeed be wrecked, but she may be terribly shaken, and her passengers made extremely uncomfortable, when prudent precaution might have kept her out of the line of the hurricane. It is not very strange that busy Americans building up national institutions and industries in hot haste, and committed to the loftiest views of rights to conscience should know little of remote histories, and should shun anything that looks like "being cool to a man on account of his religion." We too want nothing but charity and justice; but we would fain have the people who make public opinion, choose rulers and accept or reject national policies, study the past, face the facts of the case, and be on their guard against developments of fallen human nature, organized into historic agencies that have been despotic where they ruled, and that have been vexatious and disturbing where they had only partial and occasional influence.

THE PROTESTANT CHURCH AND THE APOCRYPHA.

By John Hall, D.D., LL.D., Chancellor of the University of the City of New York.

IT is interesting evidence of the quickening influence of inspired Scripture that, even when the Jews were far below the standard set up for them by the Lord, through Moses and Joshua, they yet produced and valued books of history, ethics, proverbs and religious fiction so highly prized that when the Greek translation of the Old Testament was made they were also rendered into Greek, and placed beside the divine oracles.

The Septuagint having thus given the apocryphal books a place, they passed on into the Vulgate, and were retained where the Latin Bible was the standard, even by Protestant Churches—though with such explanatory notes, or inferior type, as indicated that they did not occupy the same plane with the inspired Word.

The controversy regarding the degree of authority to be given to these sections of religious literature, of course, early engaged the attention of Christian writers, and has its place in patristic discussions. With some inconsistency—in appearance, at least—Jerome, Eusebius and Origen denied their canonical authority, although making frequent references to them of a very respectful character—one other evidence to us Protestants that we must not mix up "the Fathers" with Apostles and prophets.

Before stating the attitude of the Churches, especially of the Protestant Churches, to these books, a sentence or two may be permitted as to their worth. They differ widely As a contribution to the history of the people of Israel in the period—which Prideaux has named and written on with great learning—of the connexion between the Old and New Testaments, the books of Maccabees are of great interest and value. No one can read Ecclesiasticus without seeing what good use the writer had made of the Book of Proverbs, and of his own observation. So the author of the Book of Tobit had evidently been a diligent student of the Book of Job, and Hengstenberg valued his production so highly as a "didactic story" that, admitting geographical, chronological and historic mistakes, he would have it circulated with the canonical books. On the other hand, the Prayer of Manasses and the first and second Books of Esdras (Ezra) even the Church of Rome, in the Council of Trent, put in the doubtful place of an appendix to the Vulgate, while, curiously enough, the Church of England, in 1562 and 1571, puts I. Esdras as the "third book of Esdras," making Ezra and Nehemiah the first and second. This book Josephus used to a large extent, notwithstanding the fact that it contains blunders so gross that DeWette and Hervey describe them as hopelessly irreconcilable with historic fact. In a word, we may examine the Apocrypha, associated with the Old Testament (we do not now refer to the corresponding claimants for a place in the New), as interesting exhibitions of the mental and moral development of a people grounded in the inspired Word, but influenced by outside thought and life, these developments being by fallible men, working as did Augustine, Tertullian, Josephus, and in later times, Bunyan, Baxter and Martin Farquahar Tupper.

As to the estimate formed of the Apocrypha by the Churches, it is curious and interesting that the Greek Church —notwithstanding corruptions that are deplorable—from the time of Origen down, held to the Old Testament canon, and sometimes forbade the reading of the Apocrypha. So the Greek Church declared against the Apocrypha at the time of the Reformation, taking Protestant ground, although the need of some defence for certain views and usages akin to those of Rome has of late modified her attitude. Churches—when off the lines of loyalty to Christ—like politicians, welcome aid from any quarter, and shut their eyes to the moral disqualifications of their supporters.

The Church of Rome claims to have the unanimous approval of ." the fathers " for her doctrines, a unanimity on most subjects—like the philosopher's stone—yet Jerome, Hilary, Rufinus, Cyril, and Gregory of Nazianzen took ground against the Apocrypha, and not only so, but great men from Gregory the Great in the sixth century, Venerable Bede in the seventh, and others down to Cardinal Ximenes and Caietan in the sixteenth century, held with Jerome and shut out the Apocrypha from the canonical literature.

For the first time in the history of Christendom the Council of Trent, after much discussion, received our canonical books and the Apocrypha " with an equal feeling of devotion and reverence." History repeats itself. When the Donatists quoted II. Maccabees (xiv., 17), Augustine replied by denying its authority; but he is alleged, in three African synods, to have sanctioned the ecclesiastical use of the Apocrypha. With a like uncertain position, when the Church of Rome found Luther and his followers pronounced against the Apocrypha, and at the same time that certain parts thereof supported its policy, it went against its most influential " fathers," and put the book alongside the inspired oracle. They are made to be, like the writings of David and Isaiah, " sacred and canonical." All sorts of casuistry, special pleadings and nominal distinctions (such as between canonical and deutero-canonical) have been resorted to, and no greater mass of confused and confusing self-contradictions can be found anywhere than in the oracular utterances of so-called Roman authorities on this matter.

We shall see, later, that there was reason, avowed reason, for this human addition to the divine "law and testimony."

Now as to the Protestant Churches—in Luther's Bible the "Apocrypha" had a place as appendix, under this name with the explanation "books that are not held as equal to the Holy Scriptures, and yet are good and useful to read." While Luther's occasional lack of clear discrimination appeared here, and his course had great influence in the Lutheran Church, the Form of Concord, fifty years after the Augsburg Confession, set up the Scriptures as the only rule of faith.

The Reformed Churches took more decided ground. Westcott compliments the Calvinists for setting up the Old and New Testaments as "the outward test and spring of all truth." The French Bible (1535), while giving the Apocrypha, gives it no higher place than as found in the Vulgate. The Confession of Basle, the Helvetic Confessions, and the Belgian Confessions only recognize our Scriptures, and the French Reformed Church, in 1561, guarded itself against any appearance of evil in this matter.

The Synod of Dort (1620) characterized the Apocrypha in the severest language and raised the point, should it be translated and bound up with the Scriptures; which was decided, to put it colloquially, "It is not Scrip'ure; but let it go with it," only marked off from it by a wide fence; or, they might have said, "drain," with different paging and type, and with notes pointing out the blunders. It ended by putting it at the end of the New Testament.

The Anglican Church—the Church of England that is—occupied unique ground on this matter since 1562, the "other books," *i. e.*, than the canonical, being read for "example of life and instruction of manners," though not for the support of doctrines. Against this plan strong protests were often made; yet the Apocrypha had place in authorized English versions until 1629. In 1643 Bishop Lightfoot described the Apocrypha to the House of Commons as "wretched," a "patchery of human invention," and without formal legislation the authorized version continued to go forth without this appendix.

The controversy was revived in our century by the craving for Bibles with the Apocrypha, from communities on the continent needing aid from the British and Foreign Bible Society. Scotland revolted against this concession, and in 1819 Edinburgh took such ground that the society severed its connection with the Apocrypha in 1822, making some little compromises to the effect that any continental people who wanted it with their Bibles must pay for it themselves. But even this the Edinburgh people would not stand; and in 1827 it was decided that the society would not help anybody who put the Apocrypha with his Bible, and to prevent trickery it would only circulate "bound Bibles." The Scottish friends had such a firm hold of the Westminster decision of 1643, that "the books commonly called Apocrypha, not being of divine inspiration, are no part of the canon of Scripture; and, therefore, are of no authority in the Church of God, or to be otherwise approved of or made use of than other human writings." This part of the Confession will not, we hope, be changed by revision.

Any one anxious to study the details of this little international war, as it affected Germany, Switzerland and Great Britain, will find the details in Dr. Edwin C. Bissell's Introduction to the Apocrypha, in Lange's Commentary, of which I have made much use in this paper.

The Church of England, in her sixth article, states that the Scriptures only are to be appealed to for doctrine, but gives a list of the Apocryphal books—as of the Old Testament with this prefatory note—I quote from the English Prayer Book—"and the other books (as Hierome saith) the Church doth read for example of life and instruction of manners; but yet doth not apply them to establish any doctrine." Accordingly the books are set down in her Calendar for "Sundays and other Holydays" throughout the year, and the same in her Calendar with the table of Lessons, in which Baruch, Tobit, Wisdom, Ecclesiasticus, Judith, Bel and the Dragon stand along with Isaiah, Paul, Matthew and John.

I may add that the Book of Tobit is used twice in the Communion service in the same way as Scripture, and that in the Book of Homilies, Tobit and Wisdom are quoted as Scripture, and Baruch is called a prophet. (The American Prayer Book.)

To any policy of this kind there appear to be the following objections:

(1) The authority of the inspired Word is lowered by its being put on the same plane with the confessedly uninspired.

(2) The Apocrypha countenances, and is used to sustain, usages and views contradictory to inspired Scripture. For example, Tobit xii., 12, 15, sanctions the doctrine of the intercession of angels: there is but one mediator. Raphael is not a second. II. Macc., xv., 14, and Baruch iii., 4, put the intercession of saints in the same category, against Christ's sole priesthood.

The inherent merit of good works is taught in Tobit iv., 7–11, and Ecclesiasticus iii., 30, "alms make atonement for sin." Purgatory and the propriety of prayers for the dead are rested on II. Macc., xii., 42 and onward.

(3) And finally, there appears to be a solemn threat in the closing chapter of the inspired Apocalypse against adding to the Scriptures—whether it be that one book or the whole volume, and it is the Church's duty to avoid even "the appearance of evil," and especially when, as expressed by Tanner, the Council of Trent treated the Apocrypha as canonical because "the Church found its own spirit in these books." The Bible makes the Church, and not the Church the Bible.

THE CHARACTER AND AIM OF THE "SOCIETY OF JESUS."

By W. R. Gordon, S.T.D., of the Reformed Church of North America.

MORE books, pamphlets and paragraphs have been written about the Jesuits than about any other order of men ever formed. The reason lies not in the amount of good they have done, but in the vast amount of unmingled evil justly laid to their charge. A brief statement, therefore, is all that is necessary for our purpose.

In A.D. 1540 Ignatius Loyola, a crippled Spaniard and a fanatical, bigoted Romanist, devised the formation of a new society to help the papal cause against the progress of the Reformation. The Pope, Paul III., in due time gave it his sanction and a formal existence in a verbose bull, saying: "We will that in this society there be admitted to the number of sixty persons only, desiring to embrace this rule of living, and no more; and to be incorporated into the society aforesaid." "Given at Rome, at St. Mark's, September 27th, 1540." The limitation of the number to sixty, however, was abrogated by another bull, dated March 14th, 1543.

This society took the name of Jesuits, or followers of Jesus, but the name only; for Him they followed not at all, save in manner as did the malicious Jews who drove Him to the cross. Their history for a period of more than two centuries is most amazing. Under the autocratic power of a General to whom they made a solemn vow of blind obedience to do and dare whatever he commanded in any service assigned them, they soon became famous as the right arm of the papacy. Their number rapidly increased. Men were trained for membership with the greatest caution and subtle care, under laws and regulations the completest, most efficient and best adapted to make out of any pliable honest man the vilest villain, while wearing the livery of sanctity and essential goodness. Other and older monkish orders were content to rest in seclusion, but the object of the Jesuits was to roam the earth to gain the greatest possible influence over the persons and affairs of all men for insuring popularity, protection and support for the papal see; and that by cunning devices and false pretences, to enlist all classes in the destruction of Protestants and Protestantism by any and every means in their power. With consummate skill they managed at the same time to blind the eyes of men to the nature of their doings and the object of the designs, while making themselves the masters of the papacy. Their government was purely monarchical. Their General, elected for life, was empowered to keep and control deputies throughout all nations for consolidating Jesuitical power everywhere in the world. Their vast revenues, gained by cunning contrivances, were in his hands; in whose grip were all the cords of management worked by all the arts of treachery, through a system of espionage that eluded the wit of all who felt their power but could not discover its source.

When, however, after a successful career of two hundred and thirty-three years, the truth respecting them was revealed, it excited everywhere the intensest indignation and alarm. It was found that they had been guilty of every conceivable crime. By their means torrents of blood had been shed, the gunpowder plot had been laid, and the Duke of Alvah had been prompted to put to death thirty thousand Protestants in the Netherlands within the space of a few years, by the hands of common euecutioners. The horrid

Inquisition—a Romish institution—had destroyed, by various means of torture, a hundred and fifty thousand within the space of thirty years! These awful facts, and many more, are die-sunk into the record of Protestant experience, and can never be erased from the memory of man.

Pope Clement XIII. was a violent partisan of the Jesuits, and in answer to a thousand clamors from all quarters for their summary suppression, sent forth a bull condemnatory of the expelling decree of the French Parliament, whose act in justification of it " relates the principal works of the Jesuits, cited as extremely dangerous because of the doctrines which they professed in reference to the subjects of simony, blasphemy, magic, witchcraft, astrology, irreligion, idolatry, impurity, false witness, adultery, incest, sodomy, theft, suicide, murder, parricide and regicide. Finally, the decree concluded with a list of kings, princes, prelates and popes butchered or poisoned by the disciples of the renowned and sainted Loyola" (Bower's Hist., Vol. III., p. 350—its continuation).

The Pope, however, was too weak to withstand this pressure, and he was forced to yield to the demand for the suppression of the Jesuits, "announcing that he would formally proclaim the abolition of the order of the sons of Ignatius Loyola, in a public consistory. That announcement was the cause of his death. The Jesuits were on the watch, and during the night preceding the day appointed for that solemn act of justice, the pontiff was seized with extraordinary pains and expired in terrible convulsions, early in the morning of February 2d, 1769. The Jesuits poisoned the Pope!" (*Id.*, p. 352).

This formidable Order of " Holy Mother " has always claimed its own existence as necessary to the cause of education, and has succeeded by its blandishments in imposing large numbers of Jesuits upon the French people; for when banished from that kingdom, no less than four thousand of them were driven out of Paris alone! When their common confederacy in guilt was found out, the people soon saw what was the end of their vaunted erudition. "The boasted genius of the Jesuis for education," says M. Cousin, is "nothing but the organization of a vile system of spying into the conduct of young men, and there never was one manly course of studies in their institutions. They sacrifice substance to show, and deceive parents by brilliant and frivolous exhibitions" (*Id*, p. 353).

The Catholic Dictionary says that "at the present day the total number of the Society is believed to be about ten thousand"; and further that "Pope Clement XIV., in 1773, summarily disposed of this great society in a very unpope-like manner." He "signed the constitution, by which, on account of the numerous complaints and accusations of which the Society was the object, without declaring them to be either guilty or innocent, he suppressed the Order in every part of world." On the face of it, this account of the matter is misleading. We have open before us the bull of suppression, the Constitution of the Order, and other historical documents, by which we shall see to what extent this pretentious dictionary may be relied upon for exactitude of statement in criminating the Pope, or in vindicating "this great Order."

The Constitution of the Jesuits was first published in Latin at Rome, A.D. 1558. Our copy is one "reprinted from the original edition, with an appendix containing a translation and several important documents." (London, 1838).

By the tone of pious verbosity, well kept up throughout fifty-four chapters, in ten parts, one would judge "Constitutiones Societatis Jesu" likely to be worthy of confidence; but we are compelled to say a close perusal exhibits the exact reverse as the exact truth. This is made clear by the fact that the "Secreta Monita," or "Monita Sacra," as Giustiniani calls it—a book of rules by which the Jesuits conducted themselves, and agreeing remarkably in the style of its Latinity and drift of thought with the former, but discovered about a century previous to the expulsion of Jesuits from France, A.D. 1762—this book casts back some rays of light upon the following sentences, and others like them found scattered throughout the pages of the "Constitutiones" (Latin omitted).

1. "The Society was not instituted by human means" (p. 95). This, unfortunately, was soon shown to be true enough.

2. The members "must be gifted with a comely presence" (p. 6).

3. Men must not be admitted of "ungovernable tempers, or unavailable to the society" (p. 7).

4. They must have "a comely presence for the edification of those with whom we have to deal" (p. 7).

5. "It is necessary that all yield themselves to perfect obedience regarding the Superior (be he whom he may) as Christ the Lord" (p. 22).

6. They must not "wish to be led by their own judgment, except it agree with that of those who are to them in the stead of Christ our Lord" (p. 20).

7. They must strive to acquire "perfect denial of their own will and judgment, in all things conforming their will and judgment to that which the Superior wills and judges" (p. 22).

8. "Generally speaking, they should be taught what method should be pursued by the laborers of the Society, in securing the emoluments which contribute to the greater glory of God by employing all the means which can be possibly employed" (p. 38).

9. "They should greatly revere their Rector as one who holds the place of Christ our Lord, leaving to Him the free

dispositions of themselves and their concerns with unfeigned obedience" (p. 40).

10. "Every one must persuade himself that they who live under obedience should permit themselves to be moved and directed under Divine Providence by their Superiors, just as if they were a corpse, which allows itself to be moved and handled in any way; or as the staff of an old man, which serves him wherever and in whatsoever thing he who holds it in his hand pleases to use it" (p. 36).

11. "No one may allow himself to be examined without the license of the Superior in civil or criminal causes, unless he who can oblige him under sin should compel him, and the Superior will never grant permission except in causes which relate to the Roman Catholic religion" (p. 62).

12. "The Superiors of the Society are over them in the place of the divine majesty" (p. 64).

13. "The Society desires all its members to be secured, or at least assisted from falling into the snare of sin which may originate from the force of its constitutions or injunctions (?). It seems good to us in the Lord, that, excepting the express vow by which the society is bound to the pope for the time being, and the other essential vows of poverty, charity, and obedience; no constitutions, declarations, or any order of living can involve an obligation to sin, mortal or venial (!), unless the Superior command them, in the name of our Lord Jesus Christ, or in virtue of holy obedience; which shall be done in those cases or persons, wherein it shall be judged that it will greatly conduce to the particular good of each, or to the general advantage; and instead of the fear of offence, let the love and desire of all perfection succeed; that the greater glory and praise of Christ our Creator and Lord may follow" (?) (pp. 63, 64).

14. "Whoever is endowed with the talent of writing books conducive to the common good, and shall compose any such, nevertheless shall not publish them except the Gen-

eral shall previously see them, and subject them to the judgment and censure of others ; that, if they shall seem good for edification, they may come before the public, and not otherwise " (p. 70). (See the list of Jesuit works herein given for edification).

15. Upon the election of a General, "all shall come forthwith to do him reverence, and on both their knees shall kiss his hand" (p. 79).

16. "Among the various endowments desirable in the General, this is the most important; that he be most intimate with God and our Lord, as well in prayer as in all other actions " (p. 82).

17. "As it belongs to the General to see that the Constitutions of the Society be everywhere observed ; so shall it belong to him to grant dispensation in all classes where dispensation is necessary" (p. 85).

18. " He may send all that are subject to him to any part of the world, for any period, definite or indefinite, as he shall determine, to do any action of those which the Society is wont to exercise for the succor of souls (!). He may recall missionaries, and in short, proceed in all things as he shall think will be to the greater glory of God " (p. 85).

19. "He shall scrutinize as far as possible the consciences of those who are under his obedience" (p. 87).

20. "Obedience and reverence should always be paid him, as one who holds the place of Christ" (p. 87).

These underscored phrases—some of them blasphemous, some tyrannical, some purposely made ambiguous—occurring in a large instrument, more or less suspiciously worded throughout, are indicative of purposes that will not bear the light of a perspicuous style, while all are quite in keeping with the style and drift of the "Secreta Monita."

Soon after this Society was legalized by Pope Paul III. in 1540, it began to bring forth the fruits of iniquity, and it was long after that the people among whom it had operated found out its character by their own sufferings, were driven into exasperation, and clamored for its suppression. By heathen, as well as by Christian states; by Roman far more than by Protestant countries, the Jesuits were ignominiously expelled, as intolerably dangerous to human society.

There never was such a horrid catalogue of crime verified against any body of men, outside of Romanism, put on the records of any court since the Noachian Deluge; and this by a Parliament whose religious sentiments would have naturally biassed every member of it in favor of the accused, had it been possible to have avoided the frightful proof profusely furnished, not by Protestants, but by the Jesuits themselves in numerous books collected—one hundred and fifty, and every one of them published with the approbation and permission of their Generals.

"So atrocious, extensive, and continual were their crimes," says Mgr. De Pradt, Roman Archbishop of Malines, "that they were expelled, either partially or generally, from all the different countries of Europe, at various intervals prior to the abolition of the Order in 1773, thirty-nine times—a fact unparalleled in the history of any body of men ever known in the world. This is the seal of reprobation stamped upon Jesuitism."

The volume, published by the French Parliamentary sanction, ought to be translated into English and circulated throughout our land. It is divided into eighteen chapters, containing extracts from 150 volumes, covering the period from 1500 to 1751; and proving the various counts recited as reasons for the decree against the "Order."

· These chapters are arranged according to the following "Table of the Title of Propositions recited in this Collection":

"I. *Unity of sentiment and doctrine of those who are called the Society of Jesus.*"—Upon which topic there are extracts from five authors and eight different works, from the year

1540 to 1757. The last volume is entitled " Institutes of the Society of Jesus. By authority of the General Congregation." They inculcate these three general rules : That the spirit and character of Jesuitism are to be ascertained by the ordinances and rules composed by the superiors and most influential members ; that no book can be published by any Jesuit upon his own private responsibility, for it must be sanctioned prior to its promulgation by the Generals of the Order, as a true exposition of the avowed principles of all the members ; and that they are but "one in design, action and vows, as if they were united by the conjugal bond. At the least signal, one man turns and changes the whole Society, and determines the whole body, who are easily impelled, but with difficulty counteracted." (" Imago primi Seculi," etc., Prolog. 33, Lib. 5, 622.)

" II. *Probabilism.*—To illustrate the peculiar attributes of Jesuitism, fifty-five writers, from the year 1600 to 1759, are cited, containing about three passages, of which only one, from page 51, is selected as a specimen of that perfect adaptation of Jesuitical principles to the depraved propensities of sinners. ' The confessor, whether ordinary or delegated, under the penalty of mortal sin, is bound to absolve the penitent, who follows the probable opinion of sin, even when the confessor himself knows that it is false.' (Georges de Rhodes, Actis Humains, Disput. 2, Quest 2, Sect. 3.)

" III. *Philosophical Sin, Invincible Ignorance, Erroneous Conscience, etc.*—Forty authors are quoted as expositors of those dogmas of Jesuitism from the year 1607 to 1761 ; including 130 paragraphs.

" IV.—*Simony and Secrecy.*—To this chapter are appended the works of fourteen writers, from the year 1590 to 1759 ; and forty-one extracts from their productions.

" V. *Blasphemy.*—Five of the Jesuit commentators are

adduced, from the year 1640 to 1766; and fourteen illustrations.

"VI. *Sacrilege.*—This subject is elucidated by four passages from Francis de Lugo, of the year 1652; and three citations from Georges Gobat, 1700.

"VII. *Magic.*—To unfold that part are alleged the writings of Escobar, of the year 1663; Taberna, 1736; Arsdekin, 1744; Laymann, 1748; Trachala, 1759; and thirteen paragraphs from their works.

"VIII. *Astrology.*—Arsdekin, 1744; and Busembaum and La Croix are cited as sanctioning that impious violation of the divine law.

"IX. *Irreligion.*—Thirty-seven writers, from the year 1607 to 1759, are successively adduced, and 130 extracts from their volumes. We select one specimen: 'By the command of God, it is lawful to murder the innocent, to rob, and to commit all lewdness; and thus to fulfil His mandate is our duty.' ('Alegona. Sum. Theolog. Compend., Thom. Aquinas, Quest. 94.')

"X. *Idolatry.*—This is subdivided into three parts. The general sanction to idolatry which is given by the Order of Jesuits is proved by three extracts from Vasquez, of the year 1614; and by the quotation from Fagundez, 1640. The approbation which the Jesuits formally gave to the Chinese idolatrous ceremonies is verified by nineteen extracts from the Papal bulls and various works of those priests from the year 1545 to 1742. That they encouraged and participated in the idolatry of the Malabars is demonstrated by three extracts from Papal bulls, decrees, etc., from the year 1645 to 1745. Those mandates from the Roman court particularly interdicted the Jesuits from their open combination with those idolaters; upon which Daniel, in his 'Recucil de Divers Ouvages Philosophiques, Theologiques,' etc., Paris, 1724, thus decides: 'That article concerning idolatry, of all the provincial affairs, is the most cruel towards the Jesuits. I have often told them that it is a decisive point for all others ; for anything once having been supposed to be true, all which follows from it is credible, or at least appears not to be incredible.' (Entretien de Cleand. et d'End., 440.) According to which proposition, error or wickedness cannot possibly exist in the world.

"XI. *Licentiousness.*—This topic is illustrated by eighteen writers of the very highest authority in the Order, from the year 1590 to 1759, with fifty-one citations from their works.

"XII. *Perjury, Lying and False Witnesses.*—Twenty-nine authors, from the year 1590 to 1761, illustrating those subjects ; and 153 paragraphs are extracted from their books.

"XIII. *Prevarication of Judges.*—Laymann of the year 1647 ; Fabri, 1670 ; Taberna, 1736; Fegeli, 1750 ; and Busembaum and La Croix, 1757 ; in eight paragraphs instruct judges how to pervert law and justice.

"XIV. *Theft, Secret Compensation, Concealment, etc.*— To develop how men may steal and plunder with impunity, and without sin, by every variety of artifice, thirty-four writers, from the year 1590 to 1761, are introduced, with 149 expositions of Jesuitical knavery.

"XV. *Murder.*—Thirty-six authors, from the year 1590 to 1761, teach the various modes of violating the Sixth Commandment in 161 passages from their volumes.

"XVI. *Parricide.*—Dicastille of the year 1641 ; Escobar, 1663 ; Gobat, 1700 ; Carnedi, 1719 ; and Stoz, 1756, in twenty-nine paragraphs inculcate and justify the murder of parents and other relatives.

"XVII. *Suicide.*—Laymann of the year 1627, and Busembaum and La Croix, 1757, in fifteen passages defend suicide.

"XVIII. *High Treason and Regicide.*—Seventy-five of the most renowned Jesuit authors, from the year 1590 to 1759 : English, French, German, Spanish and Italian, all are cited ; with 221 quotations from their writings which maintain that 'Roman priests are not subject to any civil government'; Nicholas Muskza, Leg. Hum. Lib. 1, Dissert. 4, Num. 185 ; and which defend rebellon, treason, and the murder of all Protestant rulers and magistrates.

"One of the dogmas must be quoted as a specimen of the morals of Jesuits. It was the thesis of François Xavier Mamaki, Prefect of the Jesuit College of Rouen in France, in 1759 : 'Heroas faciunt, etc. Fortunate crimes sometimes make heroes. Successful crime ceases to be crime. Whom France calls by the opprobrious names of robber and pirate she will call " Alexander " if his course be prosperous. Success constitutes or absolves the guilty at its will.'"

The eleventh chapter of this volume, published by the Parliament of Paris, on the subject of licentiousness, and beginning with a quotation from Jesuit Sa., 1590, " Potest et femina quaeque, et mas, pro turpi corporis usu pretium accipere et petere ; et qui promisit, tenetur solvere " (Aphor. Luxuria, 249), is perfectly horrible. These 150 volumes were each issued with the approbation of the "General," "standing to" their author "in the place of Jesus Christ" (!!!). These books, unparalleled for intensified iniquity, afforded a mighty mass of evidence for conviction, and thoroughly justified the prompt parliamentary action.

The *arrêt*, or judicial decision, was speedily drawn up and passed so confidentially and secretly that the royal troops had surrounded the Jesuit college, and had rushed in and seized the private papers of the miserable inmates before they had become aware of the enactment of the decree relative to their banishment—subsequently and swiftly executed. Because the French Parliament was very particular to collect material sufficiently strong and unmistakably authentic to justify such expulsion to the world, in the event of their resorting to this measure, it is more important herein to relate their proceedings in the matter briefly as possible, after saying that all these documents in the case must have been before the Pope, Clement XIV., to enable him to decide upon his own duty. Never was any poor Pope more perplexed while perusing the odious mass which proved out of their own mouths what all Jesuits are bound to be and to do, and what they actually did ; and what was truly affirmed of them in the bill of indictment before a Roman Catholic parliament, upon the strength of which the suppression of the Order was clamorously demanded and righteously granted. Though " His Holiness " knew that their final suppression by his own infallible authority would be at the cost of his life, he did not flinch from his duty.

In his bull, dated July 21, 1773, Clement XIV., wrote as follows :

"That we might choose the wisest course in an affair of so much importance, we determined not to be precipitant, but to take due time not only to examine attentively, weigh carefully, and wisely debate, but also by unceasing prayer to ask the Father of lights for His particular assistance."

Thus the Pope records his decision : "The very sovereigns whose piety and liberality towards the Company were so well-known—the Kings of France, Spain, Portugal and Sicily—found themselves reduced to the necessity of expelling and driving from their states, kingdoms and provinces these very companions of Jesus ; persuaded that there remained no other remedy to so great evils, and that this step was necessary in order to prevent the Christians from rising one against another and from massacreing each other in the very bosom of our common mother, the Holy Church.

" It was very difficult, not to say impossible, that the Church should recover a firm and durable peace so long as the said society subsisted ; in consequence thereof . . . we are determined upon the fate of a society classed among the mendicant orders both by its institute and by its privileges. After a mature deliberation we do, out of our certain knowledge, and the fulness of our apostolic power, suppress and abolish the said company. . . . We declare all and all kind of authority, the General, the provincials, the visitors, and other Superiors of the said Society to be forever annulled and extinguished.

"Given at Rome, at St. Mary the Greater, under the seal of the Fisherman, the 21st day of July, 1773, in the fifth year of our Pontificate."

Notwithstanding this infallible decision, this dangerous Order was restored to life and power by another infallible Pope, Pius VII., August 7, 1814. He said : " We should deem ourselves guilty of a great crime towards God if, amid these dangers of the Christian republic, we neglected the aids which the special providence of God has put at our disposal ; and if, placed in the bark of Peter, tossed and assailed by continual storms, we refused to employ the vigorous and experienced rowers (Jesuits) who volunteer their services, in order to break the waves of a sea that threaten every moment shipwreck and death." (! ! !)

HOW CAN JESUITISM BE SUCCESSFULLY MET?

BY PRINCIPAL D. H. MACVICAR, D.D., LL.D., PRESBY-
TERIAN COLLEGE, MONTREAL.

THE question is confessedly a difficult one. To say that Jesuitism cannot be successfully met is pessimistic—equivalent to acknowledging that truth is to be ultimately overthrown by error. We cannot accept this conclusion. God is infinitely mightier than the devil, and the head of the old serpent hath been bruised under the heel of the Son of God, and, therefore, victory is sure on the side of truth and righteousness, however long delayed.

The society which is the parent and propagator of what is meant by Jesuitism has existed for more than three centuries, and, while not as strong numerically as a hundred years ago, it shows no signs of senility or lack of courage and force. In the bull of confirmation, issued by Pope Paul III., on the 27th of September, 1540, it is described as "a spiritual army under the standard of the Cross." Its members are bound by a vow of perpetual "poverty, chastity, and obedience to a General, in whom they see Jesus Christ as if He were present, and a special vow to the Pope and his successors."

Its motto is, "*Ad majorem Dei gloriam*" (For the greater glory of God). But its career, as recorded by impartial historians, Roman Catholic as well as Protestant, has long ago convinced the nations that have had most to do with it of the hollowness of these pretensions to superior piety.

At the outset it swept over Italy with wonderful rapidity.

Success marked its path everywhere, so that before the death of its first General, Ignatius de Loyola, in 1556, it had more than 1,000 members.

Its policy was, and still is, to secure the friendship and patronage of the rich and great ones of the earth, specially in educational work. In this it has often been successful, and yet eventually it became the ruler and the terror of emperors, kings and governments. For example, Jesuit colleges were opened in Portugal by Francis Xavier at the invitation of the king. Just as Jesuits accompanied Lord Baltimore to Maryland for the same purpose, and they have since so prospered that in 1876 they had seventeen colleges in the United States, including the University of St. Louis.* In Canada they have St. Mary's College, Montreal, founded in 1848, and a college at St. Boniface, Manitoba, and no doubt others are projected all under the approving smile of the pope, of politicians, and of easy-going wealthy Protestants. Spain gave the order a similarly kind reception, and by the efforts of Francis Borgia, Duke of Gandia, their prosperity was such that, in 1773, they numbered in that country alone over 6,000 members. In France their career has been checkered in the extreme; and it is a noteworthy fact that, while this country is often regarded as the very cradle of the order, no Frenchman has yet attained to the distinction of being chosen General. The University from the first, acting in self-defence, stoutly opposed their educational schemes, and in doing so it struck at the very heart of their enterprise. They lay themselves out to be educators. Their primary aim is to seize the young and saturate their hearts and minds with the principles of their system. And in every country in which their pupils in considerable numbers have grown to be men, political intrigue, religious turmoil, and national troubles have been the issue. Who does not know the treatment of

---

* See Kiddle and Schem's Cyclopedia of Education, p. 494.

Gallicans and Huguenots at their hands and the ruin which it brought upon their fair country? During the war of the League they fell into the utmost disrepute, and at length the assassination of Henry III., along with the suspicions which arose regarding the attempt made upon the life of Henry IV. by Chatell, for a time one of their pupils, led to their total expulsion from France in 1594. Being reinstated, however, in 1603, they were soon again involved in new conflicts and reproaches. The openly avowed doctrines of Mariana, a member of the society, regarding the right of revolt, caused popular indignation to settle upon them with intensity in connection with the murder of Henry IV. by Ravaillac. They were also vigorously assailed from within the Church. Jansenists, Dominicans, and Augustinians, from time to time, opened their ecclesiastical batteries upon them with galling effect. The caustic pen of the versatile Pascal, for example, in his brilliant and immortal "Lettres Provinciales," so exposed the rottenness of Jesuitical casuistry that their attempts to reply served only to cover them with greater ridicule in the eyes of educated and honest men.

Other countries, learning enough of their doings, meted out to them similar treatment. Accordingly, their entrance into Hungary, Bohemia, Moravia and Transylvania was viewed with the strongest disfavor and strenuously resisted. They also encountered the keenest hostility from the popular belief that they were the instigators of the bloody struggle known as the Thirty Years War.

Persevering, however, in the face of all forms of opposition, they claim to have gained decisive triumphs in Austria, Bavaria, and the Rhenish principalities. The story of the alleged success of their missions to the heathen in India, China and Japan was clouded with appalling disasters in the end. Even pagans gradually learned to abhor the system and to drive it from their shores with loathing. But their pristine zeal and ubiquitous spirit remained unbroken, and thirsting for new fields of conquest they pushed their way into Northern and Central America, Brazil, Paraguay, Uruguay, California, and the Philippine Islands. And so great was their success that at the first centenary celebration they reported 13,112 members; and a hundred years later they claimed to have 22,589 members, of whom 11,295 were priests, along with 24 professed houses, 669 colleges, 176 seminaries, 61 novitiates, 335 residences, and 275 missionary stations. This seems to have been the period of their greatest strength. At present it is not possible accurately to ascertain their number, but it is thought to be about 6,000 in all parts of the world. An active portion of this small but powerful army is stationed in Canada and the United States, bent upon the conquest of this continent. It surely must be possible for all lovers of truth and freedom in these two great countries to meet successfully the aggressive movements of such a handful, if the work is gone about in the right way.

And here let it be distinctly understood—

1. *That it is vain to look to the Church of Rome to terminate Jesuitism.*

The voice of history is unmistakably clear upon this point. She has signally failed wherever she has opposed and coercively touched this body. When, in 1762, F. Lavelette, the Jesuit administrator of Martinique, became bankrupt in the sum of 2,400,000 francs, it caused such a scandal that the Parliament of Paris ordered the constitutions of the society to be published, and appointed a royal commission to examine the documents. This commission called to their aid a private assembly of fifty-one archbishops, presided over by Cardinal de Luynes. This goodly company of high dignitaries, with the exception of six, condemned certain fundamental points in the constitutions and called for amendments. But it was all in vain. The defiant answer of their General, Lorenzo Ricci, was "*Sint ut sunt, aut non sint.*" Learned prelates of commanding influence are helpless when they come in collision with Jesuitical schemes. Witness the latest example of this sort in the case of Cardinal Taschereau's fruitless efforts to prevent the incorporation and subsequent endowment of the society out of public funds in the province of Quebec. In about two years, during 1887–1888, by the agency of a cunning, unscrupulous politician, a pupil of their own, who has since been covered with decorations and honors from Rome, both these ends were gained in spite of the Cardinal's opposition; and Quebec to day enjoys the unenviable distinction of having given the order what it demanded, an act of incorporation, a legal status on this continent, and of having paid out of the public purse $400,000 for its endowment and to aid the Romish Church, on the pretext of rectifying a wrong said to have been done to the society by the sovereign of England more than a century ago.

Even the remonstrances and censures of popes are disregarded by the order. According to the testimony of Clement XIV. several of his predecessors were constrained to rebuke and punish them, but to no purpose. Finally, he himself, discovering that they were hated by Spain, Portugal, France, and in fact all the nations of Europe, except the feeble kingdom of Sardinia, completely suppressed them by the brief "*Dominus ac Redemptor*," July 21st, 1773.

In this instrument they are charged, among other things, with violations of their constitutions by meddling with politics, a sin which they have not yet abandoned. They are declared guilty of insubordination to local ecclesiastical authorities, guilty of consenting to heathen practices in the East, and of disturbing in various ways the peace of the Church and bringing upon her persecutions and manifold dangers. In accordance, therefore, with the mind of bishops, cardinals and sundry other popes, and for the conservation of peace and the safety of religion, Clement declares the society suppressed, extinguished and abrogated forever, with all its rites, houses, colleges, schools and hospitals. The congregation of cardinals takes possession of all the temporalities of the order, and the unyielding General, Lorenzo Ricci, is thrown into prison in the castle of St. Angelo, where he dies in 1775.

Nothing more vigorous or drastic than this can be expected from the Vatican, and yet as a means of terminating Jesuitism it was a conspicuous failure. Other infallible popes came speedily to the rescue of the shattered order. Scarcely a quarter of a century had passed when, in 1801, a brief by Pius VII. restored it in Northern Russia; another brief did the same for it in the Two Sicilies in 1804, and, finally, in 1814 it was fully relieved of all the disabilities under which it had been placed by Clement XIV.

In the light of these transactions what is the use of looking to the Church for the removal of the evils of Jesuitism? They have their congenial home in her bosom, and thrive there when attempted to be crushed. It is often said by the advocates of peace at any price, that if Protestants would leave it alone, its incurable tendency to breed strife in the popish camp would prove its destruction. This is certainly not the lesson emphasized by the historic past. As matter of fact the thousand tumults, debates and raging controversies it has fomented among papists have not made an end of it. On the contrary it has gained additional courage and subtlety in these battles.

Besides, it is a gross mistake to suppose that the Church is the natural and uncompromising enemy of the society. Far from it. With a few notable exceptions, such as those just referred to, the society has been both tolerated and cherished as the precious child of the Church, and its spirit and methods are now dominant in the Vatican and throughout the whole body. It is too much, therefore, to expect the Church to deal unnaturally and cruelly with her own offspring. In other words, the attempt to separate Romanism and Jesuitism so as to excuse the one and condemn the other, as is the fashion with some politicians at the present time, is utter folly, and betrays surprising ignorance both of history and theology. The Jesuits claim to be most loyal sons of the Church, and they may well do so from every point of view, and she dare not disown them. They are the champions of the faith, and can fairly be counted the special apostles of Mariolatry, of the dogmas of immaculate conception and pontifical infallibility and of the indefensible notion of the divine right of the bishops of Rome to be supreme in all things temporal and spiritual. If they are to be distinguished from the Church, it can only be as the species from the genus, the part from the whole; and, in this case, the parodox is very generally allowed that the part is greater than the whole. Seeing then it cannot be doubted that, taken all in all, the Church esteems the Jesuits "very highly in love for their work's sake,' we might as well expect the Ethiopian to change his skin and the leopard his spots, or that we should gather grapes of thorns or figs of thistles, as that the Church should throw them overboard. We must look for reformation and deliverance from other sources.

2. *The sharp remedy of expulsion from different countries has proved insufficient.* It has been resorted to more than eighty times, but served only to change the domicile of the order, without terminating their machinations. And it is a significant fact that these expulsions have been in the vast majority of instances from Romish countries. No other society in the Church of Rome or out of it has received such punishment in this form at the hands of kings, popes and governments. It is wearisome and we shall not attempt here to trace the details of this method of dealing with them.* Why should

---

*They were expelled from Saragossa, 1555; La Palatine, 1558; Vienna, 1566; Avignon, 1570; Antwerp, 1578; Portugal, 1578; Segovia,

the society be hunted out of nearly every country under heaven? The members and their defenders say that it is because of their excessive piety. But surely this cannot be a reason for the Church to lay the lash upon them, and for governments under her control to visit them with such severity. The Parliament of Paris gave a very different account of the matter. In its decree enacted March 5th, 1762, it declared the doctrines of the society, as formulated at Prague, to be fitted "to destroy the law of nature," and to " break all the bonds of civil society." The same decree denounced as utterly immoral and dangerous their teachings on " secret compensation, equivocation, mental reservations, probabilism and philosophical sin." That the same views are still held and inculcated by the order admits of no doubt. As late as June, 1876, Mr. Gladstone, in the *Contemporary Review*, indicts the society on the following counts:

"(1) Its hostility to mental freedom at large; (2) its incompatibility with the thought and movement of modern civilization; (3) its pretensions against the State; (4) its pretensions against parental and conjugal rights; (5) its jealousy, abated in some quarters, of the free circulation and

---

1578; England, 1579, 1581, 1586; Japan, 1587; Hungary, 1588; Transylvania, 1588; Bordeaux, 1589; France, 1594; Holland, 1596; Toulon and Berne, 1597; England, 1602, 1604; Denmark, Thor, Venice, 1606, 1612; Japan, 1613; Bohemia, 1618; Moravia, 1619; Naples and the Netherlands, 1622; China, 1623; India, 1613; Malta, 1634; Russia, 1723; Savoy, 1729; Paraguay, 1733; Portugal, 1759; France, 1754; Spain and Two Sicilies, 1767; Malta and Duchy Parma, 1768; Russia, 1776; France, 1804; Eripou, 1804; France, 1806; Naples, 1810, 1816; Seleure, 1816; Belgium, 1818; Brest, 1819; Russia, 1820; Spain, 1826; Rouen, 1825; Great Britain and Ireland, 1829; France and Saxony, 1831; Portugal, 1834; Spain, 1835; Rheims, 1838; Lucerne, 1841, 1845; France, 1845; Bavaria, Switzerland, Naples, Papal States, Linz, Vienna, Styria, Austrian Empire, Galicia, Sardinia, Sicily and Paraguay, 1848; Italian States, 1859; Sicily, 1860. They have been several times expelled from France and other countries at later dates.

use of the Holy Scriptures; (6) the *de facto* alienation of the educated mind of the country in which it prevails; (7) its detrimental effects on the comparative strength and morality of the State in which it has sway; (8) its tendency to sap veracity in the individual mind."

We do not deny that these and other graver charges established against the order justify the action of nations in getting quit of it. It is quite possible for a body of men so to violate all the principles of the social compact as to forfeit their place in it. In self-defence the body politic may find it necessary to cast them out or to incarcerate them. These are the remedies of which the civil magistrate naturally thinks, and in using them he has justice on his side, and is commonly sustained by enlightened public opinion. But so far as the offenders are concerned his treatment is punitive, not remedial. He has not thereby improved their moral character. To turn men forcibly out of one country into another because of their alleged iniquities is not the very best thing that can be done for them. It can no more change them for the better than the imposition of a heavy fine to keep them out can do so. At bottom this treatment is thoroughly selfish in principle. It amounts to this, that we pass on to our neighbors what we find to be unbearable ourselves. Jesuitism, or any other great development of moral evil, is not to be met in this fashion. It will not do to transport our paupers, thieves, swindlers and bank-robbers to other countries, and think that we have thus fully discharged our obligations in relation to them. Evil should be fought on the soil where it grows. Thistles should be dealt with where they are indigenous instead of forcibly scattering them over the fertile fields of other lands. And so had Christian nations avoided the short-sighted selfishness of passing Jesuitism round to one another, and had they concentrated their united resources and spiritual energies upon teaching men the truth, the results would have been infinitely more satisfactory than those which historians have had to record.

3. *We discard the manipulations of mere politicians as certain to afford no solution of our problem.*

Such creatures are the puppets of Jesuits. We have not a single word of reproach to utter against true and honest statesmen, but we wish to discriminate sharply between them and quacks. The aim of the latter, so far as our present question is concerned, is so to handle Jesuitism as to gain and hold office by means of its influence. This has been the case for years in Canada, hence the obtrusive boldness of the movements of the Jesuits—and probably very many in other countries are not actuated by higher considerations. These pseudo-statesmen deem it of paramount importance always to say and do the things that please the dominant spirits in the Church, and then they try to convince the multitude that it is all for the public good. Speeches in and out of Parliament are framed accordingly. The daily editorial efforts of party journals are also governed by the same supreme motive; and the poor literary drudges who are hired to do the work are obliged to deal so recklessly with facts that, although one may read the representations on both sides of any political question he can scarcely ascertain the real state of the case. And so great is the zeal and cunning skill with which Protestant journalists plead and defend the cause of the Jesuits that one almost wonders why they should be at the trouble and expense of publishing any papers of their own. These political wire-pullers pose as great public benefactors—broad-minded, liberal and impartial—they can be Methodists, Presbyterians, Episcopalians, Baptists and Agnostics all combined—intent only upon their country's good. They detest bigotry and fanaticism. They glory in the party of peace which never stirs up race and religious animosities. And so well is this sham maintained, and so successfully do the players in the game conceal themselves behind masks that thousands of unsuspecting people are duped by them. Now and then a square issue is raised before the public when concealment by the tricksters becomes impossible. An instance of this sort recently occurred in the political history of Canada when the government of Quebec, in 1887, incorporated the Jesuits, who till then were outlawed in all parts of the British Empire, and in 1888 proceeded to endow them and the Romish hierachy of the province out of the public chest.

The case was brought before the Federal or Dominion Parliament at Ottawa on a motion, asking the Governor-General-in-Council to veto this outrageous provincial legislation. The motion was in order, perfectly constitutional, and obviously in the interests of justice and of the whole Dominion. Canada had long ago declared in favor of complete separation between Church and State, and in opposition to all public grants for sectarian purposes. This was done at the time of the secularization of the Clergy Reserves, and the principle was then incorporated in the very constitution of the country. But, on this motion to veto the question with politicans was, who shall take the responsibility of displeasing the Church and losing her support? Whoever is guilty of this temerity must speedily abandon the hope of occupying the treasury benches. And accordingly when the vote was taken thirteen incurred this risk, and 188, composed of both sides of the house, were constrained to drop their masks, and hastened to bow the knee to papal authority. No wonder that the Jesuits are jubilant. Their game, for once, has been an immense success. Canada, as represented on the floor of Parliament, has pronounced in their favor, and to the victors belong the spoils. The Church, already plethoric in wealth, is to have still greater abundance. And, as if to add insult to injustice, the 5th of November, the anniversary of the infamous gunpowder plot, was selected as the day on which the premier and cabinet ministers of Quebec, with great public ceremony in the city of Montreal, handed over to Father Turgeon, the representative of the Jesuits and the Pope, the sum of four hundred thousand dollars.

But good has already come out of this humiliating spectacle. It has demonstrated beyond the possibility of doubt what may be expected from politicians, and has opened the eyes of thousands upon a national danger the existence of which they were accustomed to ignore. The Protestant sentiment of the country has been roused as never before; and even fair-minded Roman Catholics have united with their fellow-citizens of other creeds and of both political parties in the formation of an Equal Rights' Association, which is already powerful and determined to call to account before the bar of public opinion the notorious 188. These are likely to learn in the near future that it may be worth while to think about Protestant as well as Roman Catholic votes. And whatever may be the issue at the ballot-box, one thing is certain, that all who uphold the banner of evangelical truth are convinced of the folly of looking for help from secular office-holders and office-seekers.

4. *To meet Jesuitism we must educate Protestants in certain directions.* They have themselves very largely to blame for the state of things which we are now obliged to discuss. They have been content to remain ignorant of the designs and movements of the foes of free institutions. Hence the need.

(*a*) To instruct them fully upon the true nature of the system against which they are called to contend. In this connection there is scope for the services of properly qualified lecturers; and it will be necessary to translate into English and scatter broadcast the Constitution of the Society along with many portions of the writings of standard authors such as Liguori, Gury and Busembaum. The pulpit should be the most efficient educating agency upon the moral questions at issue, and should not be silenced or abashed by the gibes of secular demagogues or the frowns of those who may be at ease in their pews.

(*b*) Very many require to be taught that truth and freedom are worth contending for—that they are really better than thousands of silver and gold. It is the lack of firm personal conviction on this point that renders it easy to make fatal concessions to error and to the secret enemies of human liberty. The heroic martyr spirit of primitive apostolic Christianity is not the overmastering force of our age. We are largely ruled by considerations of self-indulgence and a mercenary principle showing itself in every form of Mammon worship. Self-interest, and specially the hope of gain, weakens immeasurably the protest of business men against the wiles and aggressions of Jesuitism. They are peculiarly sensitive to the danger of being boycotted under ecclesiastical direction, and, therefore, will do nothing that has a tendency to withdraw traffic from their shops. It is only among agriculturists, who are not subject to such temptations, that a healthy opinion on the subject prevails. Many manufacturers are decidedly opposed to the enlightenment of the working classes and their emancipation from priest rule lest they should thus be forced to pay them higher wages. They quiet their consciences regarding the matter by the silly and oft-repeated affirmation that the religion of the Jesuit priest is good enough for people in their station so long as they are happy under its sway. They even pride themselves upon virtuous abhorrence of the mean crime of proselytism with which they charge those who seek to evangelize Romanists. They know very well that there is all the difference imaginable in the ends contemplated and the forms assumed by what is called proselytism. And they should be taught that the man who, with open Bible in hand, tries to lead his fellow-creatures in the exercise of their inalienable right of private judgment into the liberty wherewith Christ makes His people free, is not to be classed along with him who prostrates them at his feet in a confessional box and teaches them to believe in fictitious ecclesiastical miracles, in the sacrifice of the mass, in the purifying efficacy of the fabulous flames of purgatory and in the intercession of saints and the Virgin Mary—all of which is to the unspeakable detriment of the truth and dishonor of the work of our Lord and Saviour, Jesus Christ.

(c) Multitudes require to have their views greatly elevated as to the exercise of their sacred trust in electing right men to public offices. Under our free system of government the thought and moral convictions of the people are reflected in the halls of legislation; and if our rulers fall into reproach by favoring Jesuitism or otherwise, that reproach comes back with full force upon those by whom they are elected and sustained in office. There can be no doubt, in this connection, that the tyranny of partyism is a bitter curse. But how shall we get rid of it? Men are elected not because known to be persons of capacity and unswerving integrity but because they are pledged to support their party and to defend it when most deeply immersed in public iniquity. It is this, very largely, that gives Jesuitism opportunity to play its games and accomplish its ends, for it has ever delighted in political intrigues.

(d) The same system of public education should be extended to all classes, and its character should be guarded with sleepless vigilance. Poison insinuated into this fountain quickly affects the national life. If boys and girls at school and college are taught essentially different views of morals and the fundamental principles of civil government, the results cannot but be ultimately dangerous. Collision will be inevitable if, for example, the majority are instructed as to the mutual independence of Church and State in their proper respective spheres, and the minority are successfully indoctrinated in the mediæval notion that the State is merely the creature of the Church, existing only for her purposes, and thoroughly subordinate to her in all things.

To meet Jesuitism successfully this pretension must be resisted to the utmost in every legitimate form. It is in the highest degree pernicious. The maintenance of good government and the preservation of the peace and highest welfare of every country demand that the line between the civil and ecclesiastical authority should be clearly drawn and should be invariably respected in legislation and the administration of all public affairs. All branches of the Church, whatever their creeds may be, provided they are not seditious and immoral, are entitled to entire freedom and protection in their own domain which embraces all that is strictly spiritual. The State, on the other hand, must have full control in all temporal matters and cannot be domineered over by ecclesiastical persons or organizations.

We warn Protestants against the invasion of their homes by Jesuitical methods systematically pursued through parochial schools for boys and girls and through colleges and convents where education is offered to Protestants at a nominal cost. It is also represented as superior, especially with regard to accomplishments for young ladies, to what can be elsewhere obtained. This is a delusion, but one fatally attractive to many wealthy people and others who are ambitious to rise to social distinction.

The directors of these institutions make all sorts of fair promises as to non-interference with the religion of Protestant pupils. They can do so with perfect sincerity, because the current belief of Romanists and Jesuits is that Protestants have no religion to be interfered with. Here is a potent and growing danger. Thousands of families in Britain, Canada and the United States are being morally and spiritually corrupted in this manner. The remedy is mainly in the hands of faithful pastors and a vigorous, independent religious press who should warn parents against such folly and cruelty, and teach people how to meet this alarming form of Jesuitical aggression.

The public school systems of the world are at this moment in jeopardy and doomed by the Vatican. All branches of the Reformed Church, instead of dividing and contending among themselves, should close their ranks so as to meet with invincible power the subtle attacks of a common foe.

They should go farther. There is a work of emancipation to be done. The multitudes who are under the yoke of Jesuitism should be liberated. It should be put in their power to enter into the liberty wherewith Christ makes His people free. And this can best be done by the agency of colporters, missionary schools, and heroic preachers of the pure Gospel. These should be everywhere multiplied a thousand-fold; and men of the right stamp, of high intellectual and spiritual qualifications, are needed for the purpose. In Canada the Presbyterian Church carries on a noble and successful work upon these lines among the French population of the Dominion. Last year she maintained 16 colporters, 33 mission schools, and 89 preaching stations, while 19 French students are under training for the work in the Theological Seminary in Montreal. These schools are most fruitful of good results. In one of them last session as many as 36 pupils confessed their faith in Jesus Christ, and these young converts are, almost without exception, full of zeal for the propagation of the Gospel among their relatives and countrymen. And it should not be forgotten that God's remedy for all moral evil is the Gospel of His Son, Jesus Christ, and upon this we are bound to rely with unfaltering confidence. Armed with this weapon and trusting in the Almighty power of the Spirit, our victory is sure, for we have the divine promise that the Lord Jesus shall slay the lawless one with the breath of His mouth and bring him to naught by the manifestation of His coming.

[Reprinted, by request, from February "Treasury for Pastor and People," Copyrighted. $2.50 per 100, post-paid. E. B. TREAT, Publisher, 5 Cooper Union, New York.]

OPPONENTS OF CHRISTIANITY.

BY SIR WILLIAM DAWSON, PRESIDENT OF MCGILL UNI-
VERSITY, MONTREAL.

THE history of Christianity has been that of a warfare, a struggle, and though Christians may at the present time be exposed to less of actual persecution than at some former periods, they meet with quite as much of opposition. The prince of this world is by no means disposed as yet to abdicate, though he seems to have a lively conviction that his time is short. Some of our opponents are very old. Others are new or in new forms. Of the latter, perhaps the most formidable at present are materialistic and agnostic evolution and destructive historical criticism of the Bible. I use the qualifying adjectives because among the multiform and often contradicted theories grouped under the name evolution there are some that are harmless or respectable, and there is a fair and legitimate criticism to which the books of the Bible, like other books, may be subjected.

It is a favorite *ruse de guerre* with writers and speakers against Christianity to represent that these oppositions are due to modern science, meaning thereby physical and natural science; and that all or nearly all scientific men disbelieve Christianity. These, however, are groundless assertions. The experience of fifty years and acquaintance with very many scientific men of different types in different countries, enables me to say that very many of the most distinguished scientific men are Christians, and I know many others who, if not Christians, may be said to be "not far from the Kingdom of God." The utterances of a few popular or prominent men should not be taken as expressing the views of their whole class. The best and ablest of scientific men have all along been Christians, and Christianity has helped to make them what they were and are; while science itself, though it may have been used to give new forms to old objections, has been on the whole the handmaid of religion.

As examples of oppositions supposed to be based on science, we may refer to those of positivists and agnostics, as they have recently been presented so ably and clearly by Harrison and Huxley in some of the reviews, where also they have been sufficiently answered. Such discussions, I believe, must do good, and will result in a clearer perception of truth and a more intelligent faith. It is in any case encouraging that they centre around the Word of God, which is thus shown to be still a formidable power and not a thing of the past.

One curious admission which has appeared in these discussions is that of the necessity of some kind of religion or substitute for religion, while it is apparent that those who reject theism and Christianity are at variance among themselves, and fail to find any good substitute for what they avowedly reject, except by falling back on some portions of its doctrine.

In the recent articles referred to, the positivist combatant believes in the religion of humanity, that is, in setting up an ideal standard of human nature, based on historical examples as something to live up to. His agnostic opponent thinks this futile, stigmatizes man as a failure and as a "wilderness of ages," and would adore the universe in all its majesty and grandeur. They thus rehabilitate very old forms of religion, for it is evident that the most ancient idolatries consisted in lifting up men's hearts to the sun and moon and stars, and in worshipping patriarchs and heroes.

Thus we find that there can be no form of infidelity without some substitute for God, and this, necessarily, less high and perfect than the Creator Himself, while destitute of His fatherly attributes. Further, our agnostic and positivist friends even admit their need of a Saviour, since they hold that there must be some elevating influence to raise us from our present evils and failures. Lastly, when we find the ablest advocates of such philosophy differing hopelessly among themselves, we may well see in this an evidence of the need of a divine revelation. Now all this is precisely what the Bible has given us in a better way. If we look up with adoring wonder to the material universe, the Bible leads us to see in this the power and Godhead of the Creator, and the Creator as the living God, our Heavenly Father. If we seek for an ideal humanity to worship, the Bible points us to Jesus Christ, the perfect Man, and at the same time the manifestation of God, the Good Shepherd giving His life for the sheep, God manifest in the flesh and bringing life and immortality to light. Thus the Bible gives us all that these modern ideas desiderate and infinitely more. Nor should we think little of the older part of revelation, for it gives the historical development of God's plan, and is eminently valuable for its testimony to the unity of nature and of God. It is in religion what the older formations are in geology. Their conditions and their life may have been replaced by newer conditions and living beings, but they form the stable base of the newer formations, which not only rest upon them, but which without them would be incomplete and unintelligible.

The lesson of these facts is to hold to the old faith, to fear no discussion, and to stand fast for this world and the future on the grand declaration of Jesus, "God so loved the world that He gave His only begotten Son that whosoever believeth in Him should not perish, but have everlasting life."

THE RISE OF PRELACY, AND ITS GRADUAL DEVELOPMENT.*

BY PRESIDENT W. D. KILLEN, D.D., ASSEMBLY COLLEGE,
BELFAST, IRELAND.

IT is obvious from the New Testament that the primitive Church was occasionally disturbed by the teaching of errorists. We learn, however, from the testimony of the earliest witnesses, that so long as any of the inspired heralds of the Gospel survived, the propagators of false doctrine made no considerable impression on the Christian community. Hegesippus tells us that until the death of Simeon of Jerusalem—an event which occurred not long after the commencement of the second century—"the Church continued as a pure and uncorrupted virgin." "If there were any at all," says he, "who attempted to pervert the right standard of saving instruction, they were yet skulking in dark retreats; but when the sacred company of the Apostles had, in various ways, finished their career, and the generation of those who had been privileged to hear their inspired wisdom had passed away, then at length the fraud of false teachers produced a confederacy of impious errors." Celsus, an early infidel writer of the same period, gives the same report as to the primitive followers of our Lord. At first, he informs us, they were agreed in sentiment, but in his days, when "spread out into a multitude," they became "divided and distracted, each aiming to give stability to his own faction."

All accounts concur in the statement that towards the middle of the second century, or the beginning of the reign

* From advance copy of "The Framework of the Church," contributed by Pres. Killen.

of Antoninus Pius, the heretics seriously imperilled the peace
and purity of the Church. Appearing almost simultaneously
in several of the great cities of the empire, they exerted
themselves with wonderful activity to obtain positions of influence among the disciples. The dangers to be apprehended
from them were of the most formidable character. Their
leaders were men of ready eloquence and of high literary
culture; and they so mixed up their corrupt philosophical
speculations with the truths of Christianity as to render
them very attractive to many minds. In Rome, the capital
of the western world, the errorists appeared in large numbers. Here Valentine, Cerdo, Marcion, Marcus and others
were making converts. Instead of laboring diligently to
counterwork these enemies of the faith by the legitimate appliances prescribed in Scripture, the Church, in an evil hour,
proposed to put them down by a new agency of her own
devising. The Christian brotherhood had hitherto been
governed " by the common council of the presbyters"; but
it was now thought right to modify this system, so " that one
chosen from among the presbyters should be put over the
rest," " that the seeds of schism might be taken away." It
would appear that the new polity originated in the chief city
of the empire. Hence Hyginus, who was then its most influential presbyter, is said, in a book written by one of his
successors fully two centuries afterwards, to have "arranged
the clergy, and distributed the gradations."

The preservation of the unity of the Church was the
grand object contemplated by this ecclesiastical movement.
We have reason to believe that it was not accomplished
without considerable murmuring; but the influential position of the parties by whom it was inaugurated gradually
succeeded in overcoming all opposition. The presiding
presbyter now assumed the title of *bishop*, and his former
colleagues were permitted for a time to retain a large portion
of their power; but, by yielding to the principle that nothing

whatever could be done without the approval of their chief, they prepared the way for their final and complete subordination. In primitive times the Eucharist might have been celebrated at the same hour, at various places by the presbyters scattered throughout a large city; and, under such circumstances, it was difficult to prevent its dispensation to heretics by accommodating administrators. To avoid this scandal, it was now arranged that the elements should be consecrated only in the principal church, or the place where the presiding presbyter was present; and that they should be sent from thence to communicants assembled elsewhere, by the hands of trusted officials. Long afterwards this rule continued to be observed. The bishop was henceforth to be recognized as the centre of catholic unity, and his sanction was deemed necessary to give validity to all ecclesiastical ordinances. He endeavored, as far as possible, to appropriate their performance to himself. Baptism was regarded as a rite, which it was his peculiar privilege to dispense. In the sixth century the clergy of Italy complained to the Emperor Justinian, that, owing to the vacancy of sees, an immense multitude of people died without its benefit. The bishop was also most anxious to reserve to himself the blessing of the communion elements. Even in the fifth century the presbyters of Rome did not consecrate the Eucharist in their respective churches; but it was sent to them from the cathedral.

We may see from these facts that the introduction of episcopacy produced a wonderful alteration in the face of the Christian commonwealth. The presbyters became more and more subservient to the bishop, and at length almost ceased to dispute his will. That intellectual freedom, so conducive to a healthful state of public sentiment, could no longer be well asserted; for timorous presbyters were slow to ventilate convictions which might not find favor with their ecclesiastical chief. Under the very plausible pretence of conserving the unity of the Church, liberty of discussion was discouraged; and the bishop resisted with the utmost firmness all attempts to challenge or circumscribe his own newly-acquired privileges. Thus it was that at length he appropriated almost the whole of the ecclesiastical power.

It is not a little remarkable that this deviation from the primitive polity commenced in a city whose chief pastor has ever since aimed at spiritual supremacy. What was called " the Catholic Church " now took its rise. This great confederation—including all pastors throughout Christendom holding what were called catholic principles—was gradually consolidating. The leading bishops signified their adherence to it by sending the Eucharist to each other. From the very first, Rome was recognized as at the head of the organization. Irenæus, who was living at the period of its formation, shortly afterwards proclaimed the primacy of Rome in a passage which has long enjoyed historical celebrity. "To this Church," says he, "because it is more potentially principal, it is necessary that every catholic Church should go, as in it the apostolic tradition has, by the Catholics, been always preserved." The pastor of Lyons had recently been under special obligations to the Roman bishop, and he here speaks in exaggerated terms of the deference due to him. The primacy at first conceded implied nothing more than a complimentary precedence; but the Italian chief pastor and his partisans had no idea of confining it within such narrow dimensions; and not half a century had elapsed from its commencement when the imperious Victor astonished all around him by the assertion of a spiritual dictatorship. During the Paschal controversy, towards the close of the second century, he threatened with ex-communication the Churches of Asia Minor when they departed, as he conceived, from the principle of catholic unity. His arrogance surprised and irritated those who differed from him—for such a high-handed proceeding was quite unprecedented—and they treated it with contempt; but Victor could plead, notwithstanding, that he was contending for a catholic principle, as he was seeking to create and maintain unity and uniformity throughout the Catholic world. In the middle of the following century, his successor, Stephen, pursued exactly the same policy, when he excommunicated Cyprian of Carthage and others, who differed from him as to the rebaptism of heretics. Cyprian, no doubt, considered that the Roman bishop was attempting a most unwarrantable stretch of power; and yet he might have found it exceedingly difficult, in a strictly logical argument, to defend his nonconformity. Ever since the Catholic Church had been formed, ingenuity had been at work to invent plausible reasons for its constitution, and much sophistry had been permitted to pass unchallenged. A new meaning had been discovered for the text, "Thou art Peter, and upon this rock will I build my Church." These words have been expounded by a member of the Church of Rome, in a work written towards the middle of the second century; and it is there stated that the Rock is Christ; but the flatterers of the chief pastor of Christendom now extracted from it quite another interpretation, and stoutly maintained that the rock meant Peter. Cyprian incautiously accepted this foolish meaning, and thus placed himself in a position from which it was no easy matter to vindicate his consistency. For if Peter is the Rock on which the Church is built, and if the Bishop of Rome inherits his prerogatives as his successor and his representative, it may be impossible for us to tell how we are to limit the boundaries of his jurisdiction. Cyprian has made other statements from which we may see that he must have felt no small embarrassment when disputing with Stephen. He speaks of "the See of Peter" as the source "*whence the unity of the priesthood took its rise,*" and he describes the Roman bishopric as "*the root and womb of the Catholic Church.*"

We have intimated that the doctrine of ministerial parity was not relinquished without a struggle. It was not to be expected that the presbyters would all at once consent to the appointment of an ecclesiastical superior. But the dread of the spread of heresy, the hope that the new government would arrest its progress, and the influence and ability of the leading Churchmen in the great towns, eventually surmounted all opposition. Polycarp of Smyrna was still living when the system was inaugurated, and he had evidently been alarmed when he heard of this new departure in ecclesiastical discipline. He had great weight of character, as he was everywhere respected for his piety and wisdom; and there are good grounds for believing that the alteration did not meet the approval of the venerable Asiatic presbyter. Though sinking under the weight of years, he travelled all the way from Smyrna to Rome, that he might remonstrate with its bishop Anicetus Irenæus, who relates the story of this journey, but who was in favor of the new arrangements, passes over the chief cause of it in suspicious silence. He tells us that Polycarp and Anicetus "immediately agreed, without any disputation," on the Paschal question; but he acknowledges, that "as to *certain other matters they had a little controversy.*" What these " other matters " were which they left unsettled may be confidently conjectured. They plainly related to questions of ecclesiastical rank. Anicetus, we are told, tried to remove the scruples of Polycarp by inviting him to preside at the celebration of the Lord's Supper in the Roman Church. He thus obviously wished to suggest to him that he might still be considered as his ecclesiastical peer. But it would seem that the pastor of Smyrna was not content with this concession. Such a piece of courtesy was commonly rendered, as a matter of course, by one pastor to another who happened to be present in the congregation. But Anicetus on this occasion merely undertook to perform an act of condescension, in the hope of conciliating an in-

fluential stranger, at a time when the Catholic system had
not yet obtained a very firm footing. Polycarp, in consequence, returned home far from satisfied. It is a significant fact that Presbyterian Church government continued
in Smyrna for at least five-and-twenty years after his death.
When Noetus, towards the end of the second century, was
promulgating his errors relating to the Trinity, he was encountered, not by a bishop, but by the presbyters of the
place. Hippolytus, who was a contemporary, thus describes
the proceeding: "When *the blessed presbyters* [of Smyrna]
heard these things [that is, the heretical sentiments of
Noetus], *they summoned him, and examined him before the
Church.* . . . He, however, denied, saying at first that
such were not his sentiments. But afterwards, when he had
intrigued with some, and had found persons to join him in
his error, he took courage, and at length resolved to stand
by his dogma. *The blessed presbyters again summoned him,
and administered a rebuke.* But he withstood them. . . .
Then they *rebuked him, and cast him out of the Church.*"
Throughout this whole transaction no bishop makes his
appearance. Presbyterianism was evidently still the form
of government in the Church of Smyrna.

The establishment of the principle that, with a view to the
conservation of ecclesiastical unity, one of the presbyters or
elders should be set over the rest, operated somewhat differently in cities and in rural districts. In cities the presiding
presbyter, now called the bishop, acquired increased power
over a large congregation, or, it might be, over a number of
congregations; in rural districts, where the disciples were
thinly scattered, the presiding elder obtained only a small
addition to his authority as pastor of a single flock. As he
had heretofore conducted a large part of the public service,
he had already attained considerable influence, so that the
new arrangements produced no very marked change in his
situation. Meanwhile the city and the country bishops held

the same rank, and discharged the same ecclesiastical functions. But in reality they occupied very different positions. When Constantine set up Christianity as the religion of the empire, the distinction between them became still more conspicuous. The bishop of a metropolis was a rich dignitary, mingling on equal terms with the great officers of government; whilst the country bishop was not unfrequently an individual in needy circumstances, supported by the stipend of a poor congregation. Equality of ecclesiastical rank under such circumstances could not be long expected to continue. The city bishops soon began to complain of the anomaly, for they felt the country bishops to be so many thorns in their sides, curbing their ambition and preventing the enlargement of their jurisdiction. The general establishment of metropolitans, about the time of the Council of Nice in A.D. 325, prepared the way for their disappearance; for they were thus placed under the supervision of a class of prelates who looked on them with little favor. They had, shortly before, been distinguished by a new name—that of *chorepiscopi*—in token of their inferior status; and they had been forbidden, by a council held at Ancyra in A.D. 314, to ordain presbyters or deacons. Throughout the whole of the fourth century we may trace a continuous effort, on the part of city bishops, to accomplish their extinction. This was not easily effected, as their numbers rendered them very formidable. We meet with as many as fifty chorepiscopi in a single diocese. But they were gradually rooted out under the operation of canons passed by councils composed almost exclusively of city bishops. Thus, the Council of Sardica, held about A.D. 343, decreed that " a bishop be not ordained in a village or small city, *where a single presbyter is sufficient*, lest the name and authority of a bishop be brought into contempt." Again, the Council of Laodicea, held, as it is thought, about A.D. 360, enacted that " bishops ought not to be appointed in villages and rural districts, but visiting presbyters, and that those already appointed do nothing without the sanction of the city bishop." In the end they were entirely suppressed. "In the Council of Chalcedon," says Bingham, "in the fifth century, we find the chorepiscopi sitting and subscribing in the name of the bishops that sent them. But this was some diminution of their power; for in former councils they subscribed in their own names, as learned men agree; but now their power was sinking, and it went on to decay and dwindle by degrees, till at last, in the ninth century, when the forged decretals were set on foot, it was pretended that they were not true bishops; and so the order, by the pope's tyranny, came to be laid aside in the Western Church."

The Council of Nice in A.D. 325 recognized the Bishop of Rome, the Bishop of Alexandria, and the Bishop of Antioch as the three most distinguished prelates of the Church; and henceforward the status of bishops was regulated by the rank of the cities or provinces of the empire with which they were connected. When Constantinople was made the capital of the East, its bishop was not long afterwards placed almost on a level with the chief pastor of the ancient metropolis of Italy; and subsequently the struggles of these two dignitaries for superiority created confusion throughout all Christendom. Their disputes terminated in a settled estrangement of the Greek and Latin Churches.

Had the disciples continued, as at first, to be governed by the common council of the presbyters, they never could have witnessed the unseemly spectacle of two spiritual potentates contending for supremacy. By permitting one of the presbyters to be set over the rest and invested with a certain amount of irresponsible authority, the Church bartered true freedom for a mechanical and deceptive unity. It was vain to speak of unity in the midst of theological broils. In the end presbyters and people were reduced to a state of complete enslavement. The people lost the right of electing their office-bearers, and of thus controlling the government of the Church. The presbyters forfeited their most valued privileges, and even the bishops themselves were made to feel their helplessness under the pressure of an overbearing despotism. It is instructive to observe how one false step led the way to others still more dangerous. When one presbyter was raised above his fellows, arguments had to be sought for to justify his promotion. It was now discovered that the deacons, the presbyters, and the bishops had their counterparts in the Levites, the priest, and the high priest of the Jewish hierarchy. In one most important point the parallelism entirely failed, for the one high priest of Israel was matched against the countless array of city and country bishops in the Christian Church. But the advocates of the new polity attempted, by an odd style of mystical ratiocination, to get over the difficulty. They maintained that there was one episcopate, consisting of homogeneous bishops, diffused over the earth. They tried also, by changing the current terminology, to adapt present circumstances to their theory. The *presbyter* began to be called a *priest;* the *communion table* was styled the *altar;* and at length the *Lord's Supper* itself was designated a *sacrifice.* The priests and Levites had succeeded each other in the way of hereditary descent; it was now maintained that true ministers must be known by their apostolical succession. No matter what might be the excellence of a pastor, it was contended that he could not dispense valid ordinances, if he was not in communion with the bishops who presided over what was called the Catholic Church. The hierarchy was thus formed into a close corporation, claiming exclusive possession of the keys of the kingdom of Heaven; the people were reduced to such a state of impotence that they could make no movement with a view to the recovery of their ecclesiastical freedom; and they were taught to regard the clergy as mediators between God and themselves, so that without their services they were in danger of eternal perdition. The new terms descriptive of the Lord's Supper were at length literally interpreted—the sacramental elements were regarded as the real body and blood of Christ, and idolatry in its grossest form was patronized. At the time of the Reformation the Church presented a sad scene of ignorance, disorder, sensuality and will-worship. Prelacy opened the door for popery; and popery took away the Book of Life, led millions blindfolded into the house of bondage, and fed them on the husks of her own superstitions.

In discussing this subject it has been deemed unnecessary to take any notice of the epistles attributed to Ignatius. They are of the same class of writings as the spurious decretals. They appeared in the early part of the third century, along with a crowd of other forgeries evidently fabricated in the interest of prelacy. It is truly wonderful that some learned men are still befooled by these miserable impostures.

It may be well, before closing this discussion on the merits of diocesan episcopacy, to add a very few reflections. From the account just given of its rise and progress, it must be obvious that it can lay claim to high antiquity. Its germs appeared about half a century after the last survivor of the twelve Apostles had finished his career. At first it presented itself in a very elementary form, but it gradually acquired strength; and in less than three hundred years after the apostolic age, it had established itself throughout the greater part of Christendom. For well-nigh fourteen hundred years afterwards it securely retained its position. On the ground of the length of time during which it has been the recognized polity of what was called the Catholic Church, it has, therefore, an undoubted claim to respectful consideration.

It is farther noteworthy that the growth of prelacy was associated with the progress of Church corruptions. Its establishment promoted a species of artificial unity; but it also contributed to the advancement of intellectual and spiritual stagnation. The bishops soon appropriated the whole of the ecclesiastical government; the inferior clergy were obliged to obey their behests; the people were reduced to a condition of stupid serfdom, and religion was made to consist mainly in the monotonous observance of rites and ceremonies. The corruptions of the Church had reached their climax when it had attained the highest point of outward uniformity. At the dawn of the Reformation *one man* swayed his ecclesiastical sceptre over Western Christendom; *one language* was there used in the services of the sanctuary; and *one liturgy* was everywhere in use. But, meanwhile, a darkness that might be felt reigned all around.

The past history of the Church also suggests that the revival of religion appears to have been always associated with the decay of prelatic influence. Every enlightened Protestant must acknowledge that the fall of the Romish power in so many countries of Europe in the sixteenth century was the result of a remarkable outpouring of the Spirit of God; and yet it is notorious that prelacy, as well as popery, was shaken to its foundations by the great revolution. In the seventeenth century we see the same principle illustrated. In the days of the Solemn League and Covenant there was doubtless a great spiritual awakening throughout England as well as Scotland; and in many places true religion exhibited its power most significantly in a general reformation of morals, and in a thirst, before unknown, for scriptural information; but at the same time prelacy was swept away by public authority as an ecclesiastical nuisance. And in all the great revivals which have since occurred, either in Europe or America, prelacy has lost ground. The episcopal power has been often put forth to check the manifestations of religious earnestness; and the sameness of its ritual has been found to be totally unfitted for the Church when visited with times of refreshing from the presence of the Lord.

We cannot, however, conclude these remarks without admitting that, notwithstanding all the abatements we have mentioned, the Episcopal Church has produced not a few very noble specimens of vital Christianity. Who can remember the names of Ussher, and Bedell, and Bickersteth, and Marsh, and Roe, and M'Ilvaine, and a host of others, without making such an acknowledgment? Let us then beware of attaching undue importance to the fact of our ecclesiastical position. The outward framework of a Church may be constructed according to the apostolic pattern, when all within may be rottenness and death. The tabernacle of old might have been reared up in right proportions; it might have had every board, and every curtain, and every pin appointed for it; and yet had it been destitute of what did not meet the eye; had it wanted the ark, and the mercy-seat, and the cloud of the divine presence, and the comfort administered by the promises to faithful worshippers, it would have been desolate indeed. Though a Church may be fitly framed together in its ecclesiastical arrangements, still, without the indwelling of the Spirit, it wants the glory that excelleth. When it is proved that it has a form of government promulgated by the Apostles, many may not be able to appreciate the argumentation; but when it appears that its ministers are still animated by the spirit of Apostles, a testimony is presented in its favor which may be known and read of all men. Let it then be the care of all associated with a scriptural polity to furnish it with such a recommendation. Let them seek to illuminate the Church with the light of holy living, and so to execute the great commission of the ministry that onlookers may be disposed to say of them: "These men are the servants of the Most High God, which show unto us the way of salvation."

PROOFS OF A THREEFOLD ORDER OF THE CHRISTIAN MINISTRY.

BY J. F. SPALDING, D.D., PRESIDENT OF ST. JOHN'S COLLEGE AND BISHOP OF COLORADO.

THE subject is stated as assigned. I should put it differently, following the language of the preface to the Ordinal:* "It is evident unto all men diligently reading Holy Scripture and ancient authors, that from the Apostles' time, there have been these orders of ministers in Christ's Church—Bishops, Priests and Deacons." Thus, it would be more accurate to say the "three orders," rather than the "threefold order." However, the meaning intended is the same; just as we may say the threefold personality of God, or the three persons in the Godhead. It may be more than a pious fancy that the ground of a threefold ministry, as of all Fatherhood and all sonship, and indeed of society and all essential social relations and of government, is in the Godhead; as would seem to have been in the thought of that great Syrian bishop, Ignatius of Antioch, the most pronounced asserter or champion of the exclusive claims of the episcopacy. (Mag. xiii., Tral. xii., Smyr. viii.)

But it does not concern us to put forth now any doctrine of the three orders of the ministry. We are neither to show why there should be three orders, nor what doctrine or principles may be involved. Our business is only with facts. Are there three orders in the ministry? Is the threefoldness of order in the ministry a fact? Does it *characterize* the ministry? Is it, therefore, found in the Apostles'

*See Preface to Ordination Service in the American and English Prayer Books.

time, in the primitive Church, in the Church of the Nicene and the other general councils, and in all subsequent ages except so far as the unity of the Church was violated and the threefold order departed from, at and since the Reformation of the sixteenth century? We are to seek simply the proofs of the facts and not to propound theories or inferences from the facts.

It is important to observe that we are to seek the proofs of the facts concerning the ministry, whether in one order or three orders, *wherever such proofs may be found*. It is not necessary, in proving facts in regard to the beginnings or progress of Christianity, to confine ourselves to the records of Holy Scripture. Facts are just as truly facts when found recorded in what people used to call profane, as in sacred history. Proofs of facts are just as valid when derived from early ecclesiastical writers as from writers of Scripture. It is strange that so obvious a statement should need to be made or proved; and yet there are men, even in these times, who bitterly resent attempts to prove facts in the structure of the ministry, or in the customs or ritual or sacraments of the Church from any sources outside the New Testament. They will say that it is of no consequence whatever whether the *Didache* or any of the apostolic or early fathers use language that shows infants to have been baptized, for example; or Apostles to have been continued as a higher order than presbyters (presbyter-bishops). All such proofs, they contend, are irrelevant if not impertinent. "To the law and to the testimony" they urge. "The Bible and the Bible only" must be the source of all knowledge of facts pertaining to Christianity, at least in its earliest period! If I remember rightly, at least one writer in your valuable magazine manifests something of this tendency. Hence, we must remind our readers of the true relations of the Scriptures to the Church. Is it not yet generally known, that the Christian Church was most flourishing, was teaching a definite faith (creed), administering her great sacraments, preaching her Gospel of the kingdom, and extending herself throughout the world, when as yet there was no New Testament? Is it not well known that the Apostles and leaders of the Church wrote the books of the New Testament as occasion required, beginning more than a score of years after the Pentecostal baptism, and continuing till the Apostle St. John wrote his Gospel, almost at the end of the first century? The New Testament books cannot be expected to contain a prescribed constitution for the Church, or any other than incidental references to the Church and ministry as already existing. Dr. Ladd, in his recent work, "What is the Bible?" brings out clearly, what is so familiar to Churchmen, that both in the order of thought and of fact the Church is first. "The ever living Church of God is in a most important and valid meaning of these words both before and over the Bible." "The Church in the past has brought the Bible into being" (p. 415). The Church, needing the Bible, wrote it. The Bible is the invaluable, indispensable record of God's calling of His people, His revelations to them, His guidance of them through their history. The New Testament is the like record of Jesus Christ, His incarnation, teaching and works, His death, resurrection and ascension, coming, sending His Holy Spirit, His Church, the facts on which it is founded, and the teaching and life it embodies. Possibly you might be able to prove any Christian usage or any important fact about the ministry from Scripture, or you might not. The Church has had a continuous history. If you find references to the usage or fact in question, in early Christian writers, references that are clear and unmistakable, in writers of the highest character for veracity and competency of information, you must accept such proof as valid. To reject it because not scriptural proof is the height of folly and absurdity.

On this subject of the threefold ministry the proof from Scripture is abundant, and the proof from history or from ecclesiastical writers later than those who wrote the New Testament books is also abundant and equally conclusive. Both sources of proof should be considered, to give anything like an adequate impression of the full strength of the evidence.

In investigating any subject, it is necessary to proceed on some hypothesis. If the facts shall be found to be accordant with or to sustain the hypothesis, and there is no other satisfactory explanation of them, the hypothesis is considered proved. So scientists proceed in their investigations. Thus was proved the working hypothesis of the Copernican system, of the law of gravitation, of the nebular theory; and now many think that they have verified, or soon will completely verify, the theory or hypothesis of evolution.

In the same way we must pursue historical studies if we would attain the best results.

With what theory in our minds shall we undertake the investigation of the threefoldness or parity of order in the ministry? I think, taking the accepted modern historical method, we must assume as true, provisionally, or as a working hypothesis, the threefold ministry, or what is called from its highest order, episcopacy. If the facts do not bear out or substantiate this theory or hypothesis, then it must be rejected and another tried, and so on, till that hypothesis shall be found with which all the facts agree.

Why must we assume this as a working theory? Because all competent men admit that, at least from the second century, the ministry was in three orders, and that from then onwards, episcopacy was in possession everywhere. (The question only arises in regard to the highest order, everybody admitting the facts of the orders of presbyters and deacons.) The presumption certainly is that episcopacy was earlier than the second century, that it was in fact apostolic. The true historical method, therefore, requires us to examine all the facts, in view of this hypothesis, and see whether it is substantiated by them or not. It is presumptively true. The *onus* of proof is upon those who deny it. Let us test it. Let us see whether it will sustain all the facts and whether all the facts substantiate it.

Great confusion has resulted from taking an unhistorical method, and trying to fit the facts to some modern theory of what might or ought to have been the origin or character of the ministry. In such case it will be found that a large mass of facts of primary significance must be set aside and ignored. For example, Mosheim, Neander, Gieseler, Hasé, etc., ignore the apostolic office, except while the twelve and St. Paul were living, though most of these admit episcopacy to have existed under the eye and authority of the Apostles.

One of the most instructive examples of the unhistorical method of working on theoretical assumptions, which have no likelihood of truth, that I have happened to notice, is seen in the latest translation of Eusebius' Ecclesiastical History, with very full and learned notes, which forms part of the first volume of the second series of the Post Nicene Library of the Fathers. For example, he invariably translates *Paroikia* as parish. Thus he makes the writer speak of the parish of Alexandria, the parish of Antioch, the parish of Cæsarea, of Jerusalem, of Rome, etc. Thus he is guilty of a curious and amusing anachronism, if so it may be called. If the reader will examine the article " Parish " in Smith and Cheetham's Dictionary of Christian Antiquities, by E. H. (Edwin Hatch), a very free writer on ecclesiastical organization, he will see the absurdity of this apparently disingenuous attempt to carry back the modern parish into apostolic and primitive times, and thus to suggest Presbyterianism as the first form of the Christian ministry (a form which, somehow or other, very early had to be set aside, if it ever existed, though no notice or record of its having existed or been set aside has come down to us). The first meaning of the word *Paroikia* was diocese, and so it should have been translated. The second meaning was "the rural or suburban district, dependent more or less upon the bishop's church," where the presbyter or deacon was placed, and which the bishop sometimes visited. Eusebius, in several places, the Apostolic Canons, those of Ancyra, and of Nice, and a host of writers, identify the *Paroikia* with the diocese. "Where the Roman organization prevailed the parish was the *pagus, vicus* or *castellum* with its surrounding *territorium*." In England the Roman organization was swept away and "the parish was identical with the township or manor." (See art. "Parish," by E. H., as above.) The English parish, from which we get the idea and the fact of parishes, was first introduced by Archbishop Theodore in the latter part of the seventh century! This same writer makes other like blunders from his unhistorical and unproved assumptions. Thus, admitting the correctness of Eusebius' lists of the succession of bishops in all the chief apostolic sees, as at Rome, Linus, Cletus, Clement, Everestus, etc., at Alexandria, St. Mark, Annianus, Abialus, Cergon, etc., at Antioch, St. Peter, Evodius, Ignatius, Hero, etc., at Jerusalem, St. James, Symeon, etc.,admitting, too, most fully that episcopacy prevailed over the period and the areas covered by the history; that is to say, throughout the whole Christian world, at and from near the beginning of the second century onwards into the Nicene period, he yet evades the force of this evidence by the bare, unverified assertion that it was the custom of the writers of the second and third centuries to carry back the forms of organization of their own days into apostolic times. Surely such a theory might be tested. It could not be difficult, *e g.*, to examine St. Paul's Epistles to Timothy and Titus, and see whether the teaching agrees, in the matter of the orders of the ministry, with second and third century facts.

It has been attempted to deny St. Paul's authorship of the Pastoral Epistles and to place their origin in the middle of the second century for no other reason than that they assume the three orders of the ministry or episcopacy as then prevailing. But there being reasons enough outside this question for attributing these Epistles to the great Apostle, is it not far more reasonable to suppose the threefold ministry existing in St. Paul's time, rather than to deny the authenticity and genuineness of these precious documents? One or the other of these alternatives is necessary. Either that St. Paul wrote these epistles, and hence episcopacy belongs to his times, or else that episcopacy is a second century growth, and hence St. Paul could not have written these epistles. Conservative Christians much prefer, and indeed, insist upon, the former alternative.

Again, this learned translator admits that St. James had a position of eminence at Jerusalem, but asserts that he could not have been the bishop of that first see or diocese for the incomprehensible reason that he is classed with Peter and John as pillars (see page 104, note). One would think that this disciple, who was probably not an apostle in the sense of being one of the twelve, was a pillar equally with the chief of the Apostles, for the very reason that he was bishop of the earliest of the apostolic Churches or dioceses. On no other ground can we conceive it possible that he should be called a pillar of the Church.

Thus this learned, and, in the main, most accurate translator of the " Father of Ecclesiastical History," falls into the most serious mistakes from his unhistorical presumptions and inapplicable modern theories, suggesting inferences that are without plausibility, and are in the teeth of undeniable or well authenticated facts.

Others make a distinction, which is altogether without

reality, and contrary to facts, between the missionary and diocesan episcopacy, as if the same bishop could not be, and has not been, both, at one and the same time, and by turns. In every country, on planting and organizing the Gospel of the kingdom, the bishop is first an apostle, one sent, or a missionary bishop. Then as success attends his labors and those of his clergy and people, he may be able to settle down in a limited field or a diocese, or form dioceses out of his large missionary jurisdiction. An apostle, or a missionary bishop, if a missionary bishop may be called an apostle, is no different as bishop, from one who does not move about in so wide an area, but is in charge of a diocese.

The question is, Are there functions to be performed by the bishop, whether a missionary bishop like the first Apostles, a regionary bishop as some were called in the early middle ages, or bishop of a diocese, which presbyters and deacons cannot perform ? Or as St. Jerome, when angry with the bishops, and trying to disparage them, asks: "What can a bishop do which a presbyter cannot do, excepting ordination ?" He has to except ordination and all that it involves. (Ep. cxlvi. Ad. Evangelum.) For minimize the difference as he may, there is about him everywhere in the Church, east and west, in Alexandria, as everywhere else, an order of bishops, regarded as successors of the Apostles, and there has been such an order from the Apostles' times; for he attributes its institution to the Apostles, and asserts that this order has functions which distinguish it from that of presbyters. There have been many different sorts, as different titles, of bishops, bishops of large dioceses and small, of the country and the city, bishops roving and stationary, or missionary and diocesan, bishops who were princes, and bishops assistant or suffragan. But all bishops *as such* had the power to ordain ministers of all orders, as well as powers of supervision, wanting in all other ministers.

Controversial writers ought to be very careful how they

carry their modern theoretical notions, such as facts do not sustain, back into early ecclesiastical history, and attempt to interpret the fathers by these. The famous Dr. Miller, of Princeton, tried this and thought he could show the Church of Antioch and the Church of Alexandria to be Presbyterian, and Ignatius, Jerome, and one or two others like Aerius, to be advocates of ministerial parity. The terrible punishment he received from Dr. Bowden, and especially from Dr. Mines, ought forever to deter others from such unhistorical endeavors, however honest and sincere. (Bowden's letters to Dr. Miller on the Ministry, 2 vols.; Mines "Presbyterian Clergyman Looking for the Church.")

Now with the historical presumption for the threefold ministry in mind, let us examine the New Testament. What strikes us most prominently is that there is an order of apostles. This is certainly the prime fact. This is undeniable. The order of apostles is the chief and all-important order of the ministry. Then there are presbyters or elders called also bishops, and there are deacons. Here then we have on the face of the New Testament the three orders of ministers in the Apostolic Church—apostles, presbyter-bishops or elders, and deacons.

I submit it to the reader of whatever denomination to say whether or not it be true, that when it is maintained that there are only the orders of presbyters (presbyter-bishops) call them what you will, and of deacons, being as deacons clergymen or laymen, the Apostles themselves are not left entirely out of the reckoning. If so, will they also consider whether it be right thus to ignore the highest order of all, that of the Apostolate ; for clearly after Christ Himself, the Apostles are the source of ministry. "As My Father hath sent Me, even so send I you " (St. John xx. 21); and "Lo ! I am with you alway, even unto the end of the dispensation " (St. Matt. xxviii., 20); with them officially therefore, with their order, as they were not all personally to tarry till the Lord should come.

But here we encounter a peculiar theory, that there could be but twelve apostles, and that the Apostles could not have successors. They were to be witnesses of Christ's life on earth, to have known Him personally in the flesh, and to have seen Him risen from the dead. Of course in these things they could not have had successors, after the generation of Christians that was contemporary with them had passed away. But it was certainly possible, as it was also necessary and inevitable, that they should have successors in all their administrative functions, in all that was distinctive of their ministry, in teaching, governing, maintaining, perpetuating the ministry and the Church of God. And according to the inspired record they did in fact have successors. St. Matthias was made the successor of Judas, and was put in the place of his "Ministry and Apostleship" (Acts i., 25). It is too late now to say that this was a mistake. The Holy Ghost nowhere so tells us in the Acts or in the Epistles, nor was it ever suggested until the times when a sectarian motive made it desirable to show that Matthias was not an apostle, but that really St. Paul was made one of the twelve (!), a position which St. Paul evidently disclaims by insisting that he was made an apostle "not of men, neither by man, but by Jesus Christ and God the Father" (Gal. i., 1), and as much an apostle as any of the twelve who were before him. No theory can displace St. Paul from his position as the great Apostle to the Gentiles, and the head and source of lines of like apostles, beginning with his companions, whom he personally instructed and ordained.

St. James, even though not one of the twelve, was an apostle as being the Bishop of Jerusalem. As Clement of Alexandria testifies: "Peter, James and John did not contend for the honor of presiding over the Church at Jeru-

PROOFS OF A THREEFOLD ORDER IN THE MINISTRY. 83

salem, but chose James the Just to be bishop of that Church." Whatever has been or may be said to the contrary, that St. James was bishop of the mother Church, all competent modern scholars of all denominations may be said substantially to agree. All antiquity asserts this without any exception, and herein the testimony of antiquity has not been impeached.

Readers of the Greek Testament know that Barnabas, Andronicus, Junius, Epaphroditus, Timothy, Titus, Silas, Luke, are called apostles by St. Paul. There are others also, *e.g*, Dionysius, Gaius, Aristarchus, Antipas, Crescens, Evodias, Linus, Clement, Mark, Judas, Onesimus, the Angels of the Seven Churches of Asia, companions or pupils of apostles, whom early tradition, which there is no reason whatever for denying to be trustworthy, puts in the position of apostles, or successors of apostles. St. Jerome is esteemed a high authority. He was "the most learned man of the fourth century," and spent thirty years in the Holy Land. He says, speaking of James, in order to show that "others besides the twelve were called apostles," "by degrees, in process of time, others also were ordained apostles by those whom the Lord had chosen" (see in Tit. i., 5), Omnes (Episcopi) Apostolorum successores sunt. Ep. cxlvi. Ad. Evangelum.

It is supposed that the *Didache* belongs to the latter part of the first century. It is a semi-Jewish composition, probably from some obscure part of Syria, very crude, and with apparent germs of heresy in doctrine, simple even to absurdity, and not at all to be compared with any New Testament writing, nor with any of the so-called apostolic fathers; and yet this curious unauthentic document may, and doubtless does, witness to facts of custom, and even of polity, at the date to which it belongs; we find in it at any rate the three orders, apostles and prophets, apparently the same, the first and highest order, not yet in this part of the Church diocesan, but missionary in character, and with a roving commission, but who are to be "received as the Lord." Below these are the presbyters, still called bishops, as overseers of single flocks, and also deacons.

There is not time to discuss the teaching of St. Paul's Pastoral Epistles on this subject. It is sufficient to say that the Apostle enjoins upon these ministers to do, and ordains and appoints them to do, what presbyters have never been held competent to do, except post-Reformation presbyters in Presbyterian bodies; and that had any theory but the episcopal prevailed among the many congregations of Ephesus and of the hundred cities of Crete, most of which presumably had their churches, these men and their ministry would certainly have been rejected. (See the writer's work, "The Church and its Apostolic Ministry," pp. 109-113.) The writer of the article, "Bishop," in the Dictionary of Christian Antiquities, already referred to, after a most able and thorough discussion in the modern impartial historical spirit, concludes: "The episcopate, then, is historically the continuation, in its permanent elements, of the apostolate; and accordingly the reasons assigned for the actual appointment of the episcopate are (1) as given by St. Paul himself, to take the place of the apostles (Tim. i., 3; Titus i., 5), and for the better maintenance of the faith (*ib.*) and in order to a due ordination of the ministry (Titus i., 5). To these the fathers (2) add other reasons drawn apparently from their own experience of the benefits of the episcopate," etc.

So much for the highest order and its perpetuation in St. Paul's time. The second order is that of the elders or presbyter-bishops, about which, as being an order, there is no controversy.

Some recent writers against episcopacy or the threefold ministry have strangely asserted, as if it were a discovery of their own and fatal to the argument for the distinction of the first and second orders, that of late even the defenders of episcopacy have been constrained to admit that in the New Testament "bishop" and "presbyter" are used for the same persons! But this is what nobody ever denied. It is affirmed by Theodoret, Chrysostom, Hilary, Jerome, Clement, and many others, "Episcopalians a thousand years before the first non-episcopal church had been founded" (Little's Reasons). It is affirmed by all the modern Episcopal writers on this subject, Bowden, Onderdonk, Kip, Haddon, Lightfoot, Gore, Liddon, etc. It is strange indeed that there should be such lack of familiarity with the literature of the subject on the part of those who take the modern theoretical and unhistorical view as to how episcopacy may have arisen, without duly considering the facts as to its rise and prevalence.

We might go on with the New Testament proofs and show that the angels of the Seven Churches of Asia were the bishops of those Churches or dioceses. Thus there is but one angel of each church, and the responsibilities ascribed to him correspond remarkably with those which are enforced on Timothy and Titus by St. Paul in the Pastoral Epistles. They are real persons symbolized as stars, just as the churches they governed are real churches symbolized as candlesticks. They are seen to have been bishops by the analogy of Gal. i. 8, iv. 14, by their standing for and representing their several churches, by the fact credited by Clement of Alexandria, by St. Jerome, and see Eusebuis H. E. III., 23, and quite generally, that St. John is expressly stated to have appointed bishops from city to city in these very regions, and by the testimony of most of the fathers and of moderns when not writing in the interests of a theory. (See Dictionary of Christian Antiquities, art. "Angel.")

The scriptural proof ends with St. John the Apostle. The patristic begins with Ignatius, Bishop of Antioch, martyred at Rome not later than A.D. 110. Since Bishop Lightfoot's vindication, and also that of Zumpt in Germany, the genuineness of his seven short epistles can no longer be disputed. Let anyone read them without prejudice. Whoever does so must perforce admit that in his time there were the three orders which have ever since prevailed. The Ignatian bishop is not a presbyter-bishop; he is a bishop over presbyter-bishops and deacons; he is a Bishop in the historical sense.

Everybody knows the historian Gibbon's dictum—" Nulla Ecclesia, sine Episcopo " (see Cap. 15, notes 110, 111, 112). Surely, Gibbon was competent to know and was without ecclesiastical bias.

Guizot, the learned French protestant historian, says: "The Apostles themselves appointed several bishops. Tertullian, Clement of Alexandria, and many fathers of the second and third century do not permit us to doubt this fact." To sum up in the words of the learned Grotius, himself a Presbyterian: "The episcopacy had its commencement in the time of the Apostles. All the fathers, without exception, testify to this. The testimony of Jerome alone is sufficient. The catalogues of the bishops in Irenaeus, Socrates, Theodoret, and others, all of which begin in the apostolic age, testify to the same. To refuse credit in an historical matter to so great authorities and so unanimous among themselves is not the part of any but an irreverent and stubborn disposition." (See his "Annotations on the Consultations of Cassander" and his "Comments on Acts XIV.")

The challenge of the learned and proverbially judicious Hooker was never answered, " We require you to find out but one church upon the face of the whole earth that hath been ordered by your discipline or hath not been ordered by ours; that is to say, by episcopal regimen, since the time that the blessed Apostles were here conversant." Everybody interested in this subject should procure and read the latest translation of Eusebius, in the Nicene and Post-Nicene Library of the Fathers.

We will see that from Ignatius down, through Diognetus
A.D. 130, Hegesippus H. E. IV., 22; Dionysius, "the Holy
Bishop of Corinth " (H. E. IV., 23), who lived to A.D. 176;
Irenaeus, disciple of Polycarp, H. E. V., 24; Polycrates,
Bishop of Ephesus, A.D. 196, "sixty-five years of age in
the Lord "; Clement, Origen, Tertullian, Cyprian, etc., etc.,
etc., there is but one unvarying testimony, and there is
positively nothing to set against it. The threefold order is
established.

The proof of the Four Gospels and of the canon, and of
apostolic doctrine, depends on the succession of bishops in
the apostolic sees. (See Irenaeus, Haer iii., cap. iii.; Tertullian, Præscript, cap. xxxii., etc.) In reading Irenaeus and
a few other early fathers, it must be remembered that
bishops are sometimes called presbyters. In fact, every
apostle bishop is both presbyter and deacon as well, and
may be and sometimes is so called; but never does the reverse find place.

Dr. Salmon, author of the best introduction as yet to the
New Testament, writing in the *Expositor*, observes that
Church history after the time of the Apostles enters into
and passes through a tunnel, whence it emerges in the
second century; and there is only an air-hole here and
there by which the light is let in and the conditions of
progress are observable. The Church enters this tunnel
with its threefold ministry of apostles, presbyter-bishops
and deacons; shall we say at the time St. Paul wrote to
Timothy and Titus, and James, the Lord's brother, was
Bishop of Jerusalem? Or was it at the time of Symeon,
his successor, whose election and the reasons and circumstances thereof are well-known historical facts (Euseb. H.
E. iii., 4–9)? Or must it not be put still later, when St.
John comes back from Patmos and ordains bishops for
various cities, as Polycarp for Smyrna, and addresses seven
of these bishops as the angels of their churches? What-

ever moment the tunnel is entered, the train is well made up and is on schedule time. And it comes out in good condition and on schedule time on the other side, when Bishop Ignatius is being led to Rome and writes his seven short epistles, urging obedience to the bishop and the presbyters and deacons under them. Or will you put it later when Polycarp or Irenaeus or when Diognetus or Hegesippus wrote, or when the writing from which we have the "Muratorian fragment" appeared? Still it is in perfect order and on schedule time. Now shall we say that during its progress through the darkness of the tunnel it has been taken to pieces and reconstructed? Was it Presbyterian, or Congregationalist, or what not, for a brief period just before it entered or for a short space therein, though there be no record of such fact nor controversy about it? Did it get therein any new Scriptures and new doctrines and become something different from what it was, in organization and character? Or did it not rather continue what it had been under the Apostles and in the earliest authentic history that has come down to us? Why make the gratuitous and unreasonable supposition of change? It had the three orders when St. Paul, St. Peter, St. James and St. John were living. It has them in the second century. Therefore it follows that it has had them all along. Christian men lived in the second century who had been converted by Apostles. There has been no break; there is no missing link to be filled in; the memory of living men covers the whole period; there was no invention of new scriptures and doctrines. The train goes on majestically, uninterruptedly with its precious freight of scriptures, faith, government and worship. Here and there you can see it, or enough of it to know that it is unchanging, as it passes on, like the Lord Himself whom it proclaims.

The supposition that the Church of Christ which Mosheim, Hase, Neander, Kurtz, Schaff, and all the rest of the non-episcopal historians admit was episcopal almost from the beginning of the second century, and some of them much earlier, was Presbyterian or anything else in the first century, after the Apostles had departed, is without any foundation of fact to support it. It is only a theory of what might have been or what human ingenuity can conceive possible. It requires a reconstruction of the facts to suit it.

Dr. Chillingworth is much esteemed by Protestants for his famous dictum about "the Bible and the Bible only" as their "religion." The conclusion of his "unanswerable demonstration of episcopacy" is as worthy of being committed to memory and often repeated as is the last paragraph of Hooker's first Book on Law as having "its seat in the bosom of God" and "its voice" being "the harmony of the world": "When I shall see all the fables of the metamorphoses acted and prove true stories; when I shall see all the democracies and aristocracies in the world lie down to sleep and awake into monarchies, then will I begin to believe that Presbyterian government having continued in the Church during the Apostles' times, should presently after, against the Apostles' doctrine and the will of Christ, be whirled about, like a scene in a masque and transformed into episcopacy. In the meantime, while these things remain incredible and in human reason impossible, I hope I shall have leave to conclude thus:

"Episcopal government is acknowledged to have been universal in the Church presently after the Apostles' times. Between the Apostles' times and this presently after, there was not time enough for, nor possibility of, so great an alteration. And therefore there was no such alteration as is pretended, and therefore episcopacy, being confessed to be so ancient and catholic, must be granted also to be apostolic, *Quod erat demonstrandum.*"

PROOFS OF AN HISTORIC EPISCOPATE.

BY WILLIAM STEVENS PERRY, D.D., OXON., BISHOP OF
IOWA AND PRESIDENT OF GRISWOLD COLLEGE,
DAVENPORT.

THE critical examination of the New Testament writings for notices of the polity of the apostolic churches, plainly indicates that the ultimate earthly authority there recognized was that exercised by the Apostles, and that the means for the transmission of this authority was by the imposition of apostolic hands. In other words, the principle of individual overseership, or episcopacy, exercised by the Apostles first and by apostolic delegates afterwards, and gradually taking shape in more easily recognized and definite form, *is* found in the New Testament Scriptures, while we may search their pages in vain for any indication of the principle of Presbyterian parity or of Congregational democracy. Few and scattered as are the New Testament allusions to the polity of the Church in the days in which the Apostles were still present on the earth, the trend of each and all of these passages is evident. The source of power in the Church was not from the people or of the people. It was from above and in these scanty notices we see apostolic rule gradually merging into episcopal authority and power.

The exercise of the commission of their Master—"As the Father hath sent Me (ἀπέσταλκέ με), even so send I you (κἀγὼ πέμπω ὑμᾶς)"—by the Twelve, chosen not by the company of believers, but by the Lord Himself; the solemn investiture of Matthias, not by the people but by the Eleven acting under divine guidance, with the office (ἐπισκοπήν, margin, Revised Version, overseership) from which Judas fell; the choice of the great Apostle to the Gentiles by the great Head of the Church Himself—"an apostle not from men neither through men, but through Jesus Christ and God the Father";* the headship of the Church at Jerusalem, as well as the title of "apostle," so plainly accorded by St. Paul to "James the Lord's brother," who was evidently not one of the Twelve; the absence of any hint that the apostolate was to be limited to the Twelve, and on the other hand the application of the title to Barnabas,† to Andronicus and Junias,‡ probably to Silvanus ‖ and to

---

* Galatians i., 1.

† "The apostleship of Barnabas is beyond question. St. Luke records his consecration to the office as taking place at the same time with, and in the same manner as, St. Paul's (Acts xiii., 2, 3). In his account of their missionary labors he, again, names them together as 'Apostles,' even mentioning Barnabas first (Acts xiv., 4, 14). St. Paul himself also in two different epistles uses similar language. In the Galatian letter he speaks of Barnabas as associated with himself in the apostleship of the Gentiles (ii., 9); in the First to the Corinthians he claims for his fellow laborer all the privileges of an Apostle, as one who, like himself, holds the office of an Apostle and is doing the work of an Apostle (ix., 5, 6). If, therefore, St. Paul has held a larger place than Barnabas in the gratitude and veneration of the Church of all ages, this is due, not to any superiority of rank or office, but to the ascendancy of his personal gifts, a more intense energy and self-devotion, wider and deeper sympathies, a firmer intellectual grasp, a larger measure of the spirit of Christ."—Bp. Lightfoot's Epis. to the Galatians, pp. 96, 97.

‡ "On the most natural interpretation of a passage in the Epistle to the Romans (xvi., 7), Andronicus and Junias, two Christians otherwise unknown to us, are called distinguished members of the apostolate, language which indirectly implies a very considerable extension of the term."—Ibid, p. 96

‖ "In I. Thess. ii., 6, again, where . . . he speaks of the disinterested labors of himself and his colleagues, adding 'though *we* might have been burdensome to you, being Apostles of Christ,' it is probable that under this term he includes Silvanus, who had labored with him in Thessalonica, and whose name appears in the superscription of the letter."—Ibid.

others by St. Paul; the condemnation of "false apostles"; the committal by St. Paul of the charge of the churches he had founded to Timothy and Titus ; the latest messages of the Head of the Church not to the people but to the rulers, the "angels," the individually-responsible heads of the apocalyptic churches; these are each and all part of that vast net-work of scriptural testimony uniting with its countless meshes the Church's Chief Shepherd and Bishop of souls with the threefold ministry and the polity which, ere the death of the last of the Apostles, St. John, was universally established throughout the Church of Christ.

It is the judgment of the great Lightfoot, Bishop of Durham, whose recent death all good men deplore, that "history seems to show decisively that before the middle of the second century each Church or organized Christian community had its three orders of ministers, its bishop, its presbyters, and its deacons. On this point there cannot reasonably be two opinions."* The same distinguished scholar, in commenting on the position occupied by St. James, the brother of the Lord, in the Church of Jerusalem, after expressing his conviction that "he was not one of the Twelve," asserts that "the episcopal office thus existed in the mother church of Jerusalem from very early days, at least in a rudimentary form† "; while the government of the Gentile churches, though presenting no distinct traces of a similar organization, exhibits "stages of development tending in this direction." ‡ Lightfoot, who discusses this subject with singular moderation and fairness, concedes that the position occupied by Timothy and Titus, whom he styles "apostolic-delegates," "fairly represents the functions of the bishop early in the second century." ‖ Even admitting with Lightfoot that " James the Lord's brother alone,

---

*Bp. Lightfoot's Dissertation on The Christian Ministry, appended to his Commentary on the Philippians, p. 184.

† Lightfoot's Christian Ministry, p. 196. ‡ Ibid. ‖ Ibid, p. 197.

within the period compassed by the apostolic writings, can claim to be regarded as a bishop in the later and more special sense of the term," and that "as late, therefore, as the year 70 no distinct signs of episcopal government have appeared in Gentile Christendom," still it must be acknowledged, in the language of the same authority, that "unless we have recourse to a sweeping condemnation of received documents, it seems vain to deny that early in the second century the episcopal office was firmly and widely established. Thus, during the last three decades of the first century, and consequently during the lifetime of the latest surviving Apostle, this change must have been brought about." * Again and again does this great scholar refer to the fact of the early and general establishment of episcopacy "from the Apostles' times." For example, he asserts "that the evidence for the early and wide extension of episcopacy throughout proconsular Asia, the scene of St. John's latest labors, may be considered irrefragable." † And again, "these notices, besides establishing the general prevalence of episcopacy . . . establish this result clearly, that its maturer forms are seen first in those regions where the latest surviving Apostles, more especially St. John, fixed their abode, and at a time when its prevalence cannot be dissociated from their influence or their sanction."‡

And again, "It has been seen that the institution of an episcopate must be placed as far back as the closing years of the first century, and that it cannot, without violence to historical testimony, be dissevered from the name of St. John." ‖ "It will appear," continues Lightfoot, "that the pressing needs of the Church were mainly instrumental in bringing about this result, and that this development of the episcopal office was a providential safeguard amid the con-

---

* Lightfoot's Christian Ministry, p. 199.   † Ibid, p. 212.
‡ Ibid, pp. 225, 226.   ‖ Lightfoot's Christian Ministry, p. 232.

fusion of speculative opinion, the distracting effects of persecution, and the growing anarchy of social life, which threatened not only the extension but the very existence of the Church of Christ."* With this cumulative presentation of the proofs of the historic episcopate from the writings of the leading scholar of the age, we may be prepared for the Bishop's summing up of the whole matter among the closing words of his "Dissertation on the Christian Ministry": "If the preceding investigation is substantially correct, the threefold ministry can be traced to apostolic direction; and short of an express statement we can possess no better assurance of a Divine appointment or at least a Divine sanction.'† In even stronger language, this great scholar, in his sermon before the Wolverhampton Church Congress, asserts that the Church of England has "retained a form of Church government which had been handed down in unbroken continuity from the Apostles' times."

With these statements and these proofs, the language of the Ordinal of the Book of Common Prayer is in strict accord. "It is evident unto all men, diligently reading Holy Scripture and ancient authors, that from the Apostles' time there have been these three orders of ministers in Christ's Church—bishops, priests, and deacons." The full meaning of this statement appears in the fact that it is the requirement of the canon law of the Church as well as of the Ordinal that "no man shall be accounted or taken to be a lawful bishop, priest, or deacon, in this Church, or suffered to execute any of the said functions, except he be called, tried, examined, and admitted thereunto, according to the form hereafter following, or hath had episcopal consecration or ordination." In the judgment of Lightfoot, as evidently in the intention of the Ordinal, the "historic episcopate" includes the apostolic succession—the threefold

---

* Ibid.   † Page 265.

ministry communicated by the imposition of hands and continued "in unbroken continuity from the Apostles' times."

To quote the language of Mr. Gladstone, "In the latter part of the second century of the Christian era, the subject," of the Apostolic Succession "came into distinct and formal view; and from that time forward it seems to have been considered by the great writers of the Catholic body, a fact too palpable to be doubted, and too simple to be misunderstood."*

We have thus far dealt merely with the proofs of the historic episcopate as indicated in the New Testament and as existing during the lifetime of St. John. We turn to the witness of history to the fact that our Lord instituted in His Church, by succession from the Apostles, a threefold ministry, the highest order of these ministers alone having the authority and power to perpetuate this ministry by the laying on of hands.

The Church of Jerusalem, the mother of us all, as we have already seen, presents the earliest instance of a bishop in the sense in which the word was understood in post-apostolic times. The rule and official prominence of St. James, "the Lord's brother," is recognized both in the epistles of St. Paul and in the Acts of the Apostles. That which is so plainly indicated in the canonical Scriptures is supported by the uniform tradition of the succeeding age. On the death of St. James, which took place immediately before the war of Vespasian, Symeon succeeded to his place and rule. Hegisippus, who is our authority for this statement, and who represents Symeon as holding the same office with St. James and with equal distinctness styles him a bishop, was doubtless born ere Symeon died. Eusebius gives us a list of Symeon's successors. In less than thirty years,—such were the troubles and uncertainties of the

---

* Church Principles Considered in their Results. By W. E. Gladstone. p. 189.

times,—there appear to have been thirty occupants of the see. On the building of Ælia Capitolina on the ruins of of Jerusalem, Marcus presided over the Church in the Holy City as its first Gentile bishop; Narcissus, who became Bishop of Jerusalem in the year 190, is referred to by Alexander, in whose favor he resigned his see in the year 214, as still living at the age of 116,—thus in this single instance bridging over the period from the time when the Apostle John was still living to the date when, by universal consent, it is conceded that episcopacy was established in all quarters of the world.

Passing from the mother Church of Jerusalem to Antioch, where the disciples were first called Christians, and which may be regarded as the natural centre of Gentile Christianity, we find from tradition that Antioch received its first bishop from St. Peter. We need not discuss the probabilities of this story since there can be no doubt as to the name standing second on the list. Ignatius is mentioned as a bishop by the earliest authors. His own language is conclusive as to his own conviction on this point. He writes to one bishop, Polycarp. He refers by name to another, Onesimus. He contemplates the appointment of his successor at Antioch after his decease. The successor whose appointment Ignatius anticipated is said by Eusebius to have been Hero, and from his episcopate the list of Antiochene bishops is complete. If the authenticity of the entire catalogue is questionable, two bishops of Antioch, at least, during the second century, Theophilus and Serapion, are confessedly historical personages. With reference to the Epistles of Ignatius, controversy has raged for centuries. Their outspoken testimony in favor of episcopacy has been regarded by the advocates of parity or of independency as a proof of their want of authenticity. But the discussion has been practically settled in our own day, and the judgment of Lightfoot, the latest and greatest commentator on these interesting remains of Christian antiquity, will be received without question by all whose opinion is worthy of consideration. He places these epistles among the earliest years of the second century, and he regards the testimony of Ignatius to the existence and universality of the threefold ministry at the period in which he lived and wrote as conclusive. The celebrated German critic and scholar, Dr. Harnack, who characterizes Lightfoot's work as "the most learned and careful patristic monograph of the century," accepts the conclusions of the bishop and concedes that the genuineness of the Ignatian letters is rendered "certain." With such a witness, thus supported by scholars confessedly occupying the foremost place for learning and critical power, we may proceed to details.

In the Ignatian letters, the writer, the second Bishop of Antioch, appears as a condemned prisoner travelling through Asia to his martyrdom at Rome. Though each step of his progress brought him nearer to death; though the severity of his guard, "a maniple of ten soldiers," whom he designates as "leopards," makes his last days wretchedly uncomfortable, still his journey is a triumph. On his arrival at Smyrna, representatives of the churches of Ephesus, Magnesia and Tralles unite with the flock of Polycarp, the Bishop of Smyrna, to do him honor. During his stay at Smyrna the aged bishop addresses four of his extant epistles to the Ephesians, to the Magnesians, to the Trallians, and to the Romans. The remaining three epistles, those to the Churches of Philadelphia and Smyrna and to Polycarp its bishop, were written from Troas whither a deacon from Ephesus had borne him company. The saint proceeds from Neapolis to Philippi, where he is welcomed by the Church and escorted on his way, and thus he goes towards Rome. Though, in his modesty, choosing to speak of himself as "only now beginning to be a disciple," the nearness to the end evidently bringing to him new revelations of spiritual things and the life to come, he acts and writes as a man advanced in years. Doubtless he was near to man's estate when the great Apostle wrote his epistles. He must have been in full maturity when Jerusalem was trodden under foot of the Gentiles and the Church was driven from its cradle home. He in whose life all this had transpired, was now on his way to death. He fully realized that the end was near at hand. His days were numbered, and in his epistles he appears to have sought to crowd counsels of the highest moment, the dying legacy of one whose voice would soon be forever hushed in death. The points this aged saint chiefly dwells upon are two—the doctrine of the Incarnation, as an historic fact, as perpetuated in sacraments, as a fundamental principle of the faith, and the threefold ministry, the divinely-given rule for the Church, by which the Church itself would be recognized, and the religion of the Christ made known as something organic, real, lasting, disciplined.

In his statements of the prerogative of the threefold ministry, Ignatius is emphatic. "It is meet therefore . . . that being perfectly joined together in one submission, submitting yourselves to your bishop and presbytery, ye may be sanctified in all things." * " I was forward to exhort you, that ye run in harmony with the mind of God: for Jesus Christ also, our inseparable life, is the mind of the Father, even as the bishops that are settled in the farthest parts of the earth are in the mind of Jesus Christ. So then it becometh you to run in harmony with the mind of the bishop, which thing also ye do. For your honorable presbytery, which is worthy of God, is attuned to the bishop, even as its strings to a lyre." †

"Let no man be deceived. If any one be not within the

---

* Ad Eph., 2. In our citations we avail ourselves of Bishop Lightfoot's translations. † Ad Eph., 3, 4. Lightfoot's Translation.

precinct of the altar, he lacketh the bread [of God]. For, if the prayer of one and another hath so great force, how much more that of the bishop and of the whole Church. . . . Let us therefore be careful not to resist the bishop, that by our submission we may give ourselves to God. And in proportion as a man seeth that his bishop is silent, let him fear him the more. For every one whom the Master of the household sendeth to be steward over his own house, we ought so to receive as Him that sent him. Plainly, therefore, we ought to regard the bishop as the Lord Himself." *

"Assemble yourselves together . . . to the end that ye may obey the bishop and the presbytery without distraction of mind; breaking one bread, which is the medicine of immortality and the antidote that we should not die." †

"Forasmuch, then, as I was permitted to see you in the person of your godly Bishop Damas, and your worthy presbyters, Bassus and Apollonius, and my fellow-servant, the Deacon Sotion, of whom I would fain have joy, for that he is subject to the bishop as unto the grace of God and to the presbytery as unto the law of Jesus Christ. Yea, and it becometh you also not to presume upon the youth of your Bishop, but according to the power of God the Father to render unto him all reverence, . . . yet not to him but to the Father of Jesus Christ, even to the bishop of all. . . . For a man does not so much deceive this bishop who is seen, as cheat that other who is invisible." ‡

"Be ye zealous to do all things in godly concord, the bishop presiding after the likeness of God, and the presbyters after the likeness of the council of the Apostles, with the deacons also who are most dear to me, having been entrusted with the diaconate of Jesus Christ." ‖

"As the Lord did nothing without the Father, either by Himself or by the Apostles, so neither do ye anything without the bishop and the presbyters." §

---

* Ad Eph., 5, 6.   † Ibid, 20.   ‡ Ad Magn., 2, 3.   ‖ Ibid, 6.
§ Ibid, 7.

"Be obedient to the bishop and to one another, as Jesus Christ was to the Father. . . ."*

"When ye are obedient to the bishop as to Jesus Christ, it is evident to me that ye are living not after men, but after Jesus Christ. . . . It is therefore necessary, even as your wont is, that you should do nothing without the bishop; but be ye obedient also to the presbytery, as to the Apostles. . . . And those likewise who are deacons of the mysteries of Jesus Christ must please all men in all ways. . . . In like manner let all men respect the deacons as Jesus Christ, even as they should respect the Bishop as being a type of the Father, and the presbyters as the council of God and as the college of apostles. Apart from these there is not even the name of a Church." †

"This will surely be, if ye be not puffed up, and if ye be inseparable from [God] Jesus Christ, and from the bishop, and from the ordinances of the Apostles. He that is within the sanctuary in clean; but he that is without the sanctuary is not clean; that is, he that doeth aught without the bishop and presbytery and deacons, this man is not clean in his conscience." ‡

"Fare ye well in Jesus Christ, committing yourselves to the bishop as to the commandment, and likewise also to the presbytery." ||

"For as many as are of God and of Jesus Christ, they are with the bishop; and as many as shall repent and enter into the unity of the Church, these also shall be of God. . . . Be ye careful, therefore, to observe one Eucharist, for there is one flesh of our Lord Jesus Christ and one cup unto union in His Blood; there is one altar, as there is one bishop, together with the presbytery and the deacons, my fellow-servants." §

---

* Ibid, 13.   † Ad Trall, 2, 3.   ‡ Ibid, 7. || Ibid, 13.
§ Ad Philad., 3, 4.

"Shun divisions, as the beginning of evils. Do ye all follow your bishop as Jesus Christ followed the Father, and the presbytery as the Apostles; and to the deacons pay respect, as to God's commandment. Let no man do aught of things pertaining to the Church apart from the bishop. Let that be held a valid Eucharist which is under the bishop or one to whom he shall have committed it. Wheresoever the bishop shall appear, there let the people be; even as where Jesus may be, there is the universal Church. It is not lawful apart from the bishop either to baptize or to hold a love-feast, but whatever he shall approve; this is well-pleasing also to God, that everything which ye do may be sure and valid."*

"It is good to recognize God and the bishop. He that honoureth the bishop is honoured of God. He that doeth aught without the knowledge of the bishop rendereth service to the devil."†

There can be no question that the writer of these extracts held clear and well defined views both as to the existence of a visible, organized Church of Christ, and a threefold, divinely-authorized ministry ruling that Church. This he deems to be the "mind of God," this is "the commandment," and so fully does he hold these views that in his dying counsels he emphasized the idea that he who would keep the "commandment" and run in accord with the divine mind must lose sight of his very individuality in the fellowship of the Church, and unhesitatingly and without reserve submit himself in action, word, or purpose to the divinely-appointed rule and order of the Church. Nor is this all. He regards the threefold ministry as essential to the very being of the Church, for, to quote his own words, as rendered by Lightfoot, "without these three orders no Church has a title to the name." ‡ This hierarchy, this

---

* Ad Smyrn., 8. † Ad Smyrn., 9. ‡ Ad Trall., 3.

monarchical episcopate, the aged bishop of Antioch regards as " firmly rooted," as "beyond dispute," and as co-extensive with the Church. He speaks of bishops as established in "the farthest parts of the earth," * and it is evident from his language that, in his judgment, the episcopate is not an evolution from the presbyterate, but is from above, the ordering of God Himself.

To these words of Ignatius, so clear, so strong, so abundant, we turn to the testimony of Irenæus, who was born not later than A.D. 130. He asserts that in his youth he sat at the feet of Polycarp, " who had been appointed by the Apostles a bishop for Asia in the Church of Smyrna," and that he had listened to the discourses in public and private of this venerable man, whose very looks and ways, he assures us, were indelibly impressed upon his mind. Irenæus further claims that he had opportunities of instruction from Asiatic "elders," some of whom, he tells us, had been disciples of the Apostles. With these means of learning the traditions of the Church in Asia Minor as shaped by no less an authority than St. John himself, the latest living of the apostolic band, Irenæus, while yet a young man and probably prior to Polycarp's martyrdom (*circa* A.D. 155), removed from Asia to Rome. At the latest, in the year 177, when persecution visited the churches of southern Gaul, Irenæus was a presbyter of Lyons, and was elevated to the see of the martyred bishop Pothinus. There is record of his visiting Rome prior to his entrance upon the episcopal office as well as afterwards; his object in each case being to promote the peace of the Church. Thus fitted by circumstances as well as by his character to know and to maintain the "tradition of the elders," we find in his writings, to quote the language of the latest authority on this subject, Mr. Charles Gore, in his work on " The Ministry of the Christian Church," "the

---

* Ad Eph., 3.

picture of the universal Church, spread all over the world, handing down in unbroken succession the apostolic truth, and the bond of unity, the link to connect the generations in the Church, is the episcopal succession."*

The language of Irenæus is clear and determinate with reference to the succession of the bishops to the authority and rule exercised by the Apostles in the Church, and "because it would be tedious . . . to enumerate the successions of all the Churches," he gives that of the Church of Rome and records the committal of the episcopate by the Apostles SS. Peter and Paul to Linus (A.D. 68), and then the succession from him of Anencletus (A.D. 80), Clement (A.D. 92), Evarestus (A.D. 100), Alexander (A.D. 109), Xystus (A.D. 119), Telesphorus the Martyr (A.D. 128), Hyginus (A.D. 139), Pius (A.D. 142), Anicetus (A.D. 157), Soter (A.D. 168), and at length in his own day, of Eleutherus (A.D. 177).† Certain discrepancies which confessedly exist in the various lists of Roman bishops which have come down to us, may be explained by assuming the existence in the very first ages of two distinct Churches, one Jewish and one Gentile, at Rome. Lightfoot, while claiming that "no more can safely be assumed of Linus and Anencletus than that they held some prominent position in the Roman Church," ‡ adds that "the reason for supposing Clement to have been a bishop is as strong as the universal tradition of the next ages can make it." It in no way detracts from this admission with respect to Clement that Lightfoot regards him rather as "the chief of the presbyters than the chief over presbyters," and consequently not in the position of irresponsible authority occupied by his successors Eleutherus (A.D. 177), and Victor (A.D. 189) or even by his contemporaries Ignatius of Anti-

---

* Gore's Ministry of the Christian Church, chap. iii., p. 119.

† Iren. iii., 3, 3. The dates we have given to the successive incumbents of the see of Rome are from Lightfoot.

‡ Com. on the Philippians. The Christian Ministry, p. 219.

och, and Polycarp of Smyrna. With Victor, apparently the first Latinprelate who held the bishopric of Rome, a new era begins.

The line of ecclesiastical descent is now clearly defined and by the participation in each consecration of three or more of the episcopal order required by the early canons and continued with scrupulous exactness till the modern view of episcopacy as held by the papacy permitted at times the substitution of the papal authority for the presence of more than a single consecrator, there has been knitted together the meshes of that vast network which in its comprehensiveness includes the Church's chief rulers from the very first, and by the multitude of interlacing lines of succession makes any serious defect in the direct connection with the Apostles of any individual bishop well-nigh impossible. The succession of bishops from the Apostles' times is not to be regarded as a chain of single links, the whole being of no greater strength than its weakest part, but as a network, or web, of interwoven strands, now innumerable, which would hold together even if, to venture an impossible supposition, nine-tenths of these lines could be proved defective and, therefore, invalid. In other words, a possible defect in one, or in a hundred, of the different lines of succession, would in no way affect the consecration of any particular bishop of our day, so infinite in number are the interlacing strands of the great network uniting one who has been set apart for this office and administration in the Church of God, with the Apostles and, through the Apostles, with Christ the Great Shepherd and Bishop of souls.

AUTHORITIES.—In addition to the late Bishop of Durham's dissertation on " The Christian Ministry," appended to his commentary on the Philippians, and the many special treatises on the Apostolical Succession by Perceval, Haddon, Elrington, Morse, and others, the latest and most conclusive work on the general subject is that of Gore, " The Ministry of the Christian Church." James Pott & Co., N. Y., 1889. A compact treatise by the Rev. Professor J. H. Barbour, of the Berkeley Divinity School, Middletown, Conn.,* is admirably arranged and deserves general reading. Its title is, "The Beginnings of the Historic Episcopate Exhibited in the Words of Holy Scripture and Ancient Authors." Canon Liddon, in his sermon entitled "A Father in Christ" (Rivington's, London, 1875), effectually disposes of the arguments of the late Dr. Edwin Hatch, in his Bampton Lectures on the "Organization of Early Christian Churches,"† "The Growth of the Christian Church,"† and a later paper in the *Contemporary Review* from the same source. "Historical Continuity," by Dr. A. C. Garratt.† "Apostolic Succession," by Rev. A. W. Haddan.* "The Jurisdiction and Mission of the Anglican Episcopate," by Rev. T. J. Bailey.*

---

*New York: E. & J. B. Young & Co., 1887.
† T. Whittaker, New York.

THE CLAIMS OF THE HISTORIC EPISCOPATE EXAMINED.

BY PRESIDENT JAMES HARPER, D.D., UNITED PRESBYTERIAN THEOLOGICAL SEMINARY, XENIA, OHIO.

THE prelatic, or in current, though less accurate phraseology, the episcopal theory of Church government, is, in its Protestant form, to the effect that in the Christian Church there is a threefold ministry, that of deacons, of presbyters or elders, and of bishops, to all of whom belong the functions of preaching and baptizing, to the presbyters and bishops the right also to administer the eucharist, while to the bishops alone it pertains to ordain, confirm and exercise within a certain district, called a diocese, general supervision.

Among the advocates of this polity, diversity of opinion exists, some maintaining that it is of divine authority and essential to the being of the Church, others holding that it is expedient and beneficial, but not in any other sense of divine institution or obligation.

It may be noted that among Protestants the theory of prelacy by divine right is limited to the United Kingdom, with its dependencies, and the United States. Even in the ranks of Protestantism its supporters are vastly outnumbered by its opponents—a fact which might serve to abate the pretensions and supercilious tone by which many, happily not all, Episcopalians are characterized. True, they have the millions of Rome as a solace in solitude; but Rome ungraciously repudiates them because they do not go farther and admit the supremacy of the Pope.

It needs to be observed that the advocates of high-toned episcopacy contend strenuously for the doctrine of "apostolic succession," that is, the view that the official descent of bishops is, and must be, in an unbroken chain from the apostles. It is not enough that the Church be officered with the three orders aforenamed. The highest order, that of bishops, must proceed in lineal descent officially from the apostles. If, for instance, a company of men were cast by shipwreck on some lonely island, they never could be constituted as a Church of Christ and have the sacraments lawfully dispensed among them and a legitimate ministry unless they could obtain the mystic touch of a bishop's hands, who had himself been ordained by one who could trace his official genealogy to the apostles. This mechanical theory lies at the root of the full-blown prelacy of our day, and affords nurture to that baneful sacerdotalism which, it is to be feared, is gaining ground among Episcopalians in spite of manly protests made against it by many of their number.

The arguments wont to be urged by Episcopalians in favor of their theory of ecclesiastical polity are reducible to two heads, namely, considerations drawn from the Scriptures, and alleged facts of post-biblical history.

THE SCRIPTURAL PLEA FOR PRELACY.—First: It is confidently asserted that the apostolic office was meant to be in its essential features not temporary, but permanent, and that it survives in the order of diocesan bishops; the latter being stationary, whereas the apostles were "ambulatory," or itinerant bishops. Passages of the New Testament are industriously collected in which the perpetuation of the apostolic office is supposed to be indicated. For instance, in Acts xiv., 4, 14, Barnabas as well as Paul is represented to be an apostle: in Phil. ii., 25, Epaphroditus is, according to the Greek, styled an apostle; in II. Cor. viii., 23, Paul speaks of certain brethren as the "messengers [Gr. apostles] of the churches," and in the opening of several of his epistles associates others with himself, such as Timothy, Silvanus and Sosthenes. (See I. Cor. i., 1; II. Cor. i., 1; Gal. i., 1; Phil. i., 1; Col.

CLAIMS OF THE HISTORIC EPISCOPATE EXAMINED. 109

i., 1; I. Thess. i., 1; II. Thess. i., 1; Philemon verse 1. Rom. xvi., 7, and I. Thess. ii., 6, are also adduced with the same intent.)

On this branch of the argument from Scripture a few remarks are offered.

1. Beyond doubt, the word "apostle" is used in the New Testament sometimes, in its wide etymological meaning, to denote any one sent, and sometimes, in a restricted and technical sense, to signify a special functionary. A parallel usage attaches to the Hebrew word, מַלְאָךְ (malak), and its Greek equivalent, ἄγγελος (anggelos), which denote a messenger generally; but, in a limited sense, a particular kind of messenger, or agent, whom we call an angel.

2. In the special or restricted sense the title apostle is given in the New Testament to none but fourteen men, that is, to the twelve chosen by Christ to be His immediate attendants, together with Matthias, who was appointed by Christ to apostleship through the ordinance of the lot, and Saul of Tarsus, who received from the Lord an extraordinary call.

3. Among the qualifications requisite for apostleship in the limited sense were the following: Ability from personal knowledge to attest the fact of Christ's resurrection from the dead; an immediate, external call by Christ to this office; a power to work miracles as proof in part of the divine mission of the worker; and supernatural inspiration to fit for teaching the truth authoritatively and infallibly. (See Luke vi., 13; Acts i., 21, 22; xxii., 14, 15; xxvi., 16; I. Cor. ix., 1, 2; Heb. ii., 4; John xiv., 26.)

4. There is no express intimation in Scripture that the apostles, as such, were to have official successors. Appeal has been made to Matt. xxviii., 20, as proof that the apostolic order should be continued till the end of time. But this text, if interpreted with rigid literality, would teach that, till the end of the world, Christ would be with the very

individuals then addressed. The reference rather is to all those who, to the end of time, should be engaged in carrying out the great commission. According to the prelatic idea, the preaching of the Gospel pertains rather to the presbyters than to the bishops; the distinctive function of the latter being government rather than preaching.

5. There is nothing in the New Testament to show that the apostleship was actually extended beyond the number of the original twelve, together with Matthias and Saul. The case of Matthias has been urged as evidence of a purpose to perpetuate the apostolic order. But let it be noted that Matthias was simply chosen to do what Judas should have done, that is, bear witness to the fact of the resurrection of Christ, a thing which none but one who had seen Christ after His resurrection could do. But when, at a later date, James, the brother of John, was killed, no successor to him was chosen. Paul, indeed, had been called meanwhile, not only to saintship, but also to apostleship; but he speaks of himself in I. Cor. xv., 8, as attaining the latter standing irregularly as to time. He was the last to whom the Lord appeared with the view of constituting him an apostle.

In two instances Barnabas and Paul are together called apostles; but it is noticeable that Barnabas is never called an apostle previously or subsequently to the missionary tour on which he, together with Paul, had been *sent forth* by the Church of Antioch. It seems highly probable that both of these men are in the instances under notice called "apostles" in the wide sense of that word, as being in this particular tour what we would call missionaries sent out from Antioch.

In Phil. ii., 25, Epaphroditus is called an apostle, although in our authorized version and in the Revised version as well, the rendering given is "messenger." But it is observable that he is not styled an apostle of Christ, but "your" apostle, that is, the apostle of, or from, the Philippians; and in ch. iv., 18, the reason why he was called their apostle is indicated, namely, because he had acted in their behalf in carrying to Paul their gifts. The interpretation just given has the sanction of the distinguished scholar, the late Bishop Lightfoot, who, in his " Dissertation on the Christian Ministry " (p. 196), thus writes: " The true apostle, like St. Peter, or St. John, bears this title as the messenger, the delegate, of Christ Himself: while Epaphroditus is only so styled as the messenger of the Philippian brotherhood; and in the very next clause the expression is explained by the statement that he carried their alms to St. Paul. The use of the word here has a parallel in another passage (II. Cor. viii., 23), where messengers (or apostles) of the churches are mentioned."

The passing remark made in Rom. xvi., 7, respecting Andronicus and Junias that they were "of note among the apostles," can hardly mean that the persons named were distinguished apostles in the restricted sense of that word; but it rather signifies that by their character and labors they had attracted the attention and won the admiration of the apostles. It is not certain, indeed, that Junias, a masculine form, should be substituted for the feminine form, Junia, of the authorized version.

Touching the plea for the perpetuation of the apostolate drawn from the fact that in the introductory salutations of his epistles Paul associates others with himself, it may be said that Paul is careful to distinguish himself in such cases from the others whom he links with his name. For example, in I. Cor. i., 1, he writes, " Paul, called to be an apostle of Jesus Christ through the will of God, and Sosthenes our *brother*," etc. So also in II. Cor. i., 1, he expresses himself thus guardedly, " Paul, an apostle of Jesus Christ by the will of God, and Timothy, our *brother*," etc. In a like cautious way he writes in Col. i., 1, discriminating between himself as an apostle and Timothy as a *brother*. But when he conjoins himself entirely with Timothy, he uses a title common to both, namely, "servants of Jesus Christ" (see Phil. i., 1). Nor does the language used in I. Thess. ii., 6, warrant the view that Silvanus and Timothy, in common with Paul, are designated apostles; for Paul occasionally speaks of himself in the plural (see I. Thess. ii., 18), and, besides, the context, particularly verse 2, compared with the narrative in Acts xvi., forbids the supposition that Timothy at least is referred to in verse 6.

Second: By many Episcopalians great stress is laid on the alleged prelatic authority with which Timothy and Titus were clothed. "These men," it is said, "were established, the one in Ephesus, the other in Crete as bishops, to ordain to office, as occasion might demand, and to maintain supervision over presbyters, deacons, and people."

Now it is admitted that these men were invested with large authority. But they were extraordinary officers, for the circumstances in which they were called to act were extraordinary. The Church of the New Testament was then in a forming state. The apostles, as pioneers, carried the Gospel far and wide, but they could not tarry sufficiently long in every place where converts were made to organize them fully into ecclesiastical societies. Timothy and Titus, perhaps others also, were employed to complete what apostles had begun, and this in the way of establishing the faithful in the truth and carrying out in detail the organization of churches (see Titus i., 5). These men were coadjutors of the apostles, like them itinerant, not stationary, enjoying a special measure of delegated authority, and being directly instructed by apostles as to the duties to be performed. There is not the slightest evidence, but much to the contrary, that Timothy and Titus were settled as diocesan bishops in their respective fields. A disclosure of the reason why Timothy was left at Ephesus is given in I. Tim. i., 3: "As I besought thee to abide still at Ephesus, when I went into Macedonia, that thou mightest charge some that they teach no other doctrine." In II. Tim. iv., 9, 13, 21, Paul expresses the expectation and earnest desire that Timothy would come to him at Rome. And it is clear that when Paul wrote from Corinth his Epistle to the Romans, Timothy was with him (Rom xvi., 21) and that he was also with him when he wrote from Rome his epistles to the Philippians, the Colossians and Philemon respectively. If Timothy was bishop of Ephesus, he must have been sadly negligent of his diocese.

Titus was *left* in Crete, Paul intimates in his letter to him (Tit. i., 5), to attend to certain specified duties. It is not said that Titus was *established* in Crete. Besides, Paul wrote to Titus from Nicopolis in Macedonia asking that he come to him there, a procedure very singular if Crete was the proper diocese of Titus.

Third: It is claimed that James, who took a prominent part in the council, or synod of Jerusalem, was bishop of that city.

In opposition to this view, it may be urged that in the New Testament James is never styled bishop ; that the only functionaries who figured in the synod were apostles and presbyters, or elders, to whom alone appeal had been made for a decision of the question at issue; that the words of James, " wherefore my sentence is," etc , imply no assumption of authority over the others present; and that there are reasons of great weight for the belief that he was an apostle, who, though not necessarily confined to any territory, labored chiefly at Jerusalem, or at least among the Jews.

Fourth: Episcopalians have long insisted that diocesan bishops are meant by the angels of the seven churches of Asia of whom we read in the first three chapters of the Apocalypse.

A few strictures on this line in the argument for prelacy must suffice.

1. If the angels were prelates, the elders are utterly ignored. Those elders of Ephesus, for instance, whom Paul, in his parting charge to them, had led to believe that they had much to do with the oversight of the flock, are not recognized at all by Christ, if the Episcopal interpretation of the term, angel, is correct. This would be singular indeed.

2. In the course of the epistles to the Seven Churches, a particular angel is addressed, or indirectly described, as plural; a fact which favors the view that "angel" is used collectively to denote the company of elders. (See Rev. ii, 10, 13, 24, 25.)

3. John several times elsewhere in this Book of Revelation, uses the word "angel" to signify a plurality of agents. Thus, in chapter xiv., 6, it is said, "And I saw another angel fly in the midst of Heaven, having the everlasting Gospel to preach unto them that dwell on the earth," etc. Does not the angel here symbolize the ministers of the Gospel, a vast number? and may not the angel of a church denote the ministry laboring in that church? In Rev. i., 21, it is explained that a candlestick symbolized a church, which is a collective unit, and that a star symbolized an angel of a church. Might not the word "angel" also be used as a collective term to mean many?

It may be added that candid Episcopalians are beginning to admit that their cause can derive no help from the angels of the churches. Bishop Lightfoot distinctly does so. (See his "Dissertation on the Christian Ministry," p. 199.)

A few thoughts may be subjoined to our very hurried review of the argument from Scripture in behalf of prelacy.

1. It is unaccountable that in the New Testament there is no distinctive title given to the alleged third and highest order of permanent ecclesiastical officers, if such an order actually existed before the completion of the canon.

The first and second orders are distinguished respectively as deacons and elders, the latter class being also styled

CLAIMS OF THE HISTORIC EPISCOPATE EXAMINED. 115

bishops. After centuries of quibbling on the point it is now conceded by the ablest defenders of prelacy, Bishops Onderdonk and Lightfoot among them, that in the New Testament usage of the words, bishop and elder, or presbyter, are identical, or denote precisely the same kind of officer.

Is it credible that the highest permanent order would be destitute of a distinctive name? The absence of the name is a sure sign that the thing itself, the order of prelates, was absent from the arrangements of the apostolic Church.

2. It is most remarkable that, although Paul formally describes in his pastoral episties the qualifications and duties of elders, or bishops, and even those of deacons, he says nothing about the order of prelates, if such an order existed. Does not the omission indicate that such functionaries had no place in the Church of apostolic times, and that their existence was not contemplated as desirable or lawful?

3. It is highly significant, also, that in stating the duties of elders (or bishops) and deacons, Paul never enjoins it upon them to obey a superior order of officers, now called prelates, or diocesan bishops. In the letters attributed to Ignatius this duty is insisted on vehemently. But not a word on it is penned by Paul!

4. The fact that the title, bishop, was, in the course of time, appropriated to prelates, favors the view that the prelates sprang from the order of elders, and covered the usurpation of the prerogatives of the latter by retaining that title of the elders which suggested the idea of rule.

5. The elders, or Scriptural bishops, were vested with such powers as rendered needless a permanent superior order. The teaching, the ruling, the ordaining, and, so far as it pertains to any one, the confirming power was theirs (Acts xx., 28; I. Tim. iv., 14; Jas. v., 14, 15). What need, then, for a standing superior order?

6. The claim of any one in our day to be a bishop by tactual descent officially from the apostles is incapable of

proof. Archbishop Whately, with a candor creditable to him and an inexorable logic, has shown this in his "Kingdom of Christ Delineated." This idea of succession, with its correlated mysticism, has formed a bridge of passage for many Episcopalians into the realm of Rome. As already said, the mere plan or form of Church government is in the eyes of the chief sticklers for prelacy of far less moment than the fancied lineal succession.

THE HISTORICAL PLEA FOR PRELACY.—Let us now turn to the argument drawn from the condition of the Church in the second century in behalf of diocesan episcopacy. Bishop Lightfoot rests the cause of episcopacy mainly on this ground. An effort is made to prove that almost at the opening of the second century, just after the demise of the Apostle John, the prelatic form of polity prevailed generally in the Church. The inference is that this mode of government must have been established, at least sanctioned, by the apostles, or that it was the natural and purposed development of germs planted by them.

The historical evidence adduced is derived mainly from the epistles of Ignatius and the writings of Irenæus and Eusebius of Cæsarea, but from the first-named pre-eminently.

Unable to deal minutely with this line of argument, we may yet offer some criticisms upon it which may suffice to show how insecure a basis it affords for the towering fabric of prelacy.

1. The assumption that in the early part of the second century diocesan episcopacy generally prevailed in the Church is unwarranted.

Touching Ignatius, the chief voucher for the early prevalence of prelacy, it is not rash to say that his reputation for veracity is badly damaged. The real Ignatius, could we reach him, would doubtless be an unexceptionable witness; but there is room for the gravest suspicions that the epistles which bear his name have all been fabricated, tampered with at least, in the interests of the hierarchy, which, it is granted, supplanted at a very early date the primitive form of ecclesiastical polity. Any one conversant with the history of the Church in ancient and mediæval times must know how common it was to seek favor and currency for certain views by publishing them in documents purporting to have proceeded from men of high reputation in the Church. The collection of rubrics and counsels, known as "The Apostolical Constitutions," is an eminent, but by no means a solitary, instance of the practice described. Now around the name of Ignatius, probably the oldest pastor of Antioch, a halo of glory speedily gathered, both because he was reputed to have enjoyed direct apostolic instruction, and because he fell as a martyr for Christ, an event which happened probably in A.D. 115 or 116. The tradition is that, having been ordered from Antioch to Rome to suffer there, he addressed, while on his journey thither, a number of letters to individuals and churches. Of such letters, bearing the name of Ignatius, fifteen have come down to us; but that eight of the number are forgeries is now universally admitted. The remaining seven have been transmitted in Greek in a double form, a longer and a shorter, and three of them also in Syriac in an abbreviated form. By scholars in modern times it is generally held that the longer form in Greek is not genuine; and very many of the highest repute, among them Neander, regard even the shorter Greek form as much corrupted. This form, however, most Episcopalians pronounce genuine, and in this judgment Bishop Lightfoot, whose edition of the Epistles of Ignatius is a monument of fine scholarship and patient research, concurs. Some have taken the ground that all of the epistles ascribed to Ignatius are alike spurious. This we are inclined to think is an extreme view. It is most probable that Ignatius did on his way to Rome pen some letters, perhaps the seven that have found most favor; but that these have been all interpolated with the view of promoting the pretensions of an ambitious hierarchy. We know that forgeries in the name of Ignatius have been perpetrated. Then, again, suspicion is justified by the fact that these epistles have come down in a longer and a shorter form, each purporting to be genuine. Furthermore, while the external evidence in their behalf is but vague and scanty, the documents considered in themselves are fitted to beget strong suspicions that they have been corrupted for a purpose, if indeed they are not entire forgeries.

The very intensity and persistence with which the duty of revering and implicitly obeying the bishop is inculcated in these letters are fitted to rouse suspicion, and this all the more when, in other writings originating about the time of Ignatius, or even much later, the genuineness of which is hardly questioned, presbyters and deacons are brought to view, but no prelatic bishops. For example, in the lately discovered treatise entitled "The Teaching of the Apostles," which, by the most competent judges is supposed to have been composed not later than A.D. 160, possibly as early as A.D. 120, these words occur, "Choose for yourselves bishops and deacons worthy of the Lord," etc., the word "bishops" being used unquestionably, as it is in the New Testament, to denote elders. Not a hint is given in this treatise of the existence of a bishop as superior to elders.

Again, in the Epistle of Clemens Romanus written to the Corinthians about A.D. 96, while bishops (or elders) and deacons are mentioned often, not an allusion is made to a prelatic bishop; this, too, by one for whom it is claimed that he was a bishop of Rome.

The same may be said of the Epistle of Polycarp to the Philippians, written probably as late as A.D. 150. Well might Bishop Lightfoot in his notice of this letter say, "We are thus led to the inference that episcopacy did not exist at all among the Philippians at this time, or existed only in an elementary form, so that the bishop was a mere president of the presbyteral council.' ("Christian Ministry," p. 115.)

But it is said that the representations made as to Church polity in the Ignatian letters are corroborated by lists of bishops given by Eusebius. In answer it may be said that the information given by Eusebius rests largely on very hazy tradition, as he himself, in the opening of his history, candidly confesses; that the oldest presbyter in a city, or district, seems commonly to have presided in the meetings of the presbyters and to have been vested with a large measure of executive control; that by degrees he came to have the title bishop given to him by way of eminence, although theoretically he was still only the organ of the presbytery, the first among his equals; that later writers viewing the past through the customs of their own times, unconsciously in some cases, but in other cases consciously and with a view to the confirmation of hierarchal claims, transferred to the pastor, or moderator, of the early times dignity and prerogatives which only in the lapse of years had become associated with the title, bishop. These different positions can be supported by an array of evidence which it would be much easier to ignore than to encounter. Thus the assumption that diocesan episcopacy was widely established in the early part of the second century, and presumably with the sanction of at least one apostle, the saintly John, rests on grounds of a very precarious character.

2. It is a reasonable presumption that the form of Church government established by the apostles was meant to be permanent. So far as the New Testament sheds light on the point, the church wherever erected by the apostles was framed on one uniform plan. There is no evidence that one apostle organized on one plan and another on a different plan, or that in different countries divergent forms of Church government were adopted under apostolic direc-

tion. This uniformity of settlement points to purposed permanence; especially as no hint is given that in the course of time changes might lawfully be introduced. But according to Bishop Lightfoot and some other influential advocates of episcopacy, the form impressed on the Church at its organization by the apostles did not outlast the first century, nay that before the close of that century and before the death of the Apostle John, a new order of officers was created, not recognized in the book of Acts or in the epistles, for whom as yet there was no distinctive name, but corresponding to modern prelates in having jurisdiction over deacons and presbyters. The evolution, or rather revolution, resulting in the creation of this third and supreme order must have been marvellously rapid. When the curtain falls at the close of the sacred canon, the only discoverable permanent officers of the Church are deacons and elders, or presbyters, called also bishops. When it rises slightly in the first quarter of the second century, a new order has been evolved, by what authority no one can tell, but it is fondly conjectured by that of the Apostle John at least. Bishop Lightfoot says ("Christian Ministry," p. 195), "It is clear then that at the close of the apostolic age, the two lower orders of the threefold ministry were firmly and widely established; but traces of the third and highest order, the episcopate properly so called, are few and indistinct." He seems, however, to think that as circumstances changed, a new order became necessary and was added, just as the order of deacons was established when need for it arose. But he overlooks the facts, that the diaconate was established at an early date in the history of the New Testament Church; that it was not a growth, but was instituted definitely and at once by the apostles; and that a record of its institution was made in the inspired Word. If the inferior order, that of deacons was placed upon a foundation so solid, surely the order of diocesan bishops, if meant to exist in the Christian Church, the highest order, as Episcopalians think, would have been formally established by the apostles, and the fact recorded in the sacred volume.

3. Even though it could be proved that prelacy grew up under the eye of the Apostle John, it would not follow as a necessary inference that it received his approval. We know from his writings that many evils were in the Church in his time, nay that the spirit of antichrist was then at work.

4. The historic plea is faulty because it implies that the Bible is not the only rule of faith. We grant that evidence confirmatory of our faith and useful also for the interpretation of the Scriptures may be drawn from many sources, and among them from post-biblical history; but the matter and ground of our faith must be found in the Scriptures alone. Those who would have us accept the prelatic theory on the ground of post-biblical history, ask us to renounce the great Protestant position that the Bible is the sufficient, the infallible and the only rule of faith and practice. In closing this examination of the claims of the " historic episcopate " we might say in the words of Seneca, "*Inopem me copia fecit.*"

THE ONE HOLY, CATHOLIC, APOSTOLIC CHURCH.*

BY PROFESSOR JAMES HERON, D.D., PRESBYTERIAN COL-
LEGE, BELFAST.

ON the subject of "The One Holy, Catholic, Apostolic Church" there is one theory in particular so very exclusive in its claims, and also so very obtrusive at the present time, as to demand special notice. It is that theory upon which I purpose to make a few remarks to-day; and, to avoid the possibility of misrepresenting it, I will begin by stating it in the language of one of the most prominent of its recent advocates.

"As we watch the history of Christendom," says the leader of the new school of Anglican High Churchmen, "we discern a great number of organized religious bodies, owing their existence and their purpose to Christian belief and Christian ideas; but in the midst of these we discern also something incomparably more permanent and more universal —one great continuous body—the Catholic Church. There it is; none can overlook its visible existence, let us say, from the time when Christianity emerges out of the gloom of the sub-Apostolic age down to the period of the Reformation." This "Catholic Church" is described further as a visible society, possessing corporate, organic unity, historic continuity and permanence. It is "an organized society in which a graduated body of ordained ministers is made the instrument of unity"—ministers episcopally ordained, and thus, and thus only, possessing "an authoritative stewardship of the graces and truth that came by Jesus Christ, and a recog-

* Address delivered at the close of the college session, April 2d, 1891. [Copyright by E. B. TREAT.]

nized power to transmit it, derived from Apostolic descent." Access to God and all spiritual privileges depend on membership in the visible society thus organized, which is "the special and covenanted sphere of His regular and uniform operations "—" the home of the new covenant of salvation," instituted by the incarnate Son of God " for man to belong to as the means of belonging to Him " ; for " communion with God depends on communion with His Church " as thus understood.†

Here, then, we are assured, is " The One Holy, Catholic, Apostolic Church," and there is none other. The only communions that are recognized as forming part of it are the Church of Rome, the Greek Church, and the Anglican Church with its branches. The other great Christian communities, including Presbyterians (who are expressly and by name referred to), are not entitled to the name of Churches, but are—" out of communion with God, which depends on communion with His Church "—living in schism and in sin.

As, during the last two sessions, we have been tracing the history of this so-called " Catholic Church," in its rise and growth, and in the golden period, that is the medieval period, of its life, it will, I think, be no inappropriate conclusion to our studies to look at the high claim set up on its behalf, and the conception of the Church which it embodies. I can, of course, do this to-day, in the short time at my disposal, only very briefly and very cursorily.

But, before proceeding to consider the theory itself, it may be interesting to observe how far it is carried out and realized by those who advocate it. Supposing for a moment that the idea of the Church I have just presented is the true idea of it, what Church is there that can justly claim the title, " The One Holy, Catholic, Apostolic Church " ?

" The Church of Rome," it will be said by some. I shall

† " The Church and the Ministry," by the Rev. Charles Gore, M.A., pp. 11, 57, 70, 344 *et passim*.

have more to say bearing upon this answer by and by. I shall only ask at present, What about the Greek Church? Can we forget the great schism that rent these two Churches asunder in the ninth century, and that continues to this day? Can we forget how the one has excommunicated and anathematized the other, and with about equal reason, the Eastern Church denouncing the Pope himself as "the first Protestant," and the Papacy as the chief heresy of these latter days, and the Western Church paying back the compliment with interest? Can we forget the deep, wide gulf of alienation and the intense hostility that separate them; how their ecclesiastics are only kept from violent collisions and from shedding one another's blood at Bethlehem and the Holy Sepulchre by the interposition of Mahometan soldiers? Not only are they not in "organic, corporate unity"—no Churches in the world are more deeply estranged or more bitterly averse to one another. They certainly do not constitute together "One Holy, Catholic Church," for they are not one Church, but two; and with as little truth or justice can any one of them appropriate the title "Catholic" to the exclusion of the other. The theory of a visible Catholic Church "one and indivisible," with "historic continuity," has broken down, you see, in the very first attempt to apply it.

"Oh! but the Greek Church and the Roman Church have but one Episcopal form of government." Does that make them one? Has that conserved even their external unity?—and remember it is external, organic, corporate unity that the High Church theory demands. Are two nations that are at war with one another, and thoroughly antagonistic in their national traits and tendencies, one because they possess a similar form of government? The forms of government of France and Prussia at the time of the Franco-Prussian war were far more nearly akin than those of the Greek and Roman Churches. Were they, therefore, one nation? Are France and the United States one nation to-day because they have both a Republican form of government? When the same nation changes its form of government, does its national existence and identity, its existence as a State, cease? The English nation passed from a monarchy into a republic, and from a republic into a monarchy again. Did the change in the mere form of government create a break in the continuity of national existence? Did England cease to be a nation or a State under the Commonwealth? The Duke of Savoy thought otherwise when Cromwell inter'ered on behalf of the persecuted Vaudois, God's

> " Slaughtered saints whose bones
> Lay scattered on the Alpine mountains cold,"

and compelled that tyrant to desist from his barbarities. And if a particular form of government does not belong to the essence of national or State existence, I hope to show you by and by that it is still less of the essence of the Church. You might as well affirm that two hostile nations are one because they have similar forms of government, or that two men at enmity are one because they are clad in garments made by the same tailor and after the same pattern, as that the Roman and Greek Churches are one because their modes of government are somewhat similar. The one holy, Catholic Church as a visible corporate society is thus so far non-existent.

But what about the Anglican Church? What claim has she to belong to the one corporate society which Mr. Gore pictures? Having deliberately seceded and separated from the Church of Rome—that is from connection with "the one Catholic Church" of which Mr. Gore speaks—at the Reformation, and having continued separate ever since, the claim of the Anglican Church to be a part of the "one visible Catholic Church" has still less to justify it. She is certainly not a part of the corporate unity, and she is not recognized by Rome as being a Church at all. In view of that act and state of separation, how can Anglicans talk of "one holy Catholic Church"? Why the phrase, if there is any real force in it, only condemns and smites them. From the point of view of their own theory of the Church, what right had they to separate from Rome? If there is only "one visible Catholic Church," there is no right to separate from it, no matter how corrupt it may become. The moment you separate from it, you abandon the theory of the one visible Catholic Church. Augustine told the Donatists that "being separate from the body of the Church, they were *ipso facto* cut off from the heritage of the Church"; and yet those Donatists had their bishops and their Episcopal succession. It was just such considerations, Newman tells us, that drove him from Anglicanism to Rome. It was the inexorable logic of the principle of the one visible but indivisible Church body that drove him. The idea that the Roman, Greek, and Anglican communions make up one visible, indivisible Church of God he describes as "a view as paradoxical when regarded as a fact, as it is heterodox when regarded as a doctrine." "All the learning," he says, "all the argumentative skill of its ablest champions, would fail in proving that two sovereign States were numerically one State, even though they happened to have the same parentage, the same language, the same form of government;" and yet, he goes on to say, the gulf between Rome and England is greater than the demarcation between State and State. But "it may possibly be suggested," he remarks, "that the universality which the fathers ascribe to the Catholic Church lay in its Apostolical descent, or again in its episcopacy; and that it was one, not as being one kingdom or *civitas* at unity with itself, with one and the same intelligence in every part, one sympathy, one ruling principle, one organization, one communion, but because, though consisting of a number of independent communions at variance with each other, even to a breach of intercourse, nevertheless all these were possessed of a legitimate succession of clergy, or all governed by bishops, priests, and deacons. But who will in seriousness maintain that relationship, or that resemblance, makes two bodies one? England and Prussia are two monarchies; are they, therefore, one kingdom? England and the United States are one stock; can they, therefore, be called one State? If unity lies in the Apostolical succession, an act of schism is from the very nature of the case impossible. Either there is no such sin as schism, or unity does not lie in the Episcopal form, or in Episcopal ordination." "Antiquarian arguments" in favor of Apostolical succession are, he says, " altogether unequal to the urgency of visible facts;" while, with regard to the Church of England, he continues, " I cannot tell how soon there came upon me—but very soon —an extreme astonishment that I had ever imagined it to be a portion of the Catholic Church. . . . When I looked back upon the poor Anglican Church, for which I had labored so hard, and upon all that had appertained to it, and thought of our various attempts to dress it up doctrinally and æsthetically, it seemed to me the veriest of nonentities ! "*

I have thus shown how badly Mr. Gore's own Church, not to speak of others, bears the test of his own principles. But now with regard to the theory itself, I have one or two remarks to make.

I. And, first, there is no fact more distinctly revealed in history than the *genesis* of this materialistic conception of the Church—the rise of the idea that a certain piece of external organization called "the bishop" belongs to the essence of the Church—and the growth of a great hierarchical corporation after the pattern of this idea. The genesis and growth of it, and the gradual formation of the Church according to it, are apparent to every student of the literature of the second and third centuries. The idea is a complex

---

* Newman's Essays, v. i., pp. 217-220; "Development of Doctrine," c. vi., sec. 2; "Apologia," pp. 339, 340, 341, last edition.

one, involving along with other elements chiefly these two: (1) That the bishop is of a different order from the presbyter; and (2) the sacerdotal character of the ministry, with its corollary, the transmission of grace through unbroken Episcopal succession. When did these ideas begin to take visible shape? When did they attempt to "mix themselves with life"?

1. As to the first—the separation of the Episcopate from the Presbyterate, and the erection of the former into a distinct and separate order—we see the process going on in the second century, and not quite completed even towards the close of it. Not only in the New Testament, but in many sub-Apostolic writings, presbyters are bishops and bishops are presbyters. Bishop Lightfoot has clearly shown that the Episcopate was created out of the Presbyterate, that in Clement of Alexandria and Irenæus "the functions of the bishop and presbyter are regarded as substantially the same in kind, though different in degree"; that they are represented as being "not a distinct order," and that at Alexandria "the bishop was nominated and apparently ordained by the twelve presbyters out of their own number." Hilary, Jerome, Augustine and others saw this and affirmed it. "Let bishops know," says Jerome, "that they are above presbyters more by the custom of the Church than by any actual ordinance of the Lord." Under the stress and pressure of such facts Mr. Gore at one point virtually gives up the cause for which the chief part of his book is a plea—the necessity of the monarchical Episcopate. "No one of whatever part of the Church," he says, "can maintain that the existence of what may be called, for lack of a distinctive term, *mon-Episcopacy* is essential to the continuity of the Church." This, however, is what Mr. Gore himself does strenuously maintain elsewhere. But I only note that what the greater part of his book assumes as essential he here practically abandons.

2. But simultaneously with the development of one of the presbyters into a third and superior order called the bishop, another development is seen going on. The efforts of the Judaizers to preserve the distinctive features of the Jewish system, and foist them on the Christian Church, failed in the first instance. These attempts were foiled by Paul and the other Apostles, who invested all Christians with a spiritual priesthood, and clearly taught the abolition of an exclusive priesthood. As Bishop Lightfoot also shows, there is not only no trace of a sacerdotal ministry in the New Testament —there is no trace of it in any of the Apostolic Fathers. Tertullian, as he points out, is "the first to assert direct sacerdotal claims," which, however, he qualifies by his strong assertion of a universal priesthood. "The first champion of undisguised sacerdotalism," he shows, is Cyprian. "As Cyprian crowned the edifice of Episcopal power, so also was he the first to put forward, without relief or disguise, these sacerdotal assumptions," which, he adds, "were imported into Christianity by the ever-increasing mass of heathen converts, who were incapable of shaking off their sacerdotal prejudices, and appreciating the free spirit of the Gospel." Observe in passing how the growth of the Episcopate and of sacerdotalism went on together, just as they have had a peculiar affinity for each other ever since. It is not without significance that it is in Episcopal Churches, and in these only, that sacerdotalism is rampant. Archbishop Plunket must excuse us for saying that, with a most sincere desire for Christian union, this peculiar affinity which it has, and always has had for sacerdotalism, makes us wary of the so-called "historic Episcopate." For my part, I prefer the Episcopate that has the double virtue of being both historic and Scriptural.

It was under the influence of this two-fold deviation from New Testament ideas that Cyprian in the middle of the third century was enabled to take up the position, so far removed from the New Testament standpoint, that the bishop is essential to the very existence of the Church, and to be separate from the bishop is to be separate from the Church. "The true centre and living pillar of Catholicism" (says Baur), "the organizing and animating principle of the whole body corporate, is the Episcopate. Now, the early idea of the Episcopate was that the bishop was to be to the individual community of Christians, concretely and visibly, what the Jewish Messianic idea in its Christian development represented Christ as being for the Church in His heavenly dignity. And thus in the first beginnings of the Episcopal constitution we see before us the whole Papal hierarchy of the Middle Ages."* The papal supremacy is but a development of the same idea. If in the interest of external unity a diocesan bishop is necessary and a metropolitan and a national primate are also necessary, the conclusion was inevitable that a visible head and centre of the whole Church on earth, an *episcopus omnium episcoporum*, is no less essential and legitimate.

Such is the genesis of this idea of the visible Church, and of the whole Papal hierarchy in which it was embodied. It came chiefly from two sources, from Roman imperialism and from Pagan sacerdotalism. Now, if a person, whose father and mother you know to have been of humble rank, sets up a claim to royal lineage and a royal inheritance, you only laugh at his pretensions. A claim was set up some years ago to the title and estates of Sir Roger Tichborne. But when it was proved in court that the claimant had a much humbler origin, and that his proper name was Arthur Orton, an English jury made short work of his audacious pretensions. When in the Christian literature of the second, third and subsequent centuries you see, as you do see, the genesis and gradual growth of this externalistic conception of the Church, when you see the father of it to have been Roman

* Baur's "Church History of the First Three Centuries," 3d ed., p. 112.

imperialism, and the mother of it heathen sacerdotalism, your respect for it is considerably reduced, and only the large number of people who are dupes of it compels you to treat it with any seriousness.

II. But observe further that the growth of the visible Church after this pattern was but part of a general tendency to materialize and paganize Christianity. External observances took the place of spiritual and moral action. A magical efficacy in washing away sin was attributed to the external rite of baptism. The material bread in the Eucharist became the real body of Christ, and the life and aliment of the soul to him who partook of it. The repentance of the New Testament became the penance of the Vulgate— "a laborious sort of baptism" for working out sin. Pardon of sin was offered for such external acts as the payment of a sum of money, a pilgrimage to Rome or Jerusalem, or enlistment on a crusade to Palestine—acts that not only had no vital connection with morality, and no moral significance, but that were often an occasion for the indulgence of the passions. Rich nobles were enabled to reduce a fast of years to as many days, either by the payment of money or by compelling their dependants to share the fast with them. In the same way extraordinary miraculous virtue was ascribed to relics. Fabulous prices were paid for them, and fierce contests waged by monasteries to obtain possession of them. The whole forest of Lebanon would not have sufficed to produce all the wood that was brought from the East as fragments of the true cross. Fortunes were made by the manufacture of spurious relics; and image-worship was but another manifestation of the same paganizing tendency. Nay, Gregory the Great wrote in connection with the conversion of the Anglo-Saxons, that Pagan forms of worship might be profitably preserved if modified to Christian uses, and that even sacrifices of oxen might continue if they were offered on saints' days! Not only Pagans, but Pagan rites and practices were baptized.

Time won't permit me even to touch on the practical fruit borne by this system in its most palmy days. So far had men got away from spiritual Christianity and a true idea of the divine Being Himself, that when Ratherius of Verona, A.D. 974, reminded his clergy that God is a Spirit, some of them cried out, "What shall we do? We thought we knew something about God, but God is nothing at all, if He has not a head." The moral outcome was precisely what you might expect. Even the personal history of the Popes themselves during long periods, when every precept of the Decalogue was set at naught by them, and the Papal chair was occupied by the paramours or illegitimate children of three infamous women, would disgrace the annals of the most barbarous and degraded of the South Sea Islanders.

III. But the visible corporate society described by Mr. Gore "claims to have been instituted as the home of the new covenant of salvation by the incarnate Son of God" and His Apostles. Does the New Testament give any countenance to this theory of the Church? I have practically answered this question already in showing that its origin was post-Apostolic. But at least a glance must be taken at the Church delineated by our Lord and His Apostles; for the whole question turns upon this: What is the nature of the Church instituted by its authorized founders? Here to-day I can only give the heads of the statement I have prepared on this part of the subject.

1. The term *ecclesia* in the New Testament denotes (says Chremer) "the redeemed community in its two-fold aspect: (1) The entire of all who are called (*hoi cletoi*) by and to Christ's Church universal. (2) Every Church in which the character of the Church as a whole is repeated." "Where two or three are gathered together in My name there am I in the midst of them," says Christ (Matt. xviii., 20). What secures Christ's presence and constitutes the "two or three"

a Church is their being gathered together in His name, not their being in connection with an Episcopal hierarchy. "I am the door" (He says in another place—the door to the sheepfold, which is another name for the Church), "by Me if any man enter in he shall be saved, and shall go in and out, and find pasture" (John x., 9). The Church has the same broad basis in Paul's conception of it. He writes "unto the Church of God which is at Corinth, to them that are sanctified in Christ Jesus, called to be saints, with all that in every place call upon the name of Jesus Christ our Lord" (I. Cor. i., 2). All who are united to Christ by faith, all who in every place call upon His name, are recognized as members of His Church.

2. It is to the whole Christian society as thus defined that all Church power is given. The power of binding and loosing given first to Peter (Matt. xvi., 19) is extended to the disciples generally (Matt. xviii., 18). Even the words in John xx., 21–23, "Whosoever sins ye remit," etc., are shown by such expositors as Alford, Bishop Lightfoot, Plumptre, Maclear, etc., to have been addressed not to the Apostles merely, but to others as well. We thus see on what solid Scriptural ground the Reformers based their teaching that all Church power resided originally in the whole Church. It was a fundamental doctrine with the Reformers, says Principal Cunningham, that "all the power and authority necessary for the Church executing its functions, and attaining its objects, lay radically and fundamentally in the Church itself—in the company of believers; so that, when necessity required, Churches might provide and establish office-bearers for themselves, and do whatever might be needful for securing all the objects connected with their welfare, and the enjoyment of all the ordinances which Christ appointed." Even Hooker fully grants this admitting that "the whole Church visible is the true original subject of all power" (Eccl. Pol., vii., 14).

3. And now, what, in New Testament teaching, is the relation of the ministry to the Church? That a definite and permanent ministry was instituted by the Apostles, to my mind, admits of no doubt; nor, in view of this, am I able to see that the Church is now at liberty to adopt any form of ministry, any polity it pleases. But my point at present is, What relation does the ministry set up by the Apostles sustain to the Church? Is that ministry so much of the essence of the Church that a Christian society that lacks it cannot be regarded as being a Church at all? It seems to me that that question is already answered in the words of Christ, "Where two or three are gathered together in My name, there am I in the midst of them," and in Paul's synonym for the Church, "All that in every place call upon the name of Jesus Christ our Lord." Again, when the elders are told to "feed the Church of God" (Acts xx., 28); when it is said that "God hath set some in the Church, first Apostles," etc. (I. Cor. xii., 28); when bishops are represented as "taking care of the Church of God" (I. Tim. iii., 5); and Timothy is instructed "how to behave himself in the house of God, which is the Church of the living God" (I. Tim. iii., 15); in all these instances the office-bearers are distinguished from the Christian community, and the Christian community, considered apart from the office-bearers, is called "the Church." It follows that, however obligatory it is upon every Christian society to have a Scriptural ministry, and however necessary that ministry is to the well-being of the Church, it is not essential to its being. The Church exists before the ministry, and the ministry exists for the Church.

4. Another question now arises—Wherein consists the essential unity of the Church of Christ? On what does the New Testament lay special emphasis in enforcing it? Now the unity of Christians is the unity of those who have "one Lord, one faith, one baptism, one God and Father of all,"

and who are animated by one life and spirit. Adhesion to the visible society of Christians is signified by baptism, and their unity and fellowship are exhibited and promoted by their participation of one bread in the Eucharist; but the unity insisted on is mainly spiritual and moral, finding its cement and bond in love. And office-bearers are given, not, be it observed, as a part of this essential unity, but for the purpose of promoting it; "for the edifying of the body of Christ, till we all come in the unity of the faith and of the knowledge of the Son of God unto a perfect man, unto the measure of the stature of the fulness of Christ." When, therefore, Lord Bacon says, "It is good we return unto the ancient bonds of unity in the Church of God, which was one faith, one baptism, and not one hierarchy," he is strictly Pauline.

5. What has just been said with regard to the unity of the Church is in striking unison with what the Apostle teaches respecting schism: "When ye come together in the Church I hear that there be divisions (*schismata*) among you" (I. Cor. xi., 18). "I exhort you that there be no divisions (*schismata*) among you" (I. Cor. i., 10). You see, the schisms in the Church of Corinth (and they are the only schisms mentioned in the New Testament) were not secessions from the Church, but the rending of its internal unity of mind and heart by the growth of factions, and by dissensions in their Church meetings. You see from this that there may be real schism among the members of the same congregation, in the same Church, living under the same Church polity.

It is quite true that secession from a Christian society is a most grave and serious step, and requires good grounds to justify it.

"The spirit I that evermore divides"

is the delineation of Mephistopheles as given by himself in "Faust." But withdrawal from a Christian society on account of gross corruptions in doctrine, discipline and life is nowhere called schism in Scripture. On the contrary, we are to " turn away from those who have only a form of godliness, but deny the power thereof " (II. Tim. iii., 5). We are to " withdraw from them that walk disorderly and not after the tradition received from the Apostles " (II. Thess. iii., 6). Our Lord Himself informs the Church that suffers corruption in doctrine and life that unless she repents He " will fight against her with the sword of His mouth " (Rev. ii., 16). He tells another Church that except she repents He " will remove her candlestick out of its place," which means unchurching her, for the candlestick represents the Church. This yoke is not laid upon us by our Master, to live in fellowship with those who corrupt His teaching and despise His laws. Though Israel play the harlot, Judah is not to offend, nor to come to Gilgal, nor to go up to Bethhaven, to participate in his idolatrous rites—when Ephraim is joined to his idols he is to be let alone (Hos. iv., 15, 17).

The Reformers, therefore, were fully justified in withdrawing from a Church which had ceased to " walk after the tradition of the Apostles," and become thoroughly corrupt in doctrine, worship, discipline and life; justified in disencumbering themselves of the corruptions that had accumulated, and in reviving and continuing the Church of the Apostles. Even on Anglican principles they had better reason than Anglican " Catholicism." The Anglican High Churchman goes back beyond the mediæval period to the Fathers that preceded it. That surely is a tremendous breach of " historic continuity." Now, if the High Churchman may leap back over the whole Papal and mediæval period to the time of the Fathers, why should it be unlawful to go back a little farther still to the Church as founded by our Lord and His Apostles and attempt to reproduce it? The Reformers felt that in doing so they were breaking no real continuity. It was a strong point with them that they were not making a new creed or creating a new Church. The doctrines which they taught they held forth as the old doctrines of the early creeds, stripped of error and superstition, and the forms which they revived were the old forms of the Apostolic Church, freed from the corruptions that had gathered round them. They had the continuity of true Christian doctrine, and faith, and worship, and life. Does the tree, in throwing off a huge excrescence that has grown on it, and threatens its vitality, cease to be the same tree? Does the living man in ultimately getting rid of a disease or deformity that has come on him, and long afflicted him, cease to be the same?

"The One Holy, Catholic, Apostolic Church," so-called, which I have been passing in review, how little worthy of the name it is! How narrow, contracted and sectarian, how materialistic and mechanical, when brought into the light of New Testament ideas! The French academicians defined a crab as "a little red fish that walks backwards" —an admirable definition, Cuvier said, only for three slight defects. It is not a fish, it is not red, and it does not walk backwards. The title, "The One Holy, Catholic, Apostolic Church," is about equally true to what it is meant to describe. Voltaire said of the "Holy Roman Empire" that that title had a similar defect; for what it was meant to designate was not "holy"; it was not "Roman," and it was not properly an "empire." The same may be said with equal truth of what is called "The One Holy, Catholic, Apostolic Church." We may not deny it perhaps the name of "Church," but it is not "one," but several; it is not and never has been remarkable for "sanctity"; it is certainly not "Apostolic," and being of all sects the most narrow and sectarian, it is less entitled than any other to the name of "Catholic." Most fittingly it may be addressed to-day in the words which the great Cæsarean bishop Firmilian addressed to Stephen, the Roman bishop of his day, who had cut off certain churches from communion: "How great is the sin of which you have incurred the guilt in cutting yourself off from so many Christian flocks. For do not deceive yourself, it is yourself you have cut off; he is the real schismatic who makes himself an apostate from the communion of the Church. While you think that you can cut off all from your communion, it is yourself whom you cut off from communion with all."

We, too, "believe in the holy Catholic Church," but in a larger sense. We believe in it in Paul's sense, as including "all that in every place call upon the name of Jesus Christ our Lord." We believe, too, in "the general assembly and Church of the first-born which are written in heaven," the invisible Church of God, whose boundaries no human eye can trace. On the roll of its membership may our names be registered!

CHRISTIANITY versus FORMALISM.

BY PRESIDENT S. A. ORT, D.D., WITTENBERG COLLEGE, SPRINGFIELD, OHIO.

WE are living in the closing period of the nineteenth century, a century which has phases of thought, scientific, philosophical and theological, and tendencies of moment peculiar to itself. Men are pushing their investigations into every field of knowledge. They are making a resurvey of the whole territory of intelligence. They are testing the conclusions of their predecessors. They are thinking over again, in boldest manner, the problem of man; whence he is, what he is, and whither he is going. They are vigorously discussing the existence of God; who He is, and how related to the universe; whether knowable or unknowable; whether He is the fixed law of a natural world, or a personal being who has revealed Himself in a supernatural way to man. They are citing the religion of Jesus to the test of criticism and the bar of reason, and, under the claim of highest certainty, are passing judgment on its origin, whether from beneath or from above. They are seeking in nature and in the powers of the human mind, the substantial good, the eternal portion of the soul.

With all this a restless, dissatisfied spirit everywhere prevails. On the one hand, the people are not content with the teachings of skepticism. They do not find in the practice of these the satisfaction which they crave. Neither, on the other hand, do they get in the doctrinal propositions or formal statements of divine truth that rest of soul and deep assurance of union with God, which are the special promise of the Gospel. In its living the age is largely sensuous. The earth-born spirit excites its energy, governs its conduct, and directs its activity. Under the influence of naturalism the impulse is to seek the temporal as the only solid good. The chiefest aim is to live and be sensuously happy. Nothing is judged worth care, save that which helps to make man a satisfied animal.

Religion, with its eternal concerns, is deemed an idle fancy or superstition or senseless something, which, when dressed in sensuous garb, may serve to entertain and give a momentary pleasure. True, the age talks much in one way and another about moral principle and spiritual truth. It familiarly uses such words as sin and righteousness and Gospel and even salvation; but these are merely words of formal speech, repeated parrot like, with no deep sense of the realities they express. Crime of divers sort, wickedness cunning and damnable, and every ungodliness of men are described to the public mind in a mode of address and by a kind of spectacle which reveal the absence of a tender conscience that hates all vileness and loves the pure.

It is not meant that our time is worse than any period of the human past. By no means. But the meaning is, that, in our day on this western continent, materialism, with all its sequences, wields a moulding power over the life of the people, over their thoughts, over their belief and over the course of their movement. And in addition the meaning is, that rationalism is beginning to show a dominating influence in many quarters, and is gradually moving forward to a more extensive sway over the religious views and faith of the multitudes.

In consequence of these existing facts, two tendencies are clearly discernible in the evangelical Church. One is the endeavor to substitute the form of the Christian life for the life itself, or the expression of Christian sentiment for the truth in that sentiment. Emphasis is placed on the phenomenal, and, hence, a phase of religious phenomenalism is presented as the best attraction to an outside world to frequent the house of prayer, and to the inside world it is exhibited as the most acceptable way of worshipping Almighty God and being devoutly Christian. This is formalism. It may be simply intellectual or it may be chiefly æsthetic. Christian piety and true godliness are neither one nor the other in substance, though in their formal manifestation both are truly involved. The Christian religion necessarily has its forms. Every kind of life has a mode or modes of expression. Likewise the Christian. That there are forms of doctrine and forms of worship is not strange or foreign to the spirit of the Gospel. Not in the least. A living Christianity could not exist without producing and developing them. They inseparably go with the Christian life, and with its true development truly grow. But when little stress is laid on the inner life, and the outward form is taken as its equivalent, then Christian service ceases to be a worship of God in spirit and truth, and becomes a mere artificial method for meeting the obligations of a religious profession. This is easy practice for a lukewarm church and is popular with the natural man.

The other tendency is to substitute human invention for the power of divine truth. The theory is, that the preaching of the Gospel must be adapted to the sensuous taste of the day, instead of being directed to the consciences of the people. This is an age eager for show, greedy for entertainment, fond of physical excitement, intensely delighted by the extravagant. The preaching, hence, that will crowd the church and make the popular preacher, is anything which in word or manner or speech, under the semblance of Gospel truth, will beget a sensation. This is sensationalism.

And now in the face of these tendencies, with naturalism ruling the energies of the masses and rationalism beginning to reveal its presence in growing strength, what is necessary?

Answer: A deep, practical apprehension of the fundamental nature of justifying faith.

This is the vital principle of the Gospel. It is not a mere doctrine, that which is worked out in thought and given definite limit and logical form, but it is a fact revealed in Christian consciousness, and a reality known in experience. It, hence, precedes dogma, and is conditional for the framing and development of religious truth into a system of well defined statement.

As a doctrine, justifying faith stands with other doctrines in certain logical order and is, therefore, one among many, a subject for the belief and examination of the intellectual understanding. But as a principle, justifying faith is before the mental conception, the formal exhibition of saving truth, and is that according to which the construction is made. It is the light in which the spiritual understanding moves and acts. Justifying faith is the essential principle of the Gospel—it is the Gospel; for the great Apostle pointedly declares that the Gospel is the power of God unto salvation to every one who believes. Abstract this principle, or make it subordinate, or calculate it to be a part only of the body of doctrine, and you thereby either set aside entirely or push far into the background the divine plan for the recovery of sinful man. What is this plan? Salvation by faith in a crucified Jesus.

A clear, practical apprehension of justifying faith is necessary for the Christian Church to-day, because it is only by this principle *that the truth in Christianity can be known with certainty.*

Two forms of human thought are extant. One looks outward and fixes sole attention on the natural; the other directs its vision inward and recognizes supreme authority and the determiner of all certainty to be the intellectual. The first knows only nature to be real existence. Beyond this the human mind cannot go. Natural law produces everything which is—the stars, the world, man and human history with all its strange and startling facts. This law is fixed, unchangeable. No outside or superior power could anywhere, or at any time, along the course of natural development, thrust in its energy, and modify or change the facts of nature and the life of man. A union, hence, of natural with supernatural cannot occur. The miracle of incarnation is absolutely impossible. Jesus of Nazareth, like every individual of the human race, is the product of material force. Christianity, the revelation of the eternal, personal God, is made to vanish in the idle dreamings of an unsettled brain. The only religion given a weary, struggling humanity, is that which says: "Obey the laws of nature; otherwise, suffer the consequences"; a religion without love, without hope, without faith, whose only teaching is : "Eat, drink and be merry, for to-morrow you die." This is naturalism, a kind of thinking, in present time, powerful and widely influential. It reaches every sphere and grade of human life, and is the master spirit in the busy movements, the toils and struggles of a restless, disappointed humanity. It sports itself not only in an unchristian world, but also wields increasing power over the practical life of the Church and mars the faith of many. It blurs the distinction between evangelical religion and worldliness, substitutes the ways and methods of the natural man for the plain efficient means of a divine Christianity and calls man to the seeking of his destiny by appeals to his sensuous nature or æsthetic taste, instead of by a pungent preaching of the truth concerning sin to his conscience, and salvation by faith in a crucified Redeemer to his soul. According to this scheme nothing is certain except that which is determined by the fixed and final law of a natural world.

The other form of popular thought in its ultimate result is one with naturalism, just as materialism and idealism finally strike hands in pantheism. But rationalism recognizes chiefly the subject of human knowledge, and, in the solution of the question of certainty, points to reason as supreme authority. To a physical world with its fixed laws, mind is superior. Reason has power of oversight and insight for all phenomena of material existence, and hence is competent to know their truth. More than this, it is able, on account of its constitution, to look up through and beyond the natural universe to the supernatural and recognize Him as eternal, omnipotent, benevolent Deity. This is the power of intuition, in the light of which every truth in its fundamental reality must be tried and settled.

Whatever reason in the exercise of its intuitive energy cannot know, is not truth for man, in short is no truth at all. Mention a scheme of redemption, and rationalism says: "The natural powers of man alone are sufficient for the attainment of his chiefest good." Nothing pertains to this life which can prevent the ultimate reaching of his moral destiny. Sin is a sheer circumstance or accident, or at worst a misfortune, which can be easily remedied by a proper culture. Speak of the Christian religion, a revelation of the eternal God in Jesus Christ, and the New Testament as the Scripture of this revelation, and rationalism says: "This is a human book and the religion of a genius." A miracle of knowledge is impossible. Inspiration, which arises from contact between the divine and human, is inconceivable. There is but one kind of inspiration and that is the kind which distinguishes the wise and great from the common herd of mankind—the enthusiasm of genius.

Rationalism poses itself before the world as the only hope of man. It points him to a religion whose God is the human reason, whom he must implicitly trust and to whose authority he must reverently bow; a religion in which conscience is kept far in the background, and sin is made to appear simply as an unfavorable power, over which, by and by, through his own sufficiency, man will gain completest victory; a religion whose centre is the intellect and whose bulwarks are the forms of logical thought. Here truth is tested like precious metal in the crucible, and here is given the highest assurance that can ever be found in human experience.

It would be idle to close our eyes against the fact that various forms of the rationalistic spirit are manifesting themselves in the thought and life of the present generation. Everywhere almost, in school and church, in individual and social belief, their presence is evident. Not abruptly, suddenly, or in extremest form does this spirit immediately exhibit its power, but quietly, slowly, with plausible speech, it gains for itself a place in thought and belief. At length, boldly and with radical demand, it insists that the old paths be forsaken, and that Christianity, the religion of miracle and grace, be given up. What it has produced is well known : empty pews, deserted churches, pulpits turned into platforms, where every question under Heaven is discussed, except that one about which the human soul has always been most deeply concerned, "How can man be just before God?" and a people uneasy, seeking rest and finding none, reckless, miserable. These are facts which attest the products of this Christless spirit. What it has produced in a former generation and in a foreign land, it will repeat in our day and on this Western Continent. In fact, its working is already manifest and its legitimate fruits are apparent. Men are running to and fro, asking, What can I believe? Where is the truth which satisfies? The creeds are insufficient. We have thought them through in careful manner, but they do not give us what we want—peace, satisfaction. The common people go up to the house of God and listen for a message from Heaven to their weary, sin-burdened souls—a message of love, of sympathy, of gracious tenderness, but the sermon is an address to their heads, or sense of the beautiful, or appetite for entertainment, and moves at wide distance from both conscience and heart, whose chiefest aim seems to be to make Church members rather than persuade perishing sinners to become like Jesus of Nazareth and incite believers to a more unreserved dedication of their whole life to the service of a loving and most lovable God.

No wonder the plaintive cry comes up from every side, What ails thee, O Zion? and men, in boisterous manner, talk about the decay of the Church, the decline of Protestantism, and the failure of Christianity. Reason is usurping the throne of Christ and rejecting the witness of the Holy Ghost in the heart to forgiveness of sin, peace with God and assurance of eternal life. And now here are sensuous thought with its widespread influence on the one hand, and, on the other hand, the intellectual powers of man as supreme authority and sufficiency, energizing themselves to supplant the Gospel of an incarnate Redeemer, rob the world of a divine revelation and leave man without a heaven-inspired chart to steer his bark, as best he can, on a storm-tossed sea to the haven of eternal rest. What can be done to defeat these unfriendly powers and vindicate the Gospel of the crucified Nazarene? How shall the truth in Christianity be verified for this generation? By argument? By the power of logic? Does this give certainty, that kind of certainty to which clings not the slightest doubt, and is the assurance of a present, living reality? What is the sphere of logic? To settle the truth in a proposition, or to determine its form and relation to other propositions? Does it deal in any way with the thing itself, or only with the conception of the thing? Evidently the latter. True, it produces conviction of certainty, but this is a conviction which pertains to the forms of thought, and is solely for the intellectual understanding. The faith it generates is mere historical belief, which finds its limits altogether within the compass of formal thought. If inquiry be pushed beyond the forms themselves to their contents, and the demand be made to verify the truth in these, the human understanding knows no other method than that which answers for the certainty of the forms. When, therefore, the highest ground of assurance is centred in the logical understanding, the form of truth and the truth itself are confounded with each other, that is, the truth is the form, and the form is the truth. Under this conception, formal Christianity and the truth in Christianity are one and the same, and hence, certainty for the first is certainty for the second. But this means that the only faith necessary to assurance of salvation is the belief of the intellect. In this case most stress will be laid on logical propositions, and the utmost care be given to dogmatic statement. Great, massive systems of Christian thought will be developed. The historical evidences for the truth of the sacred Scriptures will be marshalled in exact order and powerful array, and every proof be furnished necessary to convince the understanding of the natural man. But though convinced, he is still the natural man. His only belief is that which he refers to the force of logic. With his intellect he knows the facts and declarations of the Scriptures, but he is yet a stranger to the saving power of the Gospel. But this is the very heart of the Gospel—Christ Jesus, who is mighty to save. This is the truth, the precious, joyful truth, which lies beyond the reach of the natural understanding, and in its reality never can be known by any sort of mental operation. It must be experienced in the heart, through the witness of the Holy Ghost, by a faith which not merely accepts the formal Scriptures as authentic and credible, but far beyond this, appropriates the saving content of the sacred Word, the living, personal Jesus, who offers Himself in this Word to the lost soul, its life and salvation. The certainty which transcends every form of doubt, and which abides the irrepressible conviction that the Christ of the Gospel is the all-sufficient Saviour, arises out of a real contact of the living, personal Word with the human soul. In this contact the heart knows Jesus, the real, personal Jesus, and not simply an impersonal statement. The formal Scriptures, the record of divine revelation, point out the way, but Jesus is the way; they give an account of the truth, but Jesus is the truth; they describe the life, but Jesus, and He only, is the life. Contact with the record is, hence, not enough. The soul and Christ must verily come together, if the great and precious truth in Christianity would be known, and a clear assurance of peace with God through the Holy Ghost would ever be a fact of personal experience. But this real contact between Christ and the human heart can only be realized through the faith which confidingly receives, appropriates the Jesus who offers Himself to the soul, its eternal portion and highest good.

In the language of Luther: "God must witness to me in my heart, that this is God's Word, else it is not determined. Through the Apostles God originally had that same Word preached, and He still has it preached. But if even the Archangel Gabriel were to proclaim it from Heaven, it would not help me. I must have God's own word; I will hear what God says. Men, indeed, may preach the Word to me, but God alone can put it in the heart, or else nothing results from it. This Word is certain, and though all the world should speak against it, yet I know that it is not otherwise. Who decides me in this? Not man, but the truth alone, which is so certain that no man can deny it." Also with the Apostle Paul we say, "I know whom I have believed, and am persuaded that He is able to keep that which I have committed unto Him against that day." It must, however, be clearly noted that this persuasion of the Apostle differs widely from that assurance which only holds that the doctrines of Holy Scriptures are true. The former is the assurance of justification and the adoption of the individual witnessed in the heart by the Holy Ghost. The latter is a conviction produced by an inference of the cause from the effect. The procedure is on this wise : Holy Scripture possesses converting, saving power. "The changed heart knows that the effect of Scripture is good." Hence the cause is divine ; in other words, inspiration of Scripture is true. This kind of assurance plainly substitutes the means of grace, word and sacrament, for the living God, and is secure in the possession of the pure doctrine.

Here is certainty of having a creed, but absence of experience in the inner life of what the creed describes. Here is possession of dogmatic formulæ, but ignorance of the vital realities denoted by the formulæ. This is the orthodoxy of two centuries ago, the orthodoxy which staked everything on the assurance of doctrine as the ultimate ground of defence, dared natural reason to combat, and at last was worsted in the fight. Scholastic orthodoxy was one-sided. It recognized chiefly the formal Scriptures, and depreciated the testimony of the Holy Ghost in the heart to forgiveness of sin; and this was its weakness. When confronted by rationalism with its high claims for the natural man and his rejection of the saving content of the Gospel, a crucified Jesus, scholastic orthodoxy had no stronger defence than the assurance of logic. In the fierce struggle which ensued, this could not avail, and utter defeat was the inevitable result. The same was true of pietistic fanaticism. It likewise was partial. It neglected the formal Scriptures as the Word of God, and hence had no fixed, invariable authority and rule for Christian faith and practice. It found assurance solely in an inner sentiment, which in itself is variable and uncertain. When called upon by rationalism to answer for the hope it professed, it could only respond in extravagant speech and wild exclamation, and was forced at last to surrender to the foe of sacred Scripture and inner experience of salvation. Justifying faith, on the contrary, lays hold of the truth in the formal Scriptures and in the creed, and makes this its own possession. It knows for itself immediately, through the witness of the Holy Ghost, what is the Word and what is not; it knows the living power of the Gospel to be, indeed, the power of God unto salvation, and that through the Christ whom it receives, it has true peace and clear assurance of eternal life. Justifying faith has the testimony to the truth in Christianity, in itself, with itself, a present fact of conscious experience; and with this most certain of all convictions, personal assurance, it is able to meet every denial of miracle, whether it be miracle of knowledge, or miracle of life. To rationalism it gives the irrepressible answer: I know that these Scriptures are the Word of God, because He has spoken their truth in my ear; and to naturalism it triumphantly replies: I know that Jesus of Nazareth is God manifest in the flesh, because He has revealed Himself to me as both the wisdom and power of God, in whom is life and light, joy and peace.

THE ENGLISH BIBLE AS A TEXT-BOOK IN THEOLOGICAL SEMINARIES.

BY PRESIDENT ROBERT GRAHAM, COLLEGE OF THE BIBLE, LEXINGTON, KY.

IT may be safely affirmed that the mental energy of our day is directedmainly to the investigation of biblical questions. Scholarship is doing its utmost to determine the exact value of the claims of the sacred writings upon human thought and their demand of devout and implicit belief, and the deepest interest centres in those discussions which vitally concern the foundations of Christian faith and worship. And this is no matter of wonder. If, indeed, it be true that "all Scripture (being) given by inspiration of God is profitable for teaching, for conviction, for amendment of life, for training in righteousness that the man of God may be perfect, thoroughly furnished unto all good works," the intellectual activity manifested in the various departments of Biblical study finds a most ample justification. "Search the Scriptures," said Jesus, "for in them ye think ye have eternal life, and these are they which testify of Me." Accordingly when Paul preached Christ to the Berean Jews it is said that "These were more noble than those of Thessalonica in that they received the word with a'l readiness of mind and searchedthe Scriptures daily to see whether these things were so, therefore many of them believed." If such be the legitimate effect of the Old Testament oracles concerning the Messiah when candidly studied, how greatly shall this intelligent belief be invigorated by proper attention to the testimony of the apostolic "eyewitnesses of His majesty"?

Nor is it merely the interest of Christian faith that is affected by the influence which the Bible exerts over individuals and nations. The interests of Christian civilization are equally involved. For the Holy Scriptures are not only "profitable for teaching" and "for conviction," but also "for amendment of life" and "for training in righteousness." As the sun both illumines the world and warms it into life, so the divine light that goes forth from the Word of God is attended by a moral power that elevates and ennobles the souls of men. A practical demonstration of this profitableness of the Holy Scriptures may be found in a comparison of the moral condition of Christian lands with that of those on which the light of divine truth has never dawned. So instructive is the result of such comparison that a distinguished skeptical writer, in concluding an article on the Christian religion, expressed with emphasis the desire that its influence should not decrease, but constantly increase from age to age, giving as his reason that the effect was the moral uplifting and purification of human thought and action. Christ then is not only "the Light of the world," but the source and sustainer of right living, and by consequence the author of true happiness.

Now from these premises the natural conclusion would be that the Bible should be used as a text-book not only in theological schools, but in all institutions of learning. Science and philosophy may minister to the intellectual progress of mankind, but the higher moral refinement of the race is due directly or indirectly to the influence of religious truth. Let the importance then of a thorough study of the Bible be emphasized as paramount. The special reason for its use as a text-book in theological seminaries is found in the latter part of the quotation given above, "that the man of God may be perfect, thoroughly furnished unto all good works." God's man or messenger or ministerial servant has certain great ends to accomplish such as teaching, convincing, correcting and training in righteousness, and for effecting these important results he is thoroughly furnished by the Holy Scriptures. In other words, the abundant provision for the accomplishment of all good works is objectively presented in the Bible, and it remains for "the man of God," the proclaimer and teacher of the divine word, to become thoroughly imbued in mind and heart with its inexhaustible riches. Whatever others may do with the Bible, if he desires to fulfil his mission with fidelity and integrity, he cannot afford to make it a mere book of reference or sort of religious armory to which he may resort for weapons in the shape of proof-texts to carry on a theological warfare. His own soul must burn under the influence of its "words of life and beauty" that he may fill others with holy aspirations after a true and righteous life.

But what is it to use the English Bible as a text-book, and what has mainly been the practice respecting this matter in theological schools? There is known to the writer only one institution that really meets this important demand. Lectures on the sacred writings, in whole or in part, and the presentation of views touching the Word of God, however excellent these might be in themselves, do not constitute a real inculcation of the Holy Scriptures. Let us illustrate this point in the first place by the correct method of procedure in the department of sacred history. When the student is made familiar with biblical events, and in the light of the Scriptures discerns their relations and especially their bearing upon the great object of divine revelation, he is using the Bible as a text-book to which he subjects his mind and heart for infallible instruction unmingled with human speculations. It is far better for example to study the character of Abraham as depicted in the Bible, to fix in the memory the events of his interesting life, and to comprehend their import as interpreted by Paul in his Epistle to the Galatians, than to be entertained by the discourse of an eloquent professor on the manliness and moral grandeur of the great patriarch. To obtain an accurate knowledge of sacred history itself, and not to receive the views of a learned lecturer respecting biblical events, is to make the Bible a text-book in this department of study.

And the great importance of such scriptural knowledge is evidenced by the fact that God has employed mainly the historical method in revealing His will and inculcating the divine lessons connected with the whole system of human redemption. The Gospel itself consists of certain great facts standing in vital relation to the spiritual interests and happiness of mankind. Even the evidence by which the reality of these facts of transcendent importance is sustained and Christian faith established comes to us in historic form. "We have not followed cunningly devised fables," says Peter, "in making known to you the power and coming of the Lord Jesus Christ, but were eye-witnesses of His majesty." "That which we have heard," says John, "which we have seen with our eyes, which we have looked upon and our hands have handled of the word of life declare we unto you. For the life was manifested and we have seen it and bear witness, and show unto you that eternal life which was with the Father and was manifested unto us." Accordingly the marvellous deeds and supernatural events that entered into the Saviour's wonderful life on earth constitute an essential element of the testimony of God concerning His Son. "The works," said Jesus, "that the Father hath given Me to accomplish, the very works that I do, bear witness of Me that the Father hath sent Me." Hence the sacred record of these events is pointed to as the ground of Christian belief. "These are written," says John, "that you might believe that Jesus is the Christ, the Son of God, and that believing you might have life through His name." In the light of all these Scriptures what can be regarded of more importance than the study of sacred history and the use of the English Bible as a text-book to this end?

But it is more in the department of biblical exegesis than in that of sacred history that the theories of men are apt to be substituted for the utterances of the Divine Word itself. All sound principles of hermeneutics conspire to one important end, to allow the Holy Scriptures to speak for themselves. It is, therefore, in the strictest sense of the word, a science whose laws cannot be safely neglected if we wish to really make the Bible a text-book in exegetical studies, and thus to ascertain what the Scriptures actually teach. A professor who would simply offer to his class his own interpretation of a given passage or present the views of a number of distinguished exegetes, leaving the student to choose the exposition which he may regard the most felicitous, is not pursuing a method that will allow the Divine Word to interpret itself. His course of procedure is not grounded on scientific principles, and cannot lead to any very profitable result. It is, indeed, the almost universal practice for men of great learning and ability connected with universities of world-wide renown to pour out their scholarly thoughts before the class in their lectures on different parts of the Bible, requiring the student to take notes on what is thus presented, and accordingly prepare for recitation. The result of necessity is a mingling of the wisdom of men with the teaching of inspiration, with perhaps a larger ingredient of the former than of the latter. And this is not the only pernicious result. The mental discipline of the student, the development of his capacity to think for himself under the guidance of principles, is here reduced to a minimum. A radical change in the method of procedure is imperatively demanded to secure a happier end, and to make the English Bible a text-book in this most interesting and vitally important department of biblical study.

And this brings us in conclusion to the consideration of

the true method of instruction in exegetical investigations. First of all the student should become thoroughly acquainted with the unalterable and self-evident principles of interpretation which cannot possibly be disregarded in exegesis without falling into error as to the teaching of the Scriptures. Then under a severe application of these laws every passage submitted for interpretation should be examined without reference to prepossessions of any kind, and the result accepted without hesitation. If, for example, sufficient light is thrown upon a passage to make its import clear by statements in the context or in passages elsewhere bearing directly on the subject in hand, these must not be neglected in the effort to determine the meaning. To do so would be far from allowing the Scriptures to interpret themselves. Without compliance with these indisputable laws of hermeneutics the correct exegesis of any passage is utterly impossible. Now the manifest duty of a professor in this department of instruction is not to present for acceptance some exposition of his own, or the views of distinguished expositors, but to require his students to test the merits of whatever view may be presented by a rigid application of the principles under the guidance of which all exegetical procedure must of necessity be conducted. This would not only lead to satisfactory conclusions as manifestly correct, but give opportunity for intelligent discipline, the expansion of mental capacity, the development of the powers of thought on the part of the learner. Hermeneutics being in reality a science, the results of a true and faithful application of its principles and laws cannot rest on mere authority or rationally be sustained by the weight of celebrated names, any more than the demonstrations of mathematics can receive force as a commendation to acceptance from the renown of distinguished mathematicians.

THE MINISTER AND HIS BIBLE.*

BY PROF. H. W. WARRINNER, B.D., CONGREGATIONAL
COLLEGE OF CANADA, MONTREAL.

I PRESUME that on such an occasion as this, it would be quite in order for the incoming professor to give an address on some feature of his own special work, even though it might be somewhat technical and abstruse; but I thought, in consideration of the general character of this audience—an audience composed not of students and ministers only, but also of the representative members of our various churches—that it would be better to choose a theme which, while it should have special reference to some phase of ministerial life and work, would also be of vital interest to every one who has the welfare of the Church of Christ at heart. I have therefore chosen for my subject, "The Minister and his Bible," and in developing this theme I propose to enquire, first of all, what the Bible is to the minister; secondly, what the college proposes to do for the minister in relation to his Bible studies, and, lastly, what the minister must do for himself.

In speaking of what the Bible is to the minister, we must remember that the minister is himself a man of like passions as his people. He is not a being of a higher or different order, removed from the common ills of humanity, the frailties and weaknesses, the temptations, the sorrows and disappointments to which flesh is heir—far from it; he is as truly human as any of his flock, and just as liable to go astray as any other Christian. And this fact is not a thing to be lamented, as if it were derogatory to the very highest success in his work: on the contrary, it is just this human

* Delivered at the opening of the college, October 2d, 1890.

element that by the grace of God may make him most successful in winning men from sin; even as the high priest of old was taken from among men, as one who could bear gently with the ignorant and erring, for that he himself also was compassed with infirmity.

Nevertheless this fact, namely, that the minister himself is beset with infirmities, necessitates on his part constant watchfulness against temptation, and persistent endeavors to build up his soul in righteousness. And how shall he do this? How shall he nourish his own soul in goodness, keep his own faith firm and true, his own heart pure and clean? How shall he obtain inspiration and strength for his own conflict with sin, if it be not at the very fountains to which he leads his people? They drink of the same living stream, the ever-blessed truth of God. The Bible must be to him inspiration and strength, just as it is to his people. It must be the bread of his life, of which he himself must first partake. The minister can no more live a Christian life without communion with God in prayer, and in the meditation of His truth, than can the weakest, the humblest, the most ignorant disciple in all his flock.

What then is the Bible to the minister? It is his life. Here he will find comfort in his sorrow, and companionship —divinest companionship—in the hours of his loneliness. Here he will gather weapons for his own spiritual warfare; sharp, keen and victorious; here he will find holiest inspiration to service, when perhaps his hands are weary, and his heart grows faint. In a word, he will meet his Lord and Saviour here, and in His fellowship find light and life.

And as a servant of the Lord Jesus Christ, co-operating with his Master in the world's salvation, he will find the Bible to be the great instrument in his life-work. If he would indeed be a successful follower of the Apostles of Christ, he must, like them, be emphatically a "minister of the Word." He must sow in the field of humanity the true seed of the kingdom, which is the "Word of God." It is to this he is called; and the obligation is laid upon him, as it was upon Timothy, to "preach the Word."

And it is by means of the preaching of this Word that he is to be successful in saving the world, "by the foolishness of preaching," as the Apostle Paul says, that is, by the preaching of the Gospel, which seemed so foolish because of its apparent inadequacy to accomplish the mighty task imposed upon it. It is not to be wondered at that the supercilious Greek and proud Roman looked upon the attempt to convert the world to the faith of a crucified Jew, through the preaching of a handful of obscure and, for the most part, uneducated provincialists, as utterly foolish and vain. And yet such was the sublime faith, yea, the divine prescience of Jesus, that He sent His followers forth to conquer the prejudices and passions of a world, by simply preaching His Gospel to every creature.

There are men to-day, even in Christian churches, I am sorry to say, who seem to have lost their faith in the power of the simple Gospel to win the affections and conquer the pride of men. There is a clamor for some new thing, some new ritual, some startling sensationalism, some eccentricity of belief, or mannerism in the pulpit; *anything* to give a little spice and flavor to a Gospel otherwise too insipid for the palled and jaded taste of this fast and full-fed age.

Thank God, we are not one of these; we still believe that the Gospel, and nothing but the Gospel, is the power of God unto salvation. That if Jesus be only truly lifted up, He will draw all men unto Himself. Depend upon it, he will be the most effective minister of Christ, who best brings Christ into living contact with men.

The preacher is not called of God to be a lecturer on social or political economy. Others, it may be, can do that better than he; or, at any rate, he may find some other platform than the pulpit from which to discourse on these themes. He is not called of God to ventilate his own peculiar theories and speculations in the realm of morals and religion. He is called to deliver a definite message, and that with the greatest urgency, because the time is short and men are dying fast.

I read, some time ago, an analysis, by an eminent leader of Christian thought, of the preaching of one of the greatest pulpit-orators of this age; a man whose mind was, perhaps, more fruitful in moral ideas than that of any other man on this side of the Atlantic. In that analysis, three steps in the development of the preacher's methods were emphasized (I quote from memory, after the lapse of two or three years):

In his earlier years, it was said, the preacher proclaimed the general truths of Christian doctrine and experience, as they came up, one by one, before his mind. Then he proceeded to systematize these doctrines and experiences, and to formulate them in logical order. Lastly, laying aside all systems, he became an explorer in new and untrodden paths. The critic held that the last development of the preacher's mind and method was the most fruitful of all. And, perhaps, in some respects, the critic was right; but, in other respects, and these the most important, the last period was the least satisfactory.

Brethren, I do not conceive the office of the preacher to be that of an explorer. I mean, that he is not called of God to lead the way into untrodden realms of speculation, or to offer for men's salvation an untried remedy. If Christ had not come; if He had not spoken; if He had not given a clear and definite message to His disciples; then indeed we might have been compelled to grope in the darkness for ourselves. But since God has spoken, it is for the preacher to hear the word at God's mouth, and declare it to the people. Since Christ has come, it is for the preacher to be simply His herald; to go forth into the world and preach

His Gospel, a Gospel which, thank God, has been fully tried by the centuries, and never found wanting yet. And if he does that, his preaching will never lose its sweetness and power, so long as sin and misery and hunger and want are in the world.

Moreover, it is only as a man's preaching is biblical that it can possess the very highest authority. A certain authority the preacher may have, apart from this, in proportion as men have faith in his sincerity, his knowledge and common sense; but if he wants to clothe himself with the authority of God, he must utter God's truth, and not his own surmisings.

The Apostle Paul realized this, as he contemplated visiting the luxurious city of Corinth. Thinking it all over in his mind, he came to the solemn conclusion not to know anything among them save Christ and Him crucified. True, he felt that he was with them in weakness, for he had voluntarily stripped himself of all the advantages of scholastic knowledge and oratory. But the power of God was on him—aye, and it was on his hearers too ; and when they believed—as they did—their faith rested, not on the persuasion of his philosophy and rhetoric, but on the very "wisdom of God." The young preacher is often tempted to despise his own youth, at least if he be rightfully modest ; he is tempted to shrink from standing before men who, in so many departments of knowledge, surpass him so very far. But he need not fear when he declares simply and truly the Word of God. The greatest and the wisest among men will bow down to that Word, though it be uttered by the lips of a child. It is, in fact, not the preacher who speaks, but God who speaks through him.

Again, this use of the Word will furnish the preacher with an endless variety of themes. I would not have you suppose, from what I have said, that I conceive the office of the preacher limited to the simple declaration of the guilt and ruin of sin, and the offer of salvation through Jesus Christ our Lord. No! Those are but the rudiments of that Gospel. It is the duty of the preacher to build up men into the fulness of the manhood of Christ. To inspire them to holy, Christ-like living in all their relationships—in the home, in business, in society, in the state. If you want to see what Paul meant by preaching Christ's Gospel, read his epistles. There was nothing of true human interest—nothing that affected the welfare of man in his whole composite nature, as body, soul and spirit—that he believed to be beyond the range of the Gospel of Christ. In his conception, it was ordained to touch and redeem all life. So that while I say it is not the minister's duty to preach social economy or politics, it is, nevertheless, his duty to preach the Gospel as it relates to these, and to every other department of human life. In a word, he is to make every man feel, whatever his circumstances may be, that Christ can be a true Saviour and friend to him that religion has to do with every concern of his life, and the cross of Christ sends its healing rays of infinite love into every avenue of human experience.

And what ample material we will find for this in the manifold fulness of the Bible! It is a world in itself. The message of the Father, not to one class of men only, nor to one age alone, but to all His children, of every condition, of every clime and every age.

The preacher who lives in sympathetic touch with his fellow-men, understanding and appreciating their perplexities, their temptations, their struggles after goodness, and who also knows something of the inexhaustible fulness of this blessed work, and how to apply the truth he finds here —incarnate, living and glorified in Jesus Christ—to the souls of men, will never want freshness or power in his preaching; nor will he lack appreciation and gratitude on the part of his fellow-men.

But we must pass on to consider the second part of our

theme : what the college proposes to do for the minister in relation to his Bible studies. Surely, if the Bible be so essential to a minister's life and work, it may well be expected to occupy the central place in every system of education which professes to have for its object the training of young men for the work of the ministry.

And yet, I dare say, many of us have met with the complaint that the Bible is not sufficiently taught in our theological seminaries ; not ours in particular, but theological seminaries in general.

Now let us look at this complaint, and see what it means, and how far it may be true, and, if true, what can be done to remedy the evil. What do men mean when they say that there is not enough of the Bible taught in the theological college ? I suppose they mean that the Bible itself as a book, is not sufficiently studied ; that men have lectures, discussing various theories about the Bible, but that the Bible itself is not brought into the class-room as often as it should be, and men taught to find out the simple facts and truths contained therein, for themselves, and how to arrange and systematize these truths in fitting forms for the practical work of saving souls. This, I think, is the meaning of the complaint, and, as you will see later on, I shall admit that there is some truth in it. But, first of all, let us bear in mind one or two things, that may help to give us a broad and rational view of the whole subject.

What then, let me ask, is the purpose of all education; whether it be given in a public or private school to our children; or in the university to our young men who are preparing themselves for the various arts and professions of life; or in the theological semirary, to students who are preparing for the special work of the ministry ? What is the broad, general and fundamental purpose of this education ? Is it to fill up the mind with an accumulation of facts ; to heap up a vast and multifarious knowledge of things ? Or is it not rather to educate the mind and heart; that is, to draw out and exercise the spiritual and mental forces which are in the scholars; and, so exercising, make them grow? I think we shall all admit that this is the true purpose of education—the development of the man himself. And if this be so, it follows that the best educated man is not the one who has stored in his memory the greatest number of facts, but the one who has his mind best trained to see, and appreciate, and use the truth.

Now for the purpose of training the mind to this masterful condition, a variety of studies is necessary; studies, some of them, that at first sight seem to have no relation to the special work of the minister. For instance, what relation does the study of mathematics sustain to the preaching of the Gospel? It has this relation that it disciplines the mind to concentration and continuity of thought; it enables a man to objectify his own thinking to himself, and see it as a thing tangible and positive; to build up idea upon idea, in continuous succession, until he has a perfect and harmonious whole. So it gives strength and vigor to his intellect, just as the exercises of the gymnasium develop muscular energy. What, it may be asked, has the leaping and vaulting of the gymnasium to do with the practical work of life. The student does not expect to make his living by these exercises. No, certainly not; but he will, by these things, have developed bodily health and muscular strength, that shall be a permanent possession, fitting him more perfectly for whatever work he may eventually undertake, whether it be mental or manual.

So in every true system of education the chief purpose is, and must always be, to produce *muscularity* of mind; strength and vigor of intellect and heart. Without this you may have fanatics—men of fiery zeal who in their narrow limits may do either a vast amount of good, or a vast amount of evil, as their inclination and prejudices may lead them—

but broad-minded, safe, reliable leaders of men you cannot expect to have.

Let us, then, not make the mistake of supposing that every item of education is lost, unless it has to do directly with the interpretation of the Bible. But while I thus speak, I will also state most emphatically that, in every well-conducted theological seminary, the Bible is made the centre around which all its studies are arranged. Every branch of study in the theological department deals expressly with some phase of Bible truth.

What are the studies usually included in the curriculum of a theological college? They may be briefly summarized as follows: The original language of the sacred Scriptures; investigations into the development of the canon, that is, an endeavor to find how, and when, and why, these Scriptures were accepted in the Church of Christ as our supreme revelation of God, and authoritative for our faith and conduct; studies in textual criticism, that is, an endeavor to find out so far as we can, what is the original and true text of the sacred Word, the exact words of Holy Writ, and their true literary meaning; studies in higher criticism, that is, an examination of the Bible in its true character, as a holy literature expressive of the life of men, under the governmental providence of God, and as God revealed Himself in that life, as it developed through successive ages; in other words, an examination of the Bible, as it is illustrated by every phase of the life of the people, by whom, and to whom, its truths were first revealed.

Then comes exegesis, or the more particular study of some selected portion of sacred Scripture, in its original tongue; endeavoring to get at the precise meaning and force of the words themselves, as they are found in that particular portion.

When all this has been done, the basis has been laid for the study of what is known as biblical theology; that is, the development of the truth, as it grew in the minds of individual writers, and advanced from age to age. It recognizes the fact, that God gave to men line upon line, precept upon precept, here a little and there a little; that He revealed Himself as they were able to bear it, speaking "by divers portions," as well as "in divers manners"; and it endeavors to trace these growing lines upon lines—to see where God gave here a little, and there a little, and how He gave it; to distinguish the divers portions, and the divers manners, that it may be able to form a true conception of the whole, and to appreciate the fulness of that revelation which, in these last days, God hath given to us by His Son.

Then, when this has been done, a safe—because an intelligent and true—foundation has been laid for the study of systematic theology; which is simply a gathering together, and an arranging in logical order, of the scattered and "divers portions" of truth. It is the gathering together of the ripe fruits of all other studies; so that they may be held in the mind in their proper order and proportion, and be most available for practical use. Then, when the Bible has been thus studied in itself, it remains to be studied in its various applications to human life.

Historic theology is the study of the doctrines of the Bible as they have been understood and dogmatically expressed in the Church throughout the centuries. Church history is the study of those same doctrines as they have become incarnate, more or less perfectly, in the organic life of the Church. Apologetics is the study of the Bible in relation to the objections of its opponents. Sacred rhetoric and homiletics treat of the Bible as the inspiration and substance of the preacher's sermons; while pastoral theology is designed to teach him how to apply the principles of the Bible to the spiritual necessities of men, as these are met with by him in his daily intercourse with them, as their spiritual leader and guide.

I do not mean to say that we are able, with our present staff, to cover all this ground; but we do as much of it as is possible in the circumstances; and we do it as well as we can. Some day we hope, through the generosity of the friends of the college, to do all this and more. At present we cover, or shall from this time onward, most of this ground. But I have described these studies especially to show how, in our theological department, the Bible is really the centre of all our operations; and no branch of study is placed in the curriculum unless it is felt to be necessary to an intelligent, and full, and practical knowledge of the Word of God. So that when men say that the Bible itself is not sufficiently studied in our theological colleges, you will see that in these important particulars the charge is not true.

And yet, as I said before, I must admit that the charge is in some sense true. The fact is, that the colleges have acted on the assumption that the men who present themselves to be educated for the work of the ministry do not need to be informed as to the simple facts of the Bible, but know these already, having learned them by previous personal study and practical Christian work. It was thought that no man would come to college who was not already a devout and successful student of the Bible, and knew how to study it. So the time—the all-too-limited time—at the disposal of the theological professor has been given to those studies in which it was thought men were most deficient, and in which they most needed that kind of help which the professor could best give. But teachers in theological seminaries are beginning to find that they have been acting on assumptions not altogether correct. The men that come up are not, save in exceptional circumstances, so well grounded in scripture truth as they thought; nor do they manifest such aptitude for the study of the Bible as has been supposed.

And so something more of this neglected work must find a place in the college. I think the colleges have presumed too much, and more than they have had any right to do in the circumstances. A man may have the natural ability in every respect, and the grace of God in his heart, to make a successful minister, and yet he may not have had time or opportunity to inform his mind with Bible facts, or train himself in the wisest methods of Bible study. Indeed, it is perhaps not too much to say that it is possible for a man to be in the ministry all his life, and yet not know how to study his Bible in a rational way.

Now, I think that there is a great and fruitful field for work; and I am glad that it falls to my lot to cultivate this field. Not because I feel myself fit for the task, but simply because I love it. To me there is no joy comparable to the joy of finding out how to get near to the very heart of the Bible. As I tell the students, I am only a student myself, and can only give to them what I find. But as it is, this keeps me happily busy.

This has been, in some measure, my work during the past four years, as I have come up to Montreal to give special courses of lectures on biblical literature. We have brought our Bibles into the classes, and studied them, not simply in the light of the original text, but also, and chiefly, as they stand before us in the English version. We have sought to find out what the Book has to say for itself, and have felt that we have been well repaid for our labors.

This work will now be enlarged, as my labors will cover the courses on the canon and criticism (both lower and higher), the examination of the text, and of the Bible as the literature of a life; the life of God in men, as that grew throughout successive ages.

We have also been able, under the new arrangement, for the first time, to classify our students according to their collegiate years; so that the studies being also graduated in logical order, the men will advance intelligently from year to year. This means more lectures for the professors, and less for the individual student; but it also means much more successful and happy work than the old system, which gathered men of all grades into the self-same class.

I think that this will give you some idea of what the college proposes to do for the minister in relation to his Bible studies.

And now, lastly, in order to do justice to my subject, and to the students who are present with us to-night, I must say a few words on what the minister must do for himself.

The college does not propose to make preachers; only to help men to do the very best possible with the talents God has given them. It does not obviate the necessity for personal effort—far from it. In fact, no truth is really known until it is apprehended as a personal experience. You cannot ladle out knowledge with a spoon. A man must work and wrestle and pray for himself. Aye, and he must live the truth, if he is really to know it. In the deepest sense, the student makes his own theology as he lives it.

What, then, must the minister do for himself? He must study the Bible for his own personal good. It is possible for the minister truly to care for the souls of others, and yet be guilty of neglecting his own; to be so busy in a multitude of Christian works as to overlook and underestimate the vital necessity of that quiet, calm and prayerful study of God's Word by which alone he can retain the freshness, and vigor, and beauty of his own heart's love for God. Yea, it is not simply possible, it is indeed one of the great temptations of the ministry to drift into a life of external activities, which may become at last a mechanical and formal routine of officialism without heart or grace.

My brethren—students for the ministry—let me urge you never to neglect to study the Bible; first, for your own good. Not to come to it simply to find material for sermons, but first, and chiefly, to find food for your own soul's life. Remember that character is more effective than eloquence. Pulpit brilliancy may attract and dazzle for awhile, but it is only the white light of a pure life that can be permanently attractive.

Barrenness of piety on the part of the minister will soon produce barrenness among the people; but if, on the other hand, you give all diligence, "in your faith, to supply virtue, and in your virtue knowledge, and in your knowledge temperance, and in your temperance patience, and in your patience godliness, and in your godliness love of the brethren, and in your love of the brethren love. If these things are yours and abound, they make you to be not idle, nor unfruitful unto the knowledge of our Lord Jesus Christ."

If you want your people to grow in goodness, you must grow yourselves. It is the growing minister whose sermons are always fresh and inspiring. His preaching can never become stale or profitless, who is always gathering to himself fresh accessions of spiritual strength, and seeing new beauties in the face of Christ. And few things can give a man such a hold of the affections and confidence of his people as the knowledge, on their part, that he himself profits by the truths that he proclaims.

Let your sermons then be the expression of your own life, as that life is nourished by the Word of God. Let the truth become incarnate in you, and it shall live in your hearers. The truth is never so persuasively eloquent as when it becomes articulate in a Christ-like life.

Again, study it patiently. Do not think to apprehend a revelation of ages in a year or two; but be glad, rather, that the Bible is so vast, so varied, so wonderful, so world-wide, that it takes you time to go over it and learn what is in it. No education can be acquired by cramming Time is needed for mind and heart to develop and quicken into receptivity and power. Experience is needed to test and prove the truth, and make it real. Not even God can teach you faster than you can learn, nor can you learn faster than you are able to assimilate the truth to your own life. You need life, years of practical Christian service, of patient, holy endeavor; and you will find, as your own life broadens and deepens, as your experience of the actual condition of humanity widens, that you will understand the Bible more and more, and see in it, ever increasingly, evidences of the manifold wisdom of God. Be patient, therefore; and, while learning with eagerness as fast as you can, be willing also to wait for the slower processes of life. You have all time and all eternity before you; and through it all your Heavenly Father will have some new revelation of His infinite wisdom, and grace, and power to show to your glad and wondering eyes.

And, lastly, study it fearlessly. Don't be afraid of the truth; no matter in what unfamiliar guise she may appear before you. The truth is God's always, however she may come. The truth is the bread of your life always. Do not for your own soul's sake turn away your face from her.

You have not come to college to be established in the dogmas of any creed—the traditionary teachings of any "father." No, thank God! You have come to a college which puts the Bible in your hand, and as you are Christian men, dares to trust you with it, and the ever-living Spirit of God.

You are not here to accept, without question, what your professors teach you. We are not here to deal out to you our opinions of God's Word, and have you accept our dicta just because they are ours. No, thank God! That responsibility is not ours. We are here simply to lead you into the presence of the Master, and help you, it may be, to catch the sound of His voice, as you sit at His feet, and look up into His face; and God forbid that we should ever come between your soul and Jesus!

Oh, brethren, this is your privilege to come, each one of you for himself, to the Great Teacher. Avail yourselves of it. Come in meekness, come in faith, come in love, come with holy boldness, and believe that Christ will lead you truly. Take His Word and trust it, whether you understand it or not; live on it, give it to others, and all your life shall unceasingly prove that this Word is the power of God, and the wisdom of God.

I congratulate you on your high and holy calling. I anticipate, with you, a most happy winter, full of helpful, holy studies. Oh, be worthy of your high vocation, and your blessed Master! Let your whole life be His entirely! Every power and faculty of body, soul and spirit train and develop to the utmost for His sake! Bring to Him who gave His life for you, no lame offering, no halting service, no poor half-educated life; but gather up all the strength of your manhood, refined, polished, fully matured, and lay it all, a willing and glad offering, at our Saviour's feet.

THE TEACHER REPRODUCED IN THE PUPIL.

BY PRINCIPAL D. H. MACVICAR, D.D., LL.D., PRESBY-
TERIAN COLLEGE, MONTREAL.

I SOLICIT consideration of this :
I. *As a fact.* What you are yourself, your pupil gradually becomes—very serious matter both to you and to him. All the relations of life are infinitely serious and pregnant with momentous issues.

We mingle in social intercourse, and life and death are the outcome of our doing so, for God says, "Evil communications corrupt good manners." We see this terribly verified when unsuspecting young persons are drawn into haunts where the wicked are supreme. It is equally true, and blessed be God for the law of His kingdom which makes it a truth, that strong intellectual and spiritual natures impress themselves upon others. If vice is contagious, virtue is undoubtedly so. If man is naturally qualified and disposed to disseminate evil, he can, by grace, attain and wield the power to propagate good. He can sow to the Spirit as well as to the flesh. If, for example, as a godly and devoted teacher, you are successful in your work, the very lineaments of your soul are being stamped more or less accurately upon your pupil. He is the index or exponent of your thinking, of your spiritual activity and intensity.

The medium upon which you thus work may be dull and comparatively unimpressible, or it may be highly sensitive and receptive, and hence, without any special fault or merit on your part, your image may reappear obscurely or vividly

—all imperfect and blurred, or accurate and clearly defined. But reappear it must in some form. You are to have immortality in your pupils. They will speak of you when you are gone, and speak and act under the controlling power of your teaching without being conscious of it, or being able to distinguish it from what they will claim to be the product of their own minds. They will be the mirrors, the reporters of your failure or success ; and well will it be with you if able to say in apostolic words, " Ye are our epistle written in our hearts, known and read of all men, being made manifest that ye are an epistle of Christ, ministered by us, written not with ink, but with the Spirit of the living God."

This fact of the reproduction of the teacher in the pupil is exemplified in the formation and history of great schools of art, poetry, theology and philosophy.

The critical, and almost the untrained eye, can easily distinguish Italian art from that which is French, German, or English. Each of these nations has had its great masters, and these have reappeared a thousand times in their admiring pupils.

So in poetry, while commonly counted a divine gift, it cannot be denied that the vast majority of the votaries of the muses sing as they are taught by loftier spirits.

Theologians follow their leaders. Great masters in Israel like Augustine, Calvin, Arminius and Luther leave their impress upon generations of feebler thinkers.

Philosophers are no exception to this rule. They may theoretically assert absolute independence of thought ; and each one who appears in an essay or voluminous treatise may promise to show the world truth never before disclosed; yet, when closely searched, what they are least remarkable for is originality. Their utterances are echoes of the near or distant past. Take but one example.

God sent Socrates into the world endowed with amazing power of thought ; and while he founded no college and presided over no great university, yet, as a teacher, he so reproduced himself in his pupils that after the lapse of more than two thousand three hundred years they have not ceased to speak of the Socratic philosophy. And so in numerous other well-known instances. Plato, Hegel, Kant, Hume and Hamilton might be mentioned. But high above all teachers stands the One who spake as never man spake —the perfect One—who is the pattern and guide of all true Sunday-school workers. They cannot improve upon His methods. Their business and wisdom is to understand and follow them. Having in Himself the fulness of the Godhead, and having come to teach our whole race, He is represented in and by His pupils in all ages and countries of the world, and will be seen in them to the end, and throughout eternity, for the *ecclesia*, the assembly, the Church or company of those whom He shall at last have effectually taught, are to continue for ever to be His very body—"the fulness of Him who filleth all in all."

The fact that the teacher reappears in his pupil is very generally acknowledged, and is made much of in educational circles. On this principle parents select the institutions in which they place their children for training and culture, and it is usual to speak of a person as well educated because he bears the imprimatur of a certain school. Witness the importance which a young man attaches to the fact of his being a graduate of Oxford, Cambridge, Edinburgh, Harvard or Yale. And he is supported in his belief by a wide-spread public opinion. He regards himself as the embodiment of the spirit and the learning of his *Alma Mater*, and he is so far right, making all due allowance for the very common danger of exaggeration as to the extent to which this embodiment has taken place. It may be conceded, with necessary limitations, that the strength and the weakness of a teaching staff can be more or less distinctly discerned in the conduct and character of those who pass through their hands. "By their fruits ye shall know them." Hence the state of the classes is the best practical test of the efficiency of Sunday-school teachers. There are, of course, exceptions to this rule for which full allowance must be made. The power of the very best teacher to stamp himself upon his pupils may be largely neutralized by noisy surroundings and lack of isolation where he is called to do his work. Then there are wayward persons, old and young, of limited capacity and abundant dulness and stubbornness. Persons whose natures are not plastic, but hard and rigid and incapable, especially because of overweening conceit, of being moulded to any considerable extent. But this is not commonly the case in childhood, at the time we have to deal with pupils; it is rather true in manhood. Then, indeed, it must be acknowledged that, in some instances, the very best teacher may fail to reproduce himself in his pupil. For example. Judas Iscariot entered the training class of Jesus Christ as a thief, and, although he listened to all the lessons of his Master against serving Mammon and as to the sin and danger of inordinate desire for riches, he closed his three years' course in the best college ever instituted, without being cured of his overmastering vice. The Teacher and the lessons were not at fault. They were most impressive and successful in the case of eleven out of twelve students, so much so that when Annas, the high priest, and his distinguished associates saw the boldness of Peter and John, as they stood before them, and "perceived that they were ignorant and unlearned men"—according to their standard of learning—"they marvelled; and they took knowledge of them that they had been with Jesus." The clearness, courage and convincing power with which they uttered their views and the spirit which governed them brought forcibly to the mind of the council the great Master by whom they were taught. They saw in Peter and John a reproduction, a fac-simile, shall I say, however imperfect, of that unequalled Teacher sent from God, as all teachers should be, who was constantly followed by multitudes.

Let this much suffice in illustration of the fact that the teacher, whether strong or weak, is more or less reproduced in the pupil.

II. *The rationale of this fact.* The question now is, by what principles or laws does it happen that the teacher reappears in the pupil? We answer, (1) the dominant thought or passion in the instructor lays hold upon and pervades his class. They are all affected in degree as he is himself. This is specially the case in teaching spiritual lessons. The sincerity and intensity of conviction with which the truth is held by the teacher is in some measure communicated to the pupils. Just as when one string upon a harp or violin is made to vibrate forcibly all the rest are moved in sympathy with it. Thus it is that a hearty burst of laughter carries a whole household into a similar state of mirth. A sudden rush of anger from one heart quickly spreads among hundreds. A piercing wail of sorrow issuing from a desolate broken heart often moves to tears those it reaches. When the Perfect Man stood by the grave of Lazarus and saw the two sisters of the deceased sobbing with grief, "Jesus wept." This is not an incidental occurrence, but is an illustration of the law of our common humanity.

The call to strike and to resist oppression uttered by the leader in tones of determined courage has inspired a whole army with the spirit of victory. Thus all experience is more or less what is originated and propagated by one.

This same law, be it remembered, is true in relation to our intellectual activity as well as our emotional nature. And, as already hinted, the depth and permanence of the experiences we cause others to have are determined by the vividness and intensity of our own mental activity. What I mean is this: when in teaching you are so controlled and absorbed by one overmastering thought that all others are necessarily excluded, and the entire force of your spiritual nature is so concentrated upon it that you can truly say "this one thing I do," that thought is sure to become the mental property of your pupil, to enter into his very being.

This law acts to a great extent irrespective of the subject-matter of what is being taught. It may be geography or geometry, history or the eternal verities of Christianity. If the soul of the teacher is burning with intense concentrated enthusiasm over the matter in hand, whatever it may be, he will lay the truth thus apprehended upon the mind of his pupil with such transforming power as to throw him, for the time being, into a precisely similar condition to his own. When this is the case, success is achieved—the work of teaching is really done. But failing to be thus borne along by a strongly dominant purpose or thought, which should always be the central or ruling thought of the lesson in the case of the Sunday-school teacher, his work is largely lost, and he but feebly and obscurely reappears in his pupil. Deservedly so, too, because he is lacking in one of the prime elements essential to success.

(2) Our passive states of mind grow weak by repetition. It is necessary to explain and illustrate this law and to show how it acts in relation to the work of the teacher.

Passive states are those induced by impressions made upon us through our bodily senses and without any effort of will on our part. The more frequently they are experienced without any active exertion of our will-power the feebler they become. For example, we witness a spectacle of deep distress and the impression made upon us the first time is strong and vivid; but we do nothing, exercise no volition to relieve the distress. Let this be repeated a sufficient number of times and the impression becomes so feeble as to be almost imperceptible. Our sensibilities are being slowly but surely deadened, or we are being hardened by the sight of distress.

Take as another illustration the case of the medical student who enters the dissecting-room for the first time. The impression made upon him by what he sees is deep and startling. He is shocked; but let him continue his visits, and pursue his work in that same place of ghastly sights for several years, and the impressions made upon him become so enfeebled by repetition that he scarcely regards his surroundings as in any sense abnormal. You see the working of this law. Look then at another correlated law.

(3) Our active mental states are strengthened by repetition. Active states are those into which we pass by volition, by the exercise of our innate will-power. Look again at a case of unmistakable distress. By a deliberate act of will you overcome a feeling of disinclination to deal with it, and you put yourself about to afford relief. That is to say, by an act of resolute choice, you turn to proper account the passive state into which you have been thrown by the sight of misery. You do so again and again, ten, fifteen, twenty times. What is affirmed is, that these repetitions give greater strength, a larger measure of ability to grant relief. Such actions become easy and natural, because a habit of virtue is gradually formed in the direction of benevolence, and thus you escape the serious danger of personal deterioration by having your feelings weakened and destroyed through frequent appeals to them without corresponding action on your part. It is under the action of these laws that the readers of sensational novels and our theatre-going population inflict irreparable mischief upon themselves. Their emotional nature is stimulated to the last degree by exaggerated representations of imaginary woes over which they weep in their boxes and on their luxurious couches while they do nothing to relieve suffering

humanity at their doors. Practical action is wholly lacking with them. Their feelings are being worn out, so that a stronger and still stronger stimulus is required to reach them, while no manly or womanly vigor is being gained by the cultivation of active habits of virtue.

But what has all this to do with teaching and with the teacher being reproduced in the pupil? Very much. These three laws, namely, that touching the diffusion of strongly dominant ideas; that under which our emotional nature may be weakened and virtually destroyed; and that by which we can gain mental strength and rise to true manhood, are all operative during the process of teaching, and success depends in a very large degree upon wise and skilful compliance with them. But this will be more apparent when we consider :

III. The opportunity and danger involved in this fact that the teacher is reproduced in the pupil. Generally speaking, privilege and responsibility go hand in hand. It is obviously so in this case. The teacher of spiritual truth has a grand opportunity of stamping his own character, views and convictions upon the minds of his pupils. Acting under the first law as to the propagation of dominant thoughts or desires he may, through the power of the Spirit of God, become to them not only the instrument of instruction but also of salvation. How so?

Let me suppose that he is, first of all, earnestly bent upon the intellectual task, by means of correct logical arrangement, lucid statement and apt illustration, to make the meaning of the lesson in hand clear, convincing and memorable. This is a commendable aim, and, when faithfully pursued, usually results in holding a class together, whether junior or senior, and evoking their interest in the study of divine truth. But, while thus intent upon the useful work of instruction, it is only a means to an end. He has one strong overmastering desire in his heart that, through this truth and the ministry of the Holy Spirit, the members of his class may be led to trust in Jesus Christ for pardon and eternal life. This feeling is so constant and vehement in his heart that he cannot conceal it. It is seen in his countenance, heard in voice, breathed in his prayers. Without perhaps making formal announcement of it, in various ways which it may be impossible to define, he convinces his pupils of the existence and the intensity of the desire. The feeling spreads among them, pervades their minds, or in other words, they respond to his dominant desire, and the result is, that it rises to God as the united wish of all in the true spirit of prayer. What then? We are assured upon the highest authority that if two or three are agreed touching what they shall ask it shall be given them; and that "whosoever shall call upon the name of the Lord shall be saved." Do not doubt the possibility of making your pupils share your feelings in their behalf, and thus drawing them after you into a praying attitude.

Witness the power exercised through intense desire in behalf of others by the Apostle Paul. You recollect how he said to the Philippians, "I have you in my heart. For God is my witness how greatly I longed after you all in the tender mercies of Jesus Christ," and to the Galatians, "My little children, of whom I am again in travail until Christ be formed in you." And this intense spiritual solicitation, this agony of soul, this ruling passion of his heart, was so reciprocated by them that he declares, "I bear you witness that, if possible, ye would have plucked out your own eyes, and have given them to me," so completely were they carried away by his travail of soul in their behalf. In another instance, you may remember, he relates that Prisca and Aquila, his fellow-workers in Christ Jesus, for his life actually "laid down their own necks." And listen to what he says respecting his Jewish fellow-countrymen : "For I could wish that I myself were anathema from Christ for my brethren's sake, my kinsmen according to the flesh."

A man thus governed by one mighty, irresistible desire could not help being influential for good among his countrymen and far beyond them. And as matter of fact he reproduced himself as to thought, energy, courage and conduct in Barnabas and Apollos and Timotheus and Titus and hundreds of men and women who caught the spiritual enthusiasm of their great teacher and leader. And thus it is in degree with every true teacher according to his ability, and in so far as the right spirit and aim are overwhelmingly dominant in him; but let the wrong spirit prevail and incalculable mischief and ruin may be the result. Whether dealing with secular or sacred subjects, the teacher should rouse his pupils to the repeated exercise of active mental states, and train them to think for themselves that they may thus develop their faculties and grow in intellectual, moral, and spiritual strength. But here, precisely, we are upon the verge of danger of the most serious nature. Instead of aiming constantly by wise forethought and preparation at awakening active mental states, the teacher may have his pupil almost habitually in a passive condition, or even in a state of active resistance, because not moving along the plane of child nature. He may deal boisterously with the child's nervous sensibilities by scolding, shouting, threatening and other methods of showing fidelity to professional duty; forgetful all the while that the feeling will not stand to be handled roughly, and that if approached in this fashion they will retreat and refuse to be dealt with. In accordance with the second law stated in another connection the longer this vicious course is pursued the feebler the impression becomes, and if persisted in for years, callousness and general mental imbecility are the results. Thus it happens that a pupil of perhaps average brightness and intelligence degenerates into a first class dunce. And usually, after having slowly and painfully passed through the deteriorating process by which the vivacity and freshness of childhood have been worn off and the power of original thinking has been effectually crippled, the unhappy victim gets credit for having been a dunce from the beginning. This is an easy way of explaining educational failures wholly from one side. I do not say that Sunday-school teachers often bring about such results. Perhaps they never do so, because half an hour of teaching per week, amid the bustle of a large school, is insufficient for the purpose. The evil can only be seen in matured form where the child is for six or eight years subjected daily to such wrong methods. Hence it is not a very uncommon thing to find boys, who have been left very much to their own resources, who have escaped the technical grind of the schools, escaped the coercion of well-meant but most unwise training, come to the front in after life just because they have been free under the influence of natural environment to exercise thought, instead of being treated as animated receptacles into which all sorts of stuff should be poured in the sacred name of education.

Finally, from this brief discussion of a single point in the philosophy of education one or two inferences are apparent.

1. The need of special training to qualify the teacher for his work. This is happily conceded by the directors of secular, and, to an increasing extent, by the managers of Sunday-schools. It is not denied that good, and in some instances a very great amount of good, is done by those who have not enjoyed the advantages of such training. It is readily admitted, indeed emphatically affirmed, that a renewed heart and a mind illumined by the Holy Spirit and guided by His infinite wisdom are of inexpressibly greater value than all that normal classes and teachers' institutes can confer upon those who attend them. But how much better is it when natural ability and high spiritual qualifications are united with the skill which technical training

imparts. The work of the Spirit of God is not hindered but helped by the superior intelligence and attainments of the devout teacher. There need be no antagonism between spirituality and educational competency. The deepest devotion in the service of God, the strongest desire to save souls, to honor the Spirit and to exalt our blessed Redeemer, may be found in minds of the highest culture and most profound and practical acquaintance with the science of education. And I feel confident that what the superintendents of the Sunday-schools of our land need in order to increase the efficiency of their great work is a large army of such persons. We should therefore urge godly young men and young women to aspire to become distinguished by the thorough mastery of the laws and best methods of teaching.

2. Teachers should always seek to be animated by the right spirit, and to have the right feeling strongly dominant. But how is this to be attained? I can only answer by hints or suggestions without elaboration. Cherish an habitual sense of the sacredness of your office and work, and of the mighty issues dependent upon it. We are working upon immortal spirits, making them more or less like ourselves, moulding them for time and eternity. This is a most serious matter.

We, the teachers of the Gospel, of God's message of love, are "a sweet savour of Christ unto God, in them that are being saved, and in them that are perishing"; that is, we represent Christ in this matter; we pray then in Christ's stead, and thus become "to the one a savour from death unto death, to the other a savour from life unto life." We, not our message or lesson, but we ourselves are this savour of life and death. "And who is sufficient for these things?"

The question may well be asked, and let it have its full force upon our hearts and consciences, that we may pray without ceasing, that we may be filled with all the fulness of God, that His Holy Spirit may be consciously our

Teacher, that, enjoying this baptism of fire from on high, being thus acted upon, we may have that love and vivid apprehension of truth, and that love of souls and intense fervor of heart which above all things qualify us to reproduce ourselves in our pupils, to the glory of God and their eternal well-being.

"Earth's crammed with Heaven,
And every common bush afire with God."

But we need to have our eyes anointed with eye-salve, that we may see and teach these wonders.

THE PULPIT AND ETHICS.

By B. P. Raymond, D.D., President of Wesleyan University, Middletown, Conn.

THE growth of our country during the century just closing has been so rapid that we have had little time for careful analysis of the facts we have gathered, or systematic study of the problems that have been multiplying about us. The growth of our population, the multiplication of large cities, the mixed character of the population, the increase of manufactures, the rapid accumulation of wealth, the emancipation of the slave, these are but suggestive of the vast mass of sociological and political facts that are to be studied and of the problems unsolved that are now beginning to press upon us for solution. In the last analysis the underlying questions are all ethical, and must be thought out from that point of view. The burning question in politics is political corruption. The solutions that are being offered are in the interest of an honest ballot. The storm centre in economics is the question of distribution. The contest between capital and labor is not between capital and labor, but between the capitalist and the laborer, and it is at last a righteous division of the products that is demanded. The temperance reform must at last depend upon the extent to which right principles can be worked into human relations and laws. The congested condition of things in our cities is on the surface, a question of security to society, of physical health, but the deeper question is one of moral health. The dynamite that threatens irreparable ruin is moral dynamite. What principles shall control conduct and determine the relation of man to his fellow-man is deeper than all other questions.

Having inherited this condition of things, a wealth of responsibilities, of liabilities and possibilities goes with it. We have not inherited the solution of the problems. No nation has applied ethical principles to our set of conditions. They are not absolutely unique but are new in many particulars. As every city must be built anew by each succeeding generation, so must each generation think out anew all the principles of life. The attention now being given to practical ethics is one of the hopeful signs of the times. It is manifest in a very marked way among writers on sociological questions and especially among the younger economists. There is an effort being made to see these questions in the light of the principle of human brotherhood.

There is a socialism which is law-abiding and righteous. It is the socialism contained in the law, "Thou shalt love thy neighbor as thyself." That is a law which cannot be ignored even in the labor problem and the question of economics. Ours cannot continue to be "the age of the first person singular," as Emerson once called it. The first person plural, we, and not I, or the possessive pronoun plural, ours, not mine, must characterize the new age. Individualism has been tried; competition has had or is having its day; monopolies cannot last. Co-operation will call out all the best powers of man. The success of the future is dependent upon it. The most potent factors at work in society to-day tend toward it. And more than all there is an ethics in it that can be justified. All questions of reform are being quickened by an appeal to ethics. So strong has this trend of thought become that in some instances, certainly, churches have become little more than an ethical society or a school of ethics.

The scientific spirit which now is brooding over every chaotic body of facts, determined to bring order out of chaos; the collision of interests made so conspicuous by the vast accumulation of material interests; and, above all, the constant pressure of the gospel of the Good Samaritan upon the thought and heart of the age; each and all of these have wrought mightily to make conspicuous all ethical questions. These are hopeful signs and the pulpit is especially concerned with the question how to make the most of them. The answer is by a many-sided development of the subject. Lotze has called attention to the fact that in heathenism there is a great preponderance of cosmological interests, and that there is such a preponderance of cosmological interests in our day. The one-sided development of principles in themselves true has compromised them and limited their influence. Church history makes prominent the tendency to asceticism, to cenobitism, and to mysticism, all of which ignore, to a greater or less extent, this world and its claims and meanings. But the peril that is imminent to-day is the peril of ignoring the unseen world, and of getting lodged in this. Partial developments of ethical principles grow almost of necessity out of the demand for specialists. Socialism shows one phase of this exaggerated tendency. The socialist "Does not propose to wait for the development of a perfect moral state before realizing his dream. Evolution is slow and manufacture rapid, he will, therefore, make the ideal state with his own hands. He will plan it and secure the popular decree that shall put it in operation. Let there be socialism, and there will be socialism—over night possibly; anarchy will put an end to the experiment in the morning." There is a disregard of property rights. There is lack of that free historic sense which always knows how to estimate the roots of things. He will saw down the tree to-day, stick down the trunk and expect it to yield fruit to-morrow. The same lack of balance which comes from a many-sided study of the subject is seen in nearly every reform. For the sake of the great cause every preacher ought to put an extension into his library for the growing literature in the field of both theoretical and practical ethics.

The preponderating cosmological trend, which multiplies questions in practical ethics, increases the demand for a wide and thorough study of the foundations of ethics. The fundamental principles must be made luminous; the presuppositions of the various systems must be brought to light; and the genetic connections between these principles and conduct made conspicuous. Not every system of thought will support the superstructure we seek to raise upon it.

Every science must deal with a distinctive body of phenomena. And the first step in the prosecution of any scientific study is to determine the subject-matter of the science, the phenomena to be treated. By the collation of the facts and the work of classification we are enabled to pass beyond the unessential differences among the facts, to the essential likenesses and to the affirmation of laws underlying all. These essential laws, thought out into harmonious relations with each other, and the forces they represent into genetic connection with the facts, constitute a science of the subject. Mr. Huxley says, "The object of science is the discovery of the rational idea which pervades the universe." The *Fortnightly Review* says, " Science is the discovery of the abstract generalities which underlie these concrete facts, and which, when fully grasped, enable us to foresee how new arrangements of facts will behave." Ethics must have to do with a definite body of facts, and conceived as a science it must seek to discover "the abstract generalities which underlie these facts." Or using Mr. Huxley's thought, it must seek to rationalize the phenomena in question.

Ethics begin by assuming man to be an ethical subject equipped with all those powers necessary for moral actions.

It assumes this as a part of the work done by psychology. As such he has knowledge of moral law, and that it is binding upon him. He has moral sensibilities, and the capacity for motives which multiply here. He is free. He has a will which puts forth volitions in execution of plans and purposes, in harmony with the right, or against it. His is a self-directed life. The forces which move him do not all work from behind, but ideals and ends are projected in harmony with reason and righteousness and he controls and directs all manner of agencies for the realization of these ideals, or he compromises both himself and them, by allowing impulses that have not been made rational and righteous by him, to control him. The moral subject has personality: eliminate either, intelligence with self-consciousness, or the moral sensibility, or will, and personality is destroyed and both moral and immoral acts are made impossible, and the word ethics might as well be dropped out of the language.

The field of absolute certainty in our conduct is a very limited one. We know to a certainty that we are under obligations to do the right, and to do it under all circumstances. We know, too, with absolute certainty the moral quality of our motives in all our acts. Did we deliberately intend the wrong? Were we indifferent? Did we intend to do the right? These questions a man can answer categorically. We know that we ought so to act as to be able to approve ourselves. No man may violate his conscience. Whether it be regarded as a power taking cognizance of the quality of motive, or of the law of right, or regarded as a sensibility, or as an impulse, moving to the doing of the right already determined by the intellect, it may never be violated. No set of circumstances arises, under which a man may say, here I may do the wrong thing, the thing which I do not approve

This all seems very clear. There is however a field of

difficulty, which is soon discerned when we come to apply the principles developed in theoretical ethics to practical life. How does this "Ought always to do right" apply in the concrete case? Do not circumstances change what I do not approve to-day into what I do approve to-morrow? What is fixed and how much of life is afloat? Has our ought no better right than that given it by Bentham? "The talisman of arrogance, indolence, and ignorance, is to be found in a single word, an authoritative imposture. . . . It is the word 'ought,' 'ought or ought not' as circumstances may be. . . . If the use of the word be admissible at all it 'ought' to be banished from the vocabulary of morals." The subject demands study from several points of view. From the study of the progress of mankind, by the widest possible generalizations, we have learned that honesty and truthfulness are obligatory in our relations with our fellow-men. The outcome of the sociological studies of Mr. Spencer and his school, in his "Data of Ethics" is the doctrine of altruism. This points toward the law "thy neighbor as thyself," however inadequate the ground of its authority as a law of duty. The subject ought also to be studied from the revelations of our own personal life. Here arise duties that are absolutely binding. The duty of unfolding this personal life, which can only be done in society, makes it necessary to determine the laws of interaction with others. By dishonesty, falsehood and selfishness I am conscious of deterioration in the quality of my personal life. I discover that certain laws of action are essential to the realization of that which I am under obligations to realize. The subject must be seen also from the point of view of my fellows. Says Coleridge, "Morality commences with, and begins in, the sacred distinction between thing and person. On this distinction all law human and divine is grounded."

Has my comrade in life's march, whom I call a slave, personality, with the same law resting upon him that holds me? And do honesty, and truthfulness, and self-sacrifice toward him contribute to the realization of the personal life, the fulfilment of the command from the throne? There are no considerations that can even be entertained as to whether I may or may not hinder or help the realization in my fellow of that command. Out from the centre of the personal life spring obligations, and with them rights, for the realization of which every moral subject may and must if need be set himself against all men and all government. The more thorough the study of ethics from these several points of view, the more clear and urgent will be the claim of that central law of society, " Thou shalt love thy neighbor as thyself."

There is a genetic connection between all ethical theories and conduct, and there is urgent necessity for the study of the subject from the point of view of utilitarianism. Mr. Spencer gives us a new study in this field in the March number of *The Nineteenth Century.* It forms a part of the work which is to treat of the " Relations between the ethics of the progressive condition and the ethics of the condition which is the goal of progress,—a goal ever to be recognized, though it cannot be actually reached." He treats in this paper of " Animal Ethics." He says, " Most people regard the subject-matter of ethics as being conduct considered as calling forth approbation or reprobation. But the primary subject-matter of ethics is considered objectively as producing good or bad results to self or others or both." " A bird which feeds its mate while she is sitting is regarded with a sentiment of approval. For a hen which refuses to sit upon her eggs there is a feeling of aversion; while one which fights in defence of her chickens is admired." No one would deny the sympathy or antipathy toward animals suggested by these illustrations. But would not every body deny that there is an ethical quality in the acts specified? Of course it is easy to apply the terminology of ethics to any subject provided you first eviscerate the terms, empty out the ethical contents, and then agree that the shell shall represent a given thing. It would be very easy to make a donkey an ethical subject, or a citizen of the republic. You have only to remember that there are a great many citizens that are donkeys, and pass up the whole class to that dignity and invest them with the rights of the franchise. The fact is, in Mr. Spencer's "Animal Ethics" we are playing fast and loose with our terminology. An animal never commits sin; cannot even rise to the dignity of a criminal. The essential powers for these acts are wanting. If we are to call the animal an ethical subject we can do it only by ignoring the essential meaning of ethics, and by changing the meaning, when we pass from the animal to the man, or *vice versa*.

But whatever the theory, its essential implications will run out into the fields of thought to which it is applied. Words are frail things, but they carry the ghosts of dead men with them, and cannot shake off the spirit of the theories which have been put into them. There can be little doubt that ethical principles are to be carried into economics. Says Prof. John B. Clark, a most suggestive writer in this field, " We may trace the economic history of Europe through a series of conditions bearing less and less resemblance to the communal ideal, until we reach the aphelion of the system, the point of extreme individualism and begin slowly to tend in an opposite direction. This turning-point may be located at a period about a hundred years ago." We have struggled through a great many experiments in the economic problem. Instead of individualism, we have had organization both on a large and small scale. Competition has had its day. Might makes right with it and the greatest monopolist is the greatest saint. The principle of co-operation is steadily advancing and moral force is to be the characteristic of the new age. The manhood of man, and the demands of the personal life are to find, progressively, the conditions of their largest development under the new régime.

But is there not a class of duties that arise in certain callings, of such a nature as to exempt them from the fundamental laws of ethics? Put in this bald way most men would probably say, No. Nevertheless, this query is often practically answered, Yes. There is a class of duties for the discharge of which professional men are responsible, and to which it is not always easy to see just how the high standards of Christian ethics, or indeed of ethics at all, are applicable. But a science never allows an outstanding class of facts which cannot be brought under the system. Such a class means a modification of the system. It is the business of science to explain facts, and if it fails in this, the so called science can only be looked upon as a working hypothesis toward a scientific theory. The ethicist can exclude no class of duties, no line of conduct from the field of ethical phenomena. Into every line of conduct, the ethical requirements of the great law, "thy neighbor as thyself," must be pressed.

The political principle, "My business is to win," has a far too wide range of application. The pulpit has no right to win, except by legitimate motives and honest arguments. The worthiness of the end does not warrant the use of an argument that has lost its force with the speaker. The effect upon the hearer may seem to be all that could be desired, but what of the mental obliquity of the preacher? What of the relation of the parties when the fraud is exposed? A man must keep on good terms with himself and with his fellows. The amusement question opens a large field of ethical inquiry for the preacher, of inquiry which concerns the arguments that may be used against questionable amusements, the motives that shall be brought to bear upon those whose spiritual life may be imperiled, and the conditions under which that spiritual life may be exercised with the best results. The ethics of reforms and of politics urgently demand the attention of the pulpit, and that too from every possible point of view.

It is not the sole business of the lawyer even to win. His obligations to his client must be determined by principles as high and holy as those that govern in any other sacred duty. That his attitude is often misunderstood is very evident. He may defend a criminal, but not in those respects in which he is a criminal. A man is something more than a criminal. He is a man and has rights as a man which have not been forfeited. There are always, perhaps, extenuating circumstances which ought to be considered, in order that injustice may not be done. It would be an injustice to hang a man for stealing a loaf of bread for his starving family. In litigation concerning property there is always a conflict of rights. But may a lawyer defend a criminal when he knows him to be a criminal? Yes, if he has rights. If he cannot defend him in the interest of justice and righteousness, then he has no ethical grounds for his defence and had better tell him so. But ought he not to state all he knows about the case in the interest of righteousness? Does he not intentionally practise a lie in such a defence? No. It is understood both by the prosecution, and the judge, and by the jury that he is responsible to defend the criminal only in so far as he has rights. No man can find any ethical ground for attempting to show that a man did not commit a crime when the criminal has confessed himself guilty of the crime. To attempt a defence of crime is immoral. Government is the institution of rights, and law is for the security of rights. The lawyer is the advocate of the principles of law for the securement and defence of rights, and never for the defence of wrong. What a revolution would be wrought if the defence of the criminal were always limited to the rights of the accused!

There is a field here for ethics the beneficial effects of which can hardly be estimated.

The want of ethical principles in the field of politics is notorious. Legislation involves insight into the profoundest and most far-reaching ethical problems. The rights of man are connected with nearly every legislative act. The Gospel has constantly exalted the ideal of human rights and extended them to all men. It must contribute to the realization of the kingdom of God among men by diligent study of the fundamental problems of ethics in their relation to all departments of life. Righteous ends by righteous means, as inspired by the law "Thy neighbor as thyself," and applied to all the relations of men in society, from the lowest to the highest, will lead steadily and surely to the goal.

SOURCES OF MORALS.

BY PRESIDENT W. M. BLACKBURN, D.D., PIERRE UNIVERSITY, DAKOTA.

THE revived demand for an education that will make good citizens has become a movement. In it is the assumption that moral teaching should have a place in every school, for the school itself, and for the later life of every pupil in society and in the State. The capacity of the child for moral ideas is admitted: they are readily received and understood when the method of teaching is wisely adapted to the moral powers of the learner. This capacity is large—wonderfully large and vigorous. What great things a little child wants to know!

In her "Lectures to Kindergartners" Miss Peabody relates certain very interesting experiments, showing that a little child craves great truths and finds delight in the knowledge of God as the good Friend, Father, Creator and First Cause. She makes this fact the mainspring of moral teaching, and goes even farther in saying " The true method of the intellect is the perpetual gift of a very present God, as much as the true method of the heart and soul."

How make this capacity a moral energy? Not solely through the emotions or feelings, for they alone do not work, conviction strong and lasting. The affections may not become a directing moral force. Love is not law although it may lead to obedience when a right law is made known.

Nor does this moral receptivity lie entirely in the realm of intellect. The moral truth should be reasonable and rationally taught. And yet the sweetest reasonableness alone will not assure duty. "You know better" is a common rebuke to the disobedient.

This receptive power is more nearly in the domain of will

There is no real morality without will—voluntariness, intention, purpose. "I did not mean to" is a child's excuse, as if non-intention were a justifying plea. Yet it is not the equivalent of "I meant not to," or "I meant to avoid the error." We want to see well-meant, well-willed deeds, for the essence of morality is in the intention. How reach the will? Through emotion, affection and reason co-operating and directed to right rules of conduct; that is, trained to obey the right laws of life. We offer, then, these four propositions:

I. Morality requires law. One expression of law is the conscience of the child. Conscientiousness is a high, noble quality in a pupil. Where you find it you expect moral earnestness. But the conscience needs to be awakened in most children, and instructed in all; as an inward law it needs to be revised, rectified and supported by some other form of law more definite and clearly stated. It is not the most trusty source, nor the ultimate standard of morals. Appeal to it always, and with as much emotion, affection and reason as every case may require; but with the appeal awaken or convey the thought of right and just law. To say "Do right" is valueless advice unless your pupils know the elementary law of right. To "put them on honor" effectively you must have an assurance that they have an adequate knowledge of the highest law of honor.

II. Law must have authority: authority to enact it and to enforce it. In morals the supreme authority is God. He has delegated the requisite amount of His authority to every parent, every teacher, and every ruler of men; in others words, the home, the school, and the State are within the dominion of God, and in them all He is the supreme author of morality. Let the teacher wisely, kindly, firmly use his own authority in the public school, with that of the State, and above all point to that of the Good Father and the Great King.

You may go into some land of ancient teachers and literatures, say India, and collect from them excellent precepts for a moral life; precepts admirably and forcibly expressed, setting forth the highest ethical virtues that come within the range of philosophy, poetry, and parable. It has been done, and a volume of them has been published for the schools of an English race. But they have long failed in India to produce the morality they commended. Why? One reason is there was in them no " Thus saith the Lord "—no authority above and beyond the human teacher; nothing to make the precepts royal and imperative to a human soul.

III. Moral law and authority must have definite and imperative expression. Where find it? Do not the Ten Commandments present paternally and royally a summary of all ethical principles and duties? The Bible interprets the Ten Commandments, out of which all others grow. Why should any one object that they are Hebrew—Israelite, Jewish? If so, they are none the worse for that. Their merit is inherent. Their worth is in the gold, apart from the coinage. But they are evidently older than Abraham, the father of the Hebrew nation, older than any known religious sect or philosophical school; so old that they were the moral law when religion was universal— the unbroken faith of the human race. Their reannouncement on Mount Sinai did not make them peculiarly Hebrew; nor did their reaffirmation by Jesus Christ render them peculiarly Christian. They are as unsectarian as the belief in one supreme God. Elements of them are in every moral system and in the laws of every civilized land. They are the original source of all our moral teachings. They have this advantage over all merely human compends of ethics, a " Thus saith the Lord."

It is a great thing for pupils to tell one another, " The teacher says so." He has a happy moral power over them when they quote his ethical precepts, refer to his good example, and gracefully admit his rightful authority. The teacher is to them a source of morality. And so is every good book which they are persuaded to read and study, every anecdote that presents a needed, or noble, trait of personal character to the child-mind, every illustration of a social grace and a civic virtue, every line, set in the copy-book, telling of imitable wisdom and excellence. We do not ignore these means of moral guidance; they are producing good results. And yet, we think it is a greater thing for teacher and pupils to unite in saying of any moral duty, "The Good Father says so"—"God says so"—or "The Bible says so"; for then they appeal to the original source of morals. This is very different from making the Church, or any form of it, or any sect in philosophy, the authority in ethics. It does not put any sort of "sectarianism" into the school-room. It recognizes in some simple, unpretentious way (I am not here saying how) the prime moral law, the Divine Author of it and the Book which contains it.

IV. The teacher of morals cannot afford to ignore a moral religion. It has never been done with safety. The separation of religion from education is a very modern thing. It would have shocked even a pagan in the times of Cyrus, Plato or Seneca. It is now an experiment, only in the earlier stage of its trial, and it has not furnished the evidence that ethics can be maintained without the help of divinely revealed truth. Morality and religion are not identical; yet morality is a part of religion; the very part which insures moral conduct, and for this reason it should enter into the teachings of the public school. It is the shortest way to teach ethics, to continue the succession of honest men and women in social life and to assure the safety of the State by the virtues and the votes of good citizens. The well that furnishes water to thirsty pupils is worthy of grateful recognition by the master of the school.

LAW AND PERSUASION.

BY PRESIDENT W. M. BLACKBURN, D.D., PIERRE UNIVERSITY, EAST PIERRE, SOUTH DAKOTA.

How are law and moral suasion related to each other? The question is timely whenever reforms are urged upon us, and different methods are proposed for effecting them. One reformer lays stress upon law as a power to remove great social evils; another insists upon the persuasive force of sympathies, facts and truths. Are not both needed? Are not both founded in the revelation which is given us concerning the divine government, and authorized by it? God has revealed a law against all sin: one that may be applied to every iniquity that exists. His Word does not specify every injurious drug or drink, every perilous indulgence and habit, and expressly forbid them, for it is not a book of special rules; but it announces principles that meet all cases of immorality with prohibitive force by bringing them under generic laws. He also offers a persuasion for every evil-doer to abandon his sins and secure the new life. The two methods are recognized in the fervent appeal of an Apostle: "Knowing the terror of the Lord [in the law by which He will judge us all], we persuade men." The assured efficiency of law in punishment—though not always in prevention of crime—does not exclude the use of persuasion. In this present world there is a place and a reason for both of them. Each is a force sent from Heaven into earthly society for the highest purpose. In each is a power for removing public evils and reforming society. How make them as efficient as possible? Is it wise, at the outset, to place them in different latitudes whose lines never meet, so that one shall be ignored, or disowned, by the other? Shall one supplant the other? Which has the right of a supplanter? Must we not recognize their mutual dependence? What can law do without love? What can love do without law? Along these lines let us consider certain possibilities.

I. Whether moral suasion would effect any permanent good in society without law—civil, moral, divine law. We mean law that has penalties, and that is not used merely persuasively. Imagine a society in which it does not exist. It has been annulled, and still the difference between right and wrong, good and evil, is not lost; the people know it, at least as a sentiment; they are conscious that virtue and vice are not the same thing in their nature and effects. The leaders wish to promote social morality, and their method is solely that of moral suasion. Nobody shall be outwardly punished for a misdeed. Then let the men of authority proclaim on the streets and in the markets that henceforth there is to be no more law. There shall be no arrests of evil-doers; no trials for injuries to person and property; no courts, no penalties; no forcible collection of debts, no recovery of damages for losses by fraud, theft or malice; no legal defence of personal character against a reckless pen or slanderous tongue, and no exaction of a guilty life for an innocent life, nor for high treason. Public economy shall be free from the expense of prisons, and public charities shall no longer be an obligation upon the state.

What would be the result of this method, if it alone were adopted? Less crime? Better morals? Nobler charities? A reign of justice, truth and beneficence? Let us think as favorably of human nature as the facts will justify, and still those facts will show that many people are restrained from crimes, not by love for the right, nor by convictions of conscience, nor by the "beauty of holiness," but by fear of the penalty. The persuasions that affect them are those of the law and the power that executes it with exactness. This is admitted in yonder court, and in the foreign land where fugitives from justice remain in exile so long as the law, which they dread, is in force. The fears of the criminal are his tribute to the civil power, and his motive for reluctant obedience to it. He knows the terrors of the law. But repeal the law, and you remove the terrors, and what can you then do with your rousing appeals to honor, and your gentlest entreaties of love? How can you guard yourselves and all that is sacred to you from an irrepressible lawlessness? How entrench yourself against the havoc by day and violence by night? On what persuasive argument can you lay hold to convince the lawless that you have rights and possessions and privileges worthy of their respect? The sheriff's warrant is cancelled, the policeman's club is broken, the jail is demolished, the penitentiary is an open retreat for wandering beggars. You may point to the worst deed of malice, or extortion, or lust, or intemperance, pleading that for the sake of personal honor, or kindred, or home, or Heaven, it never be committed again, and the guilty may reply, "There is no law against it, no penalty upon it. You are not invited to give attention to our affairs. Look to your own. Who is lord over us?"

Further, let it be taught that the moral law has come to an end, that human progress has carried us beyond it into the larger liberty of thought and life, and that we are not in the childhood of the human race, nor under the tutorage of any divine law with God for its authority, executor and judge, and with the future for complete and final reward or punishment. Teach men that the Ten Commandments are no longer laws with penalties, but merely principles of right or recommendations for general guidance, and then try to persuade them to comply with those recommendations, doing a right deed just because it is right and for the sake of goodness. What will you accomplish? They may not care for "right in itself," nor goodness by itself, and may ask, "Where is your law for it? By what authority is your moral suasion?" They may admit the reasonableness of your plea, but with no divine mandate to deepen its impression, their impulses will die away before the next temptation comes.

Experience teaches us to keep the law—civil, moral and divine—before the people: keep the lessons of it in the home, the church, the school, the court, and then we have a solid basis for the strongest persuasions that can affect the hearts of men. Little can be accomplished by moral suasion without law.

II. Whether law without persuasion will bring the desired social morality. Suppose that we have no moral force but law—rigid, unyielding, inevitable law. No entreating voice in the home reaching the impressible hearts of children, nor in the school where kindness wins more surely than severity, nor from the pulpit, where the plea, "I beseech you by the mercies of God," is always fitting; nor from the neighbor, whose kindly wishes open ways of blessedness to all who know his example. No helpful hand to lift up the fallen, nor benevolent soul to seek and teach the ignorant, nor courteous tongue to say to the erring, "Come thou with us and we will do thee good"; only law and power to enforce it upon every offender.

What may we expect in such a state of affairs? Obedience to law—ready, cheerful, complete, universal in the community? What has prepared the people for it? Not popular education, for it belongs to the persuasive agencies. Ignorance does not make her children good citizens; for, if they have any knowledge of the law, they are apt to know it only through its terrors, and grow defiant of its penalties. Why expect them to be law-abiding and obedient in a cheerful spirit? They have never been taught to love the statutes, nor the government. If arrested for crimes, they may plead their ignorance, lay the blame of it on society, and say, "None ever sought us, nor tried to convince us that our lives were wrong, and that a better way of living was open to us. None have cared for us except to punish us for evil deeds." Is the statement true? It would be true in a society which allowed the various forces of moral suasion to be unemployed.

Where persuasions are now earnestly used there is one fact prompting us to give a larger place in our higher schools to the studies relating to good citizenship: the fact that the penal side of civil government receives more attention in the courts and the public press, if not in the popular mind, than the protective and helpful side of it. Crimes are allowed columns, good conduct may beg for an item. The penalties are more conspicuous than the common benefits of law! If the disproportion seem too great, it would be far greater if moral suasion should cease; for these reports of crimes, arrests, trials in courts, and infliction of penalties need not be imported from afar to meet a demand for such news. Every locality would have a daily supply of its own, and its immoralities might seem to be past remedy by legislation alone. Wise legislators know that a statute which is extremely severe is liable to become a dead letter; or, if it be just, the people must be prepared for its execution by an advance of public sentiment. Law without moral suasion has little power to reform society.

III. Whether a union of persuasion and law be not the more excellent way. How is a community prepared to obey and execute good laws? By knowing them, receiving benefits from them, honoring and loving them; that is, by the persuasive methods of education, experience, affection and conscience. The school and church logically precede the court-house and prison. The teacher's work comes before that of the sheriff, and it may relieve the policeman of duty. The blessings of the law are set forth before the penalties (Deut. xxviii.). The people learn that they have priceless benefits in a just government, and that when a man forfeits them by lawlessness his loss is irreparable. The better the government the more certainly will privileges be assured to the obedient and punishment fall upon the guilty. Thus the same law which is a terror to evil-doers is the confidence and support of those who do well.

Ill-designing men, choosing a city where they may indulge in immoralities, do not prefer the one which has the most thoroughly executed laws, the most vigilant police, the sternest judges and strongest prisons, for the terrors are too great. But in that same city are quite certain to be schools of high moral grade, active churches, and societies promoting industry, temperance and charity, representing the suasive agencies. All these—the legal and the suasive—are attractions to those who love righteousness and hate iniquity. If you seek to know where law is best maintained, go where the brightest type of social morality prevails. There public sentiment has been created and nurtured by the persuasive agencies. There you will find efforts to reform the vicious by holding out to them the benefits of good citizenship, the persuasives to a better life, the invitations of the Gospel, the divine forgiveness, and the rest which the Christ offers to the heavy-laden when they become His disciples.

This method may be applied to any social reform. We are apt to select some one great evil at a time and try to restrain or remove it. The term "social reform" implies that the evil has gone beyond private limits and become generally prevalent, that it touches public interest and public duty, and that at least two classes of people are involved in it: those who are gainers by supplying a demand, and the losers by whom the demand originally comes; or we may say the tempters and the (usually willing) victims.

A third class seeks to bring the other two under its salutary influence and power.

The reform may become a "cause" with formulated principles and organized forces. It may grow without taking party form, or aiming at political supremacy, and still win to itself a majority in the state. As Christianity has changed the spirit and legislation of empires by moral methods (so far as human agencies are concerned), the special reform may leaven the national life; awaken, educate and direct the public conscience; propose and expect great moral changes—if not peaceful revolutions—removing vices and installing virtues; secure the enactment and execution of good laws, though not formally a law-making power, and all the while maintain itself by non-partisan methods.

The mind at once turns to a reform which has tried various methods, passed through many phases, and is still at the front with its problems scarcely solved. Is it not singular that when we wish to name it, we hesitate whether to say temperance or prohibition? One is taken to represent persuasive methods, the other legislative measures. We query whether to call the evil intemperance or the liquor-traffic, one referring to the drinker, the other to the vender. We find it questioned which of these two men is the prime sinner, the drinker who comes with the demand, or the vender who brings the supply. The whole philosophy of demand and supply enters into the discussion, and it is admitted that law is not able to remove a demand which is in an appetite (or nature), is older than the liquor-traffic, and is the real cause of it. Prohibitory laws will not remove the real cause of intemperance. This is a work for divine grace and power; all that we can do towards it must be through persuasive agencies. We may logically say, no demand, no supply; but we cannot reasonable say, no supply, no demand.

It is admitted that just law can very greatly diminish the

supply, and thus restrict the satisfaction of the demand. An appetite ungratified may annoy its possessor, but it is not likely to inflict injury upon home and society. Law may repress, if not remove, those evils which the saloon represents, and which are more public than personal drinking. But law will not produce these results until a community is educated —persuaded—and organized to maintain it.

It is little wonder that certain advocates of reform by law become intensely earnest, and see in their measures the only hope of relief. They have the sharper contest to wage because they ask for a kind of power which the people are apt to grant with reluctance. Their own method seems to them quite infallible, and other means are given a lower place or neglected. Some of them appear ready to say that temperance is not the word for them; their work is not to reform the drunkard, but to annihilate the drink, and then his sobriety will be assured; as if the drink was the cause of his imperious thirst and of intemperance, or food the cause of hunger and of gluttony.

This extreme is offset by another. In a brief notice of four "Gospel Temperance Meetings," at which 500 persons signed the total abstinence pledge, this advice is given: "If the good-meaning people who are gathered in convention to-day to devise means for the better enforcement of the prohibitory law will, on their return home, make a personal effort to save men and boys from becoming drunkards by kindness and sympathy and not rely on the law to do an impossibility, they will accomplish more for God and humanity than the law has done in the past five years in Iowa."

Such antagonism in the ranks of a great reform, which is essentially moral, is needless and dangerous. It tends to create two parties, each hurling at the other the charge of failure. That word "failure" is easily spoken. No principle, no cause, no movement has yet been fully successful anywhere on earth. Persuasion has not failed in behalf of Christianity, liberty, human rights, education, and every great element in our civilization. It has won for law its power, and given to it a field. It has still more to do in the renewal of the world. It will not gain its purpose by any sudden stroke. "It suffereth long and is kind." Its silent forces are as sure as the laws of gravitation, and its triumph is most certain when they bind us and all our efforts to the orbits fixed for us by the Sun of Righteousness, in whose kingdom there is the union of law and love. It is wrong to assume that any method of reform may not apparently fail at some time and place, yet even then we may remember that

"The good is grander in defeat
Than evil is in victory."

THE INDIAN QUESTION:—THE FRIENDLIES.

BY PRESIDENT W. M. BLACKBURN, D.D., PIERRE
UNIVERSITY, E. PIERRE, SO. DAKOTA.

THE giving of this good name to the peaceable Indians of South Dakota is a notable event in the history of a word and of a people. It originated naturally enough when they declined to join the hostiles in taking arms against the federal government. They were worthy of it.

A few months ago their position, spirit and numbers were generally misunderstood. They were almost unreported. At a distance they were classed with enemies, as if every Sioux was a foe; or regarded as exceptional—an undefined party, timid, trustless, restrained from war by coming winter, and quite ready to prove the assertion that efforts to civilize their people have been disheartening failures. In their behalf certain statements, based upon my personal observation and trustworthy replies to inquiries, are here tendered.

I. The Friendlies have been, and they now are, the vast majority. Exact figures are not now attainable, but competent teachers and missionaries make the following estimates: Ninety-five-hundredths of the Indians west of the Missouri river meant at first to be friendly, although some of them were drawn, or driven, into the hostile ranks; "a large majority in the Pine Ridge district were friendly, though some got mixed up in the last stampede; only a minority of the Rosebud Indians came into the fight"; very few from other agencies were hostile; "in general, those who had shown evidence of a real hearty acceptance of Christianity were friendly and loyal"; "you can safely say that the effect of Protestant Christian missions has been to cut the nerve of the war instinct"; "the Indians among whom the Gospel has had time to work were not in these troubles." East of the Missouri river there were no fighting hostiles. It was not a war upon settlers, although foraging bands carried off property. Instances of kindly warning given by Indians to white ranchmen are noteworthy. The main conflict was centred at one point, near Pine Ridge, and the military reports, when published, will probably show the comparatively small number of Indians engaged in it.

II. The Friendlies were artfully tempted, and their loyalty was severely tested. The hostiles, whatever the purpose at first, sought to arouse their pride of race, their spirit of clanship, their respect for the chiefs, their sense of deprivation and poverty, and their love for the old freedom, customs and associations. The dance was fascinating, and why should it be thought uncivil or unchristian if white people could have a "ball" upon so many public occasions without relapsing into barbarism? The Messiah dance appealed to their Christian hope until it bewrayed itself as the old ghost-dance, or war-dance. Its tendency was to mislead and "enthuse" the young men and "the Sioux of the old style." It drew hundreds away from their homes, broke up schools, depopulated villages, and brought excited bands together in threatening wildness. The religious nature of the craze was tempting even to the more civilized Indians, so long as the pagan and disloyal elements of it were concealed. The purpose of the leaders seems to have been to restore the old spirit of independence and the glory of nationality in a people who have had a pride in being called "the Sioux nation." As earnest was the effort of the hostile chiefs to nurture discontent on account of alleged ill-treatment, reduction of rations, and non-fulfilment of pledges by the Government. The Indian would naturally look at these alleged wrongs from his point of view. The Friendlies were thus tempted to revolt and resistance by an appearance (at least) of reasonable grievances; and writings from white hands could be quoted to inflame their minds and give them "bad hearts." Let those who stood such tests and remained loyal have large credit for their fidelity.

III. When the moral line was drawn between the hostiles and the peaceful, the Friendlies refused to cross it. The real causes of the outbreak seem to have been opposition to Christianity and to the civilization produced by it. Aversion to the Severalty Bill, which requires the Indians to abandon their tribal relations, take lands, cultivate them, gradually attain self-support and become citizens, had its effect. "It figured considerably," says a missionary who ought to know. When Sitting Bull, the archconspirator, said, "as a citizen I must be no more than any other man; as Indian chief, I am big man," he expressed the ambition of the hostile chiefs. Other leaders were probably more pagan in their sentiments. The natural Indian is very religious in his way. Every day he "sees God in clouds, or hears Him in the wind," regards himself as under the control of a spirit whom he consults, and from whom his enthusiasms are supposed to come. He is a spiritist without intentional imposture. When hostile to the Government, his old religion moved him to revolt. His recent war, then, has a parallel in the spasmodic reaction or paganism against Christianity in the times of the Roman Emperor Julian, of the fiery Penda in Mercia, of the Saxons under Charlemagne, and of a modern queen in Madagascar. A competent witness wrote: "This is not a race war. It is a war of barbarism against civilization."

The Friendlies resisted this complex hostility. They valued the benefits already received from "the pale faces." In their dress, their houses, their furniture, their farms and their modes of life, they were conforming to those of the white people. They were using the sewing-machine and the reaper. They were becoming useful citizens of the State, patrons of the schools, supporters of the Church, some of them contributing annually eighty cents a member to missions. They proved the elevating power of Christianity. It had not been a failure. It did not fail them when the test of religion came. When the Messiah craze proved to be the heathen war-dance, it had no charm for them. As a rule, no Indians at any mission station joined the hostiles. Where a village had a missionary the villagers remained friendly. Out of 1100 communicants in a single denomination, only one is known to have been hostile. Out of 127 young people, who had been in the Indian school at Carlisle, Pa., only seven became ghost-dancers. These are samples of fidelity.

IV. The resumption of civilizing work. During the conflict nearly all the village schools on the reservation west of the Missouri river were suspended. The prospect of resuming them was dark and doubtful. A letter of the time ran thus: "How long it will take to recover from so great a drawback in the work of civilizing the Indians!" But the recovery has already begun. The Friendlies have had "light in their dwellings." They want the schools restored, and where it has been possible in the winter they have been resumed. The missionary schools, of at least one denomination, are better attended than last year. The new Indian school (government) at Pierre is daily receiving new pupils. One overseer of mission work says that the demand for churches is increasing, and that there have lately been more applicants for admission to church membership than at any time for years. Thus the pagan reaction has "stirred up the Friendlies to a higher appreciation of education and Christianity," and been the storm before a revival of light and life. These encouraging facts have parallels in the history of successful missions.

The much-discussed Indian question will never be justly solved unless the Indians become active and influential in its solution. They must be kept from pauperism and from sole dependence on the Government. They must learn to labor, engage in various employments, earn a living, gain property, know the value and right uses of wealth, understand their real needs and be free to supply them in all honest ways. The aversion to work is not so peculiar to them, nor so inveterate, as most people suppose. The obstacles to labor and its profits come mainly from the old tribal relation or clanship. This relation gives undue power to the chiefs and to men ambitious to maintain the tribe as a sort of nation with which the Government must continue to make treaties for the purchase of peace ; it nurtures pride, prejudice and ignorance: it makes labor appear contemptible, and so long as it exists there must be trouble. Destroy it, not by proclamation, but by persuasive measures (rather strictly urged), so that land will be taken by individuals or families who will settle on it and thus become separate from the tribe. Kinship will thus give way to neighborhood, or grow into it, as it did among the Anglo-Saxons when the tun, or clan-village, became the township with its organized society, meetings, and laws.

Who of the Sioux are most ready for all these changes? Evidently the Friendlies. The civilizing movement depends on them. They have begun it. The school and the Church have led them to it. Many of them are now settled on farms and ranches ; others are locating lands. Neighborhoods of farmers are forming ; the township, school district, village, voting-places and due number of elect officials will follow. Pride of tribe will yield to privilege of town. The leading Friendlies perceive this result of the severalty law, if it be wisely carried out, and they wish it for their children. Their eye is upon citizenship. Through them, under the educative and Christianizing agencies at hand, the law may become effective. It is a timely, wise and great law ; just, generous, protective and competent to solve the Indian problem. The Friendlies can give it power. It can give them power, for under it a citizen will be mightier than a chief.

TEMPERANCE IN ALL THINGS—BIBLICAL TEACHINGS AND MODERN METHODS.

BY PROF. E. J. WOLF, D.D., LUTHERAN THEOLOGICAL SEMINARY, GETTYSBURG, PA.

HOW the good old words are changing ! And our ideas too ! The changes in the latter are, in fact, so rapid that words cannot be created fast enough to keep pace with them. Old terms have to serve in a new capacity. They stand for a meaning quite different from that which historically belongs to them. Old clothes are fitted to new ideas. Sometimes the relationship between the new thought and the thought they formerly invested is scarcely discernible, yet as these appear successively in the same well-known garment they may be easily mistaken for each other, like two individuals whose personal features bear hardly any resemblance, but who in turn wear the same dress.

Open any standard dictionary and "temperance" is defined as moderation in the indulgence of the natural appetites and passions, freedom from excess, self-restraint, continence. And the Bible as well, whenever it uses this expression or its synonyms, inculcates unmistakably the observance of due limits in our gratifications ; the curbing of one's passions, moderate indulgence, self-government, with no reference to the subject now commonly understood by the term temperance. Yet were you to speak in a modern Christian assembly of men who moderately gratify the appetite for strong drink as temperance men, you would so shock the sensibilities of many good people as to expose your reputation if not your head to serious injury.

No indulgence whatever, total abstinence, nay, with many the absolute prohibition of all intoxicants is the only principle that is now recognized in the noble old-fashioned garb of temperance. Underneath a well-worn robe pulsates an idea that is practically new. Our fathers did undoubtedly preach temperance, but they meant something altogether different from the reform now agitated; while the sturdy, ancient virtue of temperance which they emphasized, and which has the sanction alike of heathen and Christian morality, so far from being earnestly advocated, has almost disappeared from the ethics of the hour. A reformation apparently in direct conflict with it has boldly usurped its place.

I have no quarrel with this reformation. Inappropriate and misleading as the designation may appear, I will not even question its right to be entitled " temperance," although it obviously violates the acknowledged, well-defined and lofty meaning of the word. I am persuaded that the Gospel in its essential spirit justifies the most radical opposition to the drinking customs which have become an unmitigated curse to society. Let the iniquitous traffic be abolished. Let the infamous and infernal business which submits to neither regulation nor reform be crushed under the iron heel of the State. Let prohibition come, the sooner the better.

But while we invoke the secular power in this crusade, let us also call up from the past that inestimable, comprehensive, now almost obsolete virtue of temperance. Having, not without some misgivings, recourse to the State in behalf of a moral reform, let us at the same time remember the cardinal law of Christianity, which imposes upon its disciples the culture of internal spiritual strength, and fortifies them with the power of inward principles, the bulwark of conscience and the firmness of the will. These are ever to be recognized as mightier weapons than the sword.

It is at all events to be feared that many are making the fatal mistake of overestimating the scope and power of prohibition. It is no panacea. It makes no one inherently better. The utmost it can do is to create for some the possibility of improvement. Unspeakably better would it be, if men could protect themselves against the temptation, if by the energy of their moral nature they could enforce prohibition on themselves. Self-restraint is certainly and always superior to outward and forcible regulation. The wise parent would choose to have his son saved from youthful enticements by self-imposed moral restrictions rather than by the vigilance of the police. Prohibition is a police measure. Temperance is self-restraint. One is the government of the State, the other is self-government.

Men and women are conquered by other appetites as well as by that for drink, appetites quite as powerful, as vicious and as ruinous as the thirst for an intoxicating beverage. To cut off the supply of this thirst will save them from this form of perdition, but it makes them no stronger, it imparts to them no virtue, it does not affect their moral nature and does not furnish them with any armor against other foes that plot and work their destruction as certainly and as effectively as the fiend of the bar-room. Evil is hydra-headed and the excision of a single head does not slay the monster. The enemy is driving on us from every quarter, and it happens too often that just as we are bearing down vigorously on one of his strongholds, he forces the lines at another point and gets possession of the field.

Intoxicating liquors of every description may be done away. Excepting only cold water the country may be turned into a Sahara, yet men are still exposed to temptations without number. And if they are not panoplied in the steel of moral firmness, if they have not attained to a supreme self-command, if they cannot pronounce a prompt, resolute and unalterable " No," they will inevitably be overborne in the conflict. Splendid youths who have never "tasted a drop" are lured by the enchantment of other sirens and swept headlong upon the rocks. They are not on the lookout. They are defenceless against the approaches of evil.

They are weak, without self-government, without armor. They have not mastered their passions. They are strangers to self-denial. And when the real test of virtue comes they have no power of resistance and succumb to the destroyer almost without a struggle. Had their moral attributes been rightly developed, had they been schooled to self-discipline, had they been shielded by the old-time virtue of temperance, they might have withstood every fiery assault. But without this iron mail of inherent moral power the overthrow of the tempted is inevitable. If they do not "walk in the spirit" men will sooner or later be overpowered by "the lusts of the flesh."

Unless the whole life is governed by a supreme moral principle enthroned on the heart, what is to save our youth from the wily blandishments and allurements of impurity? Of what avail is the feeble show of virtue when one is overborne by the power of unbridled passion? No vice is more prevalent, none more besotting and blasting than the social evil. None makes greater havoc of body and of soul, of individuals and of homes, of personal interest and of personal character; and the one sole bulwark against it is found in that resolute, sturdy self-possession or self-control which in olden times men called temperance.

Observe the rage for gambling, the towering passion for some species of gaming or chancing which involves from day to day the wreck of thousands in fortune and character. Measures for its suppression were instituted by Imperial Rome, and our statute-books are covered over with prohibitory enactments, but the State finds itself confronted here with one of those natural immoralities which no law can suppress except the law of self government by which the individual may control the strongest and most depraved propensities.

It is the same with the immoderate pursuit of pleasure, the inordinate and irrational craving for personal gratification, by which the noblest intellectual and moral energies are corroded and the soul delirious goes whirling down the inexorable abyss.

And it is just the same with the mad chase after fashion —that goddess so fascinating and yet so corrupting, so dainty and yet so hideous and heartless, to whose iron sceptre a whole sex yields remorseless slavery and on whose altars are consumed the spiritual affinities and the sacred affections of woman. When one considers to what crimes of embezzlement and forgery men are driven to pay for the finery and extravagance of the household, he may justly raise the question: Which is the greater foe of human society, the Saloon of strong drink or the Salon of fashion? Which does more to overturn the financial, social and moral foundations?

And there is the insatiate greed for wealth. How universal amongst us is this passion! And how base, how depraving and hardening. It slays one by one the better instincts of humanity and ruthlessly extinguishes benevolence, equity, justice, honesty and every other virtue. A casual observer may exclaim: The love of drink is the root of all evil. An inspired Apostle says the love of money is. And it is this lust of gain, the same moralist affirms, which "drowns men in destruction and perdition."

And thus the black catalogue continues with its lusts of the flesh and lusts of the eye, multifarious and possessed of the strength of giants, directed, it would seem, by some infernal will and exposing especially the young to omnipresent and innumerable perils.

Now that which gives to these elements of evil their terrific power is the peculiar affinity for them in men's own hearts. The objective evil is only the correlative of our moral organism. The saloon, the gambling den, are indeed very wicked places, but it is mainly what is in us that makes them so wicked. Men have a morbid inclination for evil, as the sparks have a propensity for flying upward, and it is the torch within them that sets on fire of hell the objects around them. The law of action and reaction is of course at work here, but the vileness of outward things would be inconsiderable were it not for the vileness of inward depravity. It's man that's vile. The gilded portals to ruin which open everywhere so temptingly would offer little danger to any one but for the attraction felt for them within his own heart. Men are swift to run into them. When legal force even closes them, they are not slow in looking out a back entrance.

Change this inward trend and those doorways may stand open night and day without harm. Quench "these fires that within my bosom burn" and the hells of which we hear so much will die out of themselves. Purge out the filth that reeks in your breast and all the putrid dives of vice will be no more contaminating to you than so many drifts of snow. There is no surer method of abolishing the saloon and every kindred evil than by the repression of sensual appetites and the readjustment of the affections. Secure a change in the spirit of men's minds, let them be "strengthened with might in the inner man," fortified by the inherent power of self-discipline and self-dominion, and these haunts of sin will crumble away for want of support. There is, after all, no mightier remedy against intemperance than just temperance. Bring the drinker, the one that is tempted by any lust, to enforce prohibition on himself, and the process of his deliverance is not only amazingly simplified but at the same time made doubly sure. Power over one's self is the most effective power in the world. He that ruleth his own spirit is better than he that taketh a city.

When two persons are set on marrying and their union is viewed as a calamity by the parents, there is only one measure which never fails to prevent it. Effect, if possible, a change of mind in one of the parties, a change sustained by a firm purpose and a resolute will, and you can dispense with bolts and police and detectives. The girl is safe. No expedient of her suitor can make any impression upon the impregnable defence of her own fortitude.

How much superior, then, is this old-time, sturdy, stalwart, temperance to every modern reform that passes under that name. As long as men and women are so lacking in moral fibre as to be capable of but feeble resistance to the pressure of temptation, as long as they are morbidly inclined to wrong-doing and wrong-going, and possessed of a depraved eagerness to compass their ruin, no power on earth can save them alike from inebriety and impurity, from the spell of the dice, the grasp of Mammon and the lures of fashion. But with the character changed, the heart drawn to spiritual objects, with inward strength replenished and moral principle made firm, all forms of evil lose at once their attractions, or if they still wear an enticing garb, there is inherent moral power to withstand them. The danger is at the worst reduced to a minimum. One becomes so thoroughly fortified in grace and virtue as to be made proof against all temptation. For real temperance is a comprehensive virtue, directed not, like prohibition, against a single vice, but against every vice. It is a safeguard against every foe. It is essentially the rule of one's spirit under every excitement or provocation, and makes one safe in the midst of the aggression and whirl and tumult of the hosts of sin. Nor is it, like prohibition, a merely negative expedient. It is the positive exercise of moral principle. It is self-acting, self-enforcing prohibition by virtue of which a man curbs his headlong passions, denies to himself every indulgence that undoes the soul and keeps at a safe distance all the countless forms of evil.

Arrayed in this panoply the youth may enter the city where temptations roll around him like the waves of the sea. Bacchus may lure him to halls of revelry, pleasure spread her silken toils, beauty may assail him with her meretricious charms and gold may offer the world for his soul,—he cannot be moved. He stands like a rock amidst the breakers. "Though devils all the world do fill" he is protected by an armor that quenches all the fiery darts of the wicked one. Temptation has, indeed, strength. It is the fierce power of hell. But virtue sustained by grace is yet stronger. It is the power of God.

And this method of reform, finally, accords with the genius of Christianity. Our efforts for good are certainly most efficacious when directed upon the line of divine methods. The Gospel goes below the surface and lays the axe upon the root. It deals not so much with the outward manifestations of evil as with its hidden sources. Its process is from within outward. It saves men not by the abolition of temptation, but by the renewal of their natures and by the upbuilding of a character that firmly resists evil. The devil, for some good reason, has not been chained. And the new convert in religion is not taken out of the world where temptation is rife, but he is transformed internally and thereby the world is disenchanted.

"The weapons of our warfare are not carnal," was the confession of one of those men who were charged with turning the world upsidedown, and those weapons proved their power in "the pulling down of strongholds." It did not occur to those single-minded pioneers of reform to invoke the assistance of the empire for the suppression of drunkenness, licentiousness and idolatry. They might have owned even to the conceit of wielding armor at which satanic interests trembled more than at the fiats of emperors or the decrees of senates. The state is no doubt of divine appointment as a terror to evil-doers, but as a positive means of saving and training men the family has been instituted, and the Church. And more can be done for temperance at a mother's knee and through the means of grace than by the combined power of the legislation and police of the world.

WHAT IS TRUTH?*

BY PRESIDENT FRANCIS L. PATTON, D.D.,LL.D., PRINCETON COLLEGE, N. J.

PILATE said unto Him, What is truth? (John xviii., 38.) I did not hear Pilate say these words and I do not know whether he was jesting, as Bacon says, or not. Much depends, as we all know—and this is just as true of written as of spoken utterances—on emphasis and accent, on tone and qualifying phrases, and this is something that both readers and writers would do well always to bear in mind. The speaker will probably show the spirit he is of in the way he asks the question.

But Pilate altogether apart this famous interrogation may at the present day pass from the lips of the philosopher, the religious inquirer, or the scoffer. Each will probably show the spirit he is of in the way he asks it. What is truth? What meaning do you impose upon this word? The answer leads so rationally to suggestions that are eminently appropriate to all the circumstances of to-day that I think we may spend a few moments in its consideration.

"What is truth?" Truth is the correspondence between thought and reality. A fact in the outward world or an event, is not truth. The river or the wind-mill which you pass during an evening's drive, the events of history, are all facts but not truths. The world we live in might have been as full of material for thought as it now is, but had no thinker appeared there would have been no truth. Our thought relation implies the great thinker whom we call

* Abstract of Baccalaureate sermon, delivered May 7th, 1891.

God. That, indeed, is the great inference to which we are led in our attempt to impose a meaning upon this word truth. In every case the endeavor is, to bring the mind into harmony with the actual, so that there shall be the closest consonance between the thought of the thing and the thing itself. Truth is not the thing; it is the accurate thought of the thing. Truth is thought's relation to reality, truth is the word we use when we wish to say that thought and things match each other perfectly. There is no truth where there is no thought. No man has truth imparted to him. He may swallow facts and repeat formulas, but until he thinks he is a stranger to truth. Your text-book will do you as much good in your pocket, as in your memory, if you have not thought over its statements for yourself.

The training you have received here will prepare you for putting a proper valuation upon some rhetorical statements about truth that are so common as to be misleading, for men write truth in capitals, speak of her in the feminine gender, and say she is relative and partial; and that what passes for truth in one age is discarded in the next; or indeed that the question," What is truth ?" if by it, you mean, what are the contents of your knowledge chest, is one that cannot be answered. Of course truth is relative ; that is, one man knows one thing and another knows something else. Truth being the consonance of my thought with reality, it must be relative. It must be relative, for my range of vision is limited, and I trouble myself about some things, and let others severely alone. Then what is truth ? The question is asked this time in a tone of anxiety that betrays a personal interest. It is now a question of religious truth. There is no way of keeping young men from coming in contact with the religious problems of the age. They cannot well be educated men without coming in contact with them, for the open questions in science and philosophy involve them. It is not unnatural for young men to think that the old is false and the new is to supersede it, and that this should have a disturbing influence upon the early faiths of educated young men. I am sorry for the young man who feels that his faith is undergoing eclipse ; and that his education is lifting a barrier between him and those who are most dear to him, by preventing him from sharing their religious faiths in the fulness of the old and unhesitating confidence. I pity the man who feels as he leaves college that he has more philosophy and less Bible than when he entered. Far sooner would I, that a son of mine should never enter a college door, than that his college learning should be gained at the cost of his Christian faith. And yet I suppose there is a quiet process of reconstruction of religious faith that goes on in the minds of a great many young men, and an anxiety, consequently, of which very few of us have any idea. There are flippant men who ask, " What is truth ? " as though they did not care. But the men of whom I am speaking now, are speaking soberly. Would to God I could speak a helpful word to such to-day—the last time I may have a chance to answer the question, " What is truth ? "

Your college training has done either of two things for you in a greater or less degree. It has increased your love for truth or lessened it, for I am a full believer in the truth that men get good in college that does not show in classroom. Now, young men, I tell you that you may be earnest, charitable, and full of good works, but unless Jesus of Nazareth is distinguished both in person and in work by marked supernaturalism your Christianity with all its earnestness is only a baptized paganism.

When I see young men can carry the Christian name and really illustrate so many of the features of Christian life, and yet make a positive denial of essential truth, or, by their indifference to it, sacrifice the dearest interest of Christian truth, I am disheartened. I am not contending here for a sectarian theology. I am preaching to you on the broad lines of Catholic Christianity, and am trying to present to you the essence of Christian faith. I only wish that you should realize that Christianity, if it is anything, if it deserves any enduring place, if it has any exceptional claims, if it brings any word of comfort, if it has any voice of authority, rests upon the doctrine that Jesus Christ was delivered for our offences, and raised again for our justification. It is not true that Christianity is a life and not a doctrine. It is a life because it is a doctrine. A religion that sees only the human side of Christ always calls him Jesus; the religion that looks only upon ethical states and preaches only the moralities of life, a religion that holds that love is the greatest thing in the world, and is satisfied with the sweetness and tenderness of Christian feeling, is a religion of which the best that you can say is, that it is trying to keep the fruits of Christianity living, while it lays the axe at the root of the tree which bears them.

Now I say, I dare to say—would to God that men would heed me—that if I must choose between life and dogma, I will say that Christianity is not a life, but a dogma. You cannot live the Christian life without holding the Christian dogma, the one emanates solely from the other. This dogma's great supposition is, that man is a sinner and that without the shedding of the blood there is no remission of sin. Its great fact is that Jesus was the propitiation of our sins, and not for ours only, but for the sins of the whole world. It comes to us saying in a thousand ways that we cannot be justified by the works of the law, but that being justified by faith, we have peace with God. Its one shining and conspicuous miracle is the resurrection of Christ. Its doctrine of the incarnation separates it from all the religions in the world.

If you are in earnest, my friends, and you want to know what you shall do to keep your Christian faith on rational grounds, I will tell you how to get at the heart of the question without delay. You believe in God. Add to your theism the Incarnate Christ, and you have found the truth. The pitched battle of unbelief is here. It is history *versus* philosophy. Settle with yourself whether you will let your rationalistic philosophy settle your history; or whether you will make history qualify your philosophy. Will you permit theory to make fact, or fact to make theory? This is the crucial question of theological debate; not the inspiration of the Scripture nor the authorship of the Pentateuch.

Young men of the senior class, you lately won a battle in athletic games, then remember that ordinary events in life are often parables to us. There are battles we have to fight and victories we hope to win all through life. You know how you did it. You know the patience, you know the training and the faith that entered into it. Self-confidence is the beginning of great acts. You contested that you might win an earthly crown; but do not forget, my friends, that there is a crown of righteousness that fadeth not away. Go forth to-day in the strength of Christian character, stand like true soldiers on the battlefield and fight your hardest.

HIGHER CRITICISM.

BY PROF. MILTON S. TERRY, D.D., GARRETT BIBLICAL INSTITUTE,
EVANSTON, ILL.

WITH hundreds of devout biblical scholars it is a matter of profound regret that the term "Higher Criticism" should be confounded with destructive rationalism. Not that the term in itself is of any great importance, but the mistaken sense of it has been employed to fill the popular mind with narrow prejudice against critical research. The "higher critic" is referred to with a sneer, and it is implied that he gives himself this title, and thereby assumes a higher grade of knowledge and ability than other men. Those who are guilty of this misuse of language ought to know that the term "Higher Criticism" held an honorable place in biblical science some years before they were born. It has served a most convenient purpose in distinguishing historical and critical inquiries into the age, authorship and contents of the sacred writings, from similar inquiries after the exact original texts of those writings, which latter is known as "Lower Criticism." Perhaps the misuse and abuse of the term may lead to the adoption of another word. Some writers of distinction are already substituting such synonyms as "biblical criticism," and "historical research."

But this kind of criticism is nearly as old as Christianity. Eusebius tells us that many in his day had questioned the authorship of Hebrews, and James, and II. Peter, and Jude, and the Revelation of John. Porphyry assailed the genuineness of Daniel, and Jerome and others defended it. The last century has, indeed, brought out libraries of literature on both sides of these questions, and comparatively little that is really new has been brought forward within the last fifteen years, and yet, within that time, "Higher Criticism" has been denounced as a monstrous hydra, aiming to destroy the faith once delivered to the saints. But the defenders of traditional views, who have maintained a learned opposition to rationalism, are as truly "higher critics" as the neologists. Neander distinguished himself in higher criticism as truly as did Strauss. All who search in a true scientific manner to ascertain the facts touching date, authorship and character of the books of the Bible are students in higher criticism.

It is the infirmity and misfortune of some minds to suppose that everything of importance in religion must be *settled* by outward authority. The Epistle to the Hebrews loses all its interest to them when told that it was probably not written by Paul. They suspect the piety and honesty of one who affirms that, in his judgment, the internal evidence against the Isaiahan authorship of Isa. xl.–lxvi. outweighs the external evidence in favor of such authorship. Such minds are apt to rush at certain conclusions much as Don Quixote attacked the windmills, and when one affirms his conviction that Moses did not write the Pentateuch, they hasten to class him with infidels, and sometimes indulge in pitiful commiseration over his lack of understanding, and perversity of heart. Surely, they say, he ought to know that he is openly contradicting the Lord Jesus Christ!

But in the interest of piety, and fairness, and honor, let us calmly consider the nature and issues of one or two of the unsettled questions of higher criticism. Take first the question of the date and authorship of Isa. xl.–lxvi.

I. The thoughtful reader finds in xliii., 14; xlvi., 1; xlvii., 1–7; xlviii., 14–20, passages in which Babylon is mentioned in a manner very unnatural for a writer living more than a hundred years before the Babylonian exile.

II. He finds in xlii., 22–25; xliv., 26–28; lii., 2–11; lxiii., 18; lxiv., 9–11, passages which show the Jewish people in exile, Judah a desolation, and Jerusalem and the temple in ruins. "Our holy and beautiful house, where our fathers praised Thee, is burned with fire, and all our pleasant things are laid waste."

III. He also finds passages which mention or refer to Cyrus as a well known conquerer. In xli., 2, 25; xlv., 13; xlvi., 11, he is referred to as one so well known as not to need naming in order to be recognized, and in xliv., 28, and xlv., 1-4, he is explicitly named and titled.

These three classes of passages resolve themselves into one united testimony to show that the standpoint of the writer is the time of the Babylonian exile. The ruin and desolation of Jerusalem and Judah are not predicted as something yet to be, but assumed as already existing. To imagine, as some have done, that the prophet transports himself to a future age, and from that future standpoint predicts a future still more distant, is a most violent and unnatural assumption. Passages like Isa. v., 13; ix., 1-7, in which we meet with what is called the "prophetic perfect" in the use of the verbs, furnish no true parallel. Their context and historical background abundantly explain them, and they contain no such sustained and continuous picture.

Moreover, the mention of Cyrus by name, and the manner in which he is repeatedly referred to, would be utterly unnatural in a prophet writing more than a century before the conquerer appeared. The mention of Josiah by name in I. Kings xiii., 2, is not parallel, for there we have a definite prediction; but here Cyrus is first referred to without mention of his name, xli., 2, 25, as a person supposed to be known, and when he is named, xliv., 28; xlv., 1, it is not done after the manner of prediction. It is amazing to find an exegete like Cowles declaring that such language in a writer of the exile time would be "false and even blasphemous" (*Bibliotheca Sacra*, 1873, p. 532). Forbes also makes the bold assertion that such language "would be utterly ludicrous if made by one who wrote at the close of the Babylonian captivity" (*Servant of Jehovah*, p. x). The prophet does not claim, as these writers assume, to name Cyrus before he has appeared, but he points to him rather as one who has already taken his place upon the stage of history. He has appeared, and is marching on to conquest, as a chosen vessel of Jehovah. "I have called thee by thy name," He says; "I have surnamed thee (*i. e.*, called him His *shepherd* and *messiah*, in xliv., 28, and xlv., 1), though thou hast not known Me." Cyrus did not know or worship Jehovah, but was employed as His agent to say of Jerusalem, "she shall be built, and to the temple, thy foundation shall be laid."

These are specimens of evidence in the book itself bearing directly on the question of date. To many of the most devout students of the sacred Word they have more weight and cogency, to prove the exile date, than all the arguments from other sources to prove a date a century before the exile. But, whatever one's judgment as to that, what are we to think of the fair mindedness of a writer who sets out to discuss this subject, and totally ignores all this internal witness to the exile date? Is it honest to say that higher criticism claims that these chapters were written after Cyrus? If such a charge is made in ignorance, then the ignorance is culpable. Is it pious to say that those who deny the Isaiahan authorship are anxious to get rid of the supernatural? Such a charge is little less than a violation of the Ninth Commandment. No; not the supernatural, but the *unnatural*, is what most recent critics seek to avoid. The dating of these prophecies in the closing years of the exile (not after the exile) does not in the least diminish their power as inspired oracles of God. The glorious Messianic future, as outlined in these wonderful chapters, has the exile for its background, just as the Messianic glory of Isaiah xi. follows in prophetic vision immediately upon the fall of Assyria.

But, writers who identify higher criticism with rationalism

are not only guilty of misrepresenting the issues of criticism on this subject, but they prejudice fair-minded students by irrational methods of defending what they hold to be the truth. What must a well-informed student of the Bible think of proving the author of Isaiah lxii., 4, to be a contemporary of King Hezekiah because he chances to use the word *Hephzibah*, which was the name of Hezekiah's wife? The Hebrew scholar will be asking why the symbolical name Hephzibah should be allowed such an historical reference, rather than *Azubah* and *Shemamah* and *Beulah*, which occur in the same verse. It is also claimed that these chapters exhibit a notable play on the name of Hezekiah by means of various forms of the Hebrew verb *hhazaq*, and *therefore the prophet was a contemporary of that king!* But these logicians seem never to have noticed that the Hiphil form of this verb occurs more times in the short book of Nehemiah than in all the sixty-six chapters of Isaiah.

It is not the purpose of this paper to argue for or against any particular theory of the authorship of Isaiah, or of the Pentateuch. We have written the foregoing to show the false and self-destructive methods often conspicuous in some who assume to confute "higher criticism." We enter an emphatic protest against current indiscriminating denunciations of men who see good reason to reject some of the traditional notions of the Bible. Whatever may become of the term "higher criticism," its age-long work will go right on. Centuries of patient research may not settle a number of interesting questions, but it is noticeable that the defenders of the Pauline authorship of Hebrews are becoming fewer, while those who adopt the exile date of Isaiah xl.-lxvi. are becoming more numerous every year. All such questions should be calmly left to the most rigorous criticism. There is no probability that the great body of biblical critics will be willing to persist in any palpable sophistry. If the analysis of the Pentateuch, now prevalent among the best biblical scholars, has no valid foundation in fact, it will surely come to nought. But, if it is true, there is no more wisdom in fighting against it than in fighting against God.

It should be added that no sound criticism will ignore the weight and importance of a unanimous tradition. One of its settled axioms is that such a fact has "the right of way," until offset by controlling evidence to the contrary. But a uniform tradition of centuries may have originated in error, and, having so begun, centuries of repetition do not add one whit to its correctness. Age cannot make an error truth.

But what about our Lord and His disciples endorsing such a tradition? So far as this question touches the traditional authorship of Old Testament books, the naked proposition, fairly stated, is: Does the quotation of a book, or a reference to it or its traditional author, after the current and popular methods of quotation, commit the person making such reference to an authoritative verdict on the questions of date and authorship? Sober and thoughtful minds will hesitate before affirming such a proposition. We quote with approval and conclude this article with the following words of Prof. Stevens, in his opening address before the Rochester Theological Seminary:

"Does the language of our Lord forever debar a Christian scholar from raising the question whether the Pentateuch is a composite document, or wholly the work of Moses? I have learned the danger of taking any passage of Scripture to teach that which it was not originally intended to teach. One of the most difficult tasks of the interpreter is to distinguish between the teaching of Scripture and his own inferences from that teaching. Hence in this, and in all similar cases, in order to know what our Lord's conception of the fact was, what He meant to say and what He did say, it is first incumbent upon us by all possible research to ascertain what the given fact was."

INSPIRED FICTION.

By Prof. Milton S. Terry, D.D., Garrett Biblical Institute, Evanston, Ill.

TO some minds the two words in the title of this article may seem preposterous. The Holy Scriptures, given by inspiration of God, are assumed to be the written embodiment of truth, without any admixture of error, and to say that they contain works of fiction is to put a heavy burden upon the evangelical faith. Such inspired oracles must needs confine themselves to the realm of sober fact.

But is it not rather preposterous to set up such a presumption in advance? Who is qualified to say *a priori* what form the written Word of God must take on? Is it not the wiser way to examine carefully the writings as they are, and suspend judgment on questions of form and method until we have all the facts before us?

Looking into these sacred writings we find not only the record of facts, and laws, and counsels, and exhortations, and predictions of what shall certainly come to pass, but also riddles, fables, enigmas, proverbs, poems, parables, allegories and symbols. Is there anything absurd in the thought of an inspired riddle, or an inspired parable? What are the parables of Jesus but inspired fictions? The parable of the good Samaritan begins: "A certain man went down from Jerusalem to Jericho and fell among thieves." Are these statements and the rest of the parable fact or fiction? We hesitate not to pronounce it fiction. Scores of men may have made such a journey and fallen into similar misfortunes; although it may be doubted whether any Samaritan ever really did what is here written.

But even that is not impossible. Whatever may be supposed of the actual occurrence of such an affair, no evangelical interpreter deems it important to maintain such a proposition in order that the parable may be made to serve its highest purpose. The same may be said of all the parables of Scripture, for it is the nature of a parable to move in the realm of supposable reality. Herein the parable differs from the fable. But Gotham's story of the trees choosing a king, Judges ix. 7-15, is a pure fiction. Will anyone maintain that *therefore* it is not inspired and has no place in the oracles of God?

Some four hundred years before Christ we find Plato writing his philosophical treatises and putting them in the form of conversations between Socrates and his friends. Does any scholar believe that those dialogues are accurate transcriptions of what Socrates said? It goes without saying that such "Socratic method" was only Plato's chosen way of writing his philosophy. Socrates may indeed have taught in that manner, and many of his teachings are doubtless correctly represented in the dialogues of his peerless disciple, but it would be a waste of time and words to argue that the Platonic dialogues are accurate reports of conversations of Socrates. Why, then, should it be deemed a thing incredible that the teachings of the ancient Scriptures should be also cast in a like fictitious form?

In the Book of Job we seem to have a most notable example of this. The book is a magnificent poem, cast in dramatic form. Like many of Shakespeare's dramas, it may or may not have been based on historical fact. But so far as its great lessons are concerned, it matters not whether Job be a real person of history or the creation of the poet's genius. The reader who most fully takes in the divine lessons of the drama cares as little about that question as the appreciative reader of Shakespeare cares about the question whether "Hamlet, Prince of Denmark," was a real person. He knows in any case that the work is essentially a fiction, and such works, even the most ephemeral novels of modern times, usually select some historic names and places as a background.

It has become the all but unanimous opinion of the best biblical scholars that the author of Ecclesiastes was not Solomon, but a much later writer who personates Solomon and speaks as "king over Israel in Jerusalem." According to this view, the author puts what he wishes to say in the form of what he assumes "the Son of David, king in Jerusalem," might have said. He does what Plato has done in presenting his philosophy as the wise discourses of Socrates. Such dramatic personation has been, in various times and countries, a favorite method of communicating instruction. The apocryphal book entitled the "Wisdom of Solomon" assumes this form, as, for example, when its author writes, ix. 7, 8 : " Thou hast chosen me to be a king of thy people, and a !udge of thy sons and daughters. Thou hast commanded me to built a temple upon thy holy mount, and an altar in the city wherein thou dwellest." Men who insist that the Solomonic authorship of Ecclesiastes must be held because the writer assumes to speak in the name of Solomon, must also expect to show convincing reasons for rejecting the Solomonic authorship of that magnificent apocryphal book just quoted, which makes the same claim.

But many among us feel that such concessions are virtually a surrender to the demands of a destructive rationalism. Such turning from traditional views always starts the question, " Where will this procedure end?" If the books of Job and Ecclesiastes are works of fiction, who knows what other books will soon be swept into the same category ?

Such questions evince a prudent caution, and every wise man forecasts to see the probable outcome of marked tendencies of thought. But other important questions demand for their answer equal caution. Must free inquiry touching the date and authorship of a book be overruled by an *ab extra* command of "thus far and no farther"? Is it compromising the evangelical faith to hold that the Bible contains works of fiction? Is our faith in a divine revelation to depend on *a priori* assumptions of what forms its written documents must take? We believe the best minds of the modern Church are coming to see the peril of such assumptions as these questions suggest. There is wide room for differences of opinion on the great questions of biblical criticism. I may be persuaded in my own mind that the traditional authorship of Ecclesiastes is too well established to be overthrown by valid criticism. But I should cheerfully concede that hundreds of the most devout students of the Word believe it to be a work of fiction, and no more intended to deceive its readers than Plato's Apology of Socrates. I should be broad enough to see that no essential doctrine which it teaches and no important truths of religion suffer by such concession.

But many will feel that this matter takes on a more serious aspect when one thinks he discovers the elements of a fiction in such a book as Daniel. This hits at once upon the question of the evidential value of prophecy, and sets aside what many have long regarded as one of the central pillars of divine revelation. But must this fact stop free and full investigation? It is possible that an argument, or even a series of arguments, in apologetics, may become obsolete, because of the discovery of a latent error therein. Suppose it should be shown, by evidence impossible to refute, that the Book of Daniel originated in the time of Antiochus Epiphanus (about 170 B.C.), would the book thereby be made worthless and lose its right to a place in the volume of inspiration? There are those who answer this question affirmatively. They may, perhaps, allow that Job, and Ecclesiastes, and the Song of Songs are works of fiction, but they will not permit the Book of Daniel to be so regarded. But why may we not have genuine prophecy, as well as genuine philosophy, set in a fictitious background? The difficulty which dogmatic theologians find in allowing such a range of biblical fiction is only the outcome of their own unproven assumptions. They assume that all fiction is false, and the Word of God must needs be given in a form of absolute fidelity to historical fact. Other literatures may embody art and fiction and sentiment, but the Scriptures of God must not employ anything so common and unclean.

But we may respond: "What God has sanctified, call thou not common or unclean!" The Holy Spirit has chosen fable, and riddle, and allegory and parable, and symbol as vehicles of divine revelation. Why should He not also sanctify any other forms of literary fiction which might be made to serve the purpose of "instruction in righteousness"? Whether the narrative portions of the Book of Daniel be fact or fiction, the sublime prophecies of the future of the Kingdom of God remain the same. In no other book of the Old Testament have we so unique a picture of the coming Messiah, or so impressive a revelation of the innumerable company of angels that minister before God. If the story of the fiery furnace and the den of lions be a fiction, it still remains a fact that those fictitious creations of inspired genius have cultivated the true martyr spirit, and served to strengthen thousands who have been tested by fire and thrown to the wild beasts.

Now there are many among us who have no trouble in accepting all the miraculous narratives of Daniel as facts, and who hold to the genuineness of the entire book, and defend its historical and prophetical character after the manner of the fathers. But we believe that such defenders of the traditional view go too far when they assume to proscribe that large number of devout and truth-loving scholars who see no reason for adopting a different opinion. To make the faith of the Church and the value of the Scriptures depend on such a doubtful question as that of the date, authorship and historical accuracy of the Book of Daniel is, to our thought, a most hazardous procedure. The bare fact that the arguments against the traditional view have been "answered so many times" (!), and yet will not stay answered, is an admonition to be less presumptuous. The number of those who reject the traditional arguments seems to be constantly increasing.

We exult in the manifoldness, nay, more, the infinite suggestiveness, of the inspired oracles which were given to the fathers "in many parts and in many forms," Heb. i. 1. Their imperishable value does not depend on critical questions of literary form, and dates, and chronologies, and human authorship. The minister of the Gospel, who is impelled by an all-controlling call to "preach the Word," should not make such questions prominent in his proclamation of God's truth. The great spiritual lessons, the correction, the rebuke, the warning, the doctrine of salvation in Christ, the consolation and comfort, the promise and eternal hopes—these are the great pulpit themes. And these are illustrated and enhanced by divers forms of literary art in the Bible. These the preacher should employ, but without distortion or abuse. "Let him speak as the oracles of God." These seem so utterly indifferent about the questions of their date and authorship, that a large number of them make no mention of the time and place of their composition. It is not the province of the preacher to discuss such questions before the promiscuous assembly. He may study them for himself. He should make himself acquainted, so far as opportunity is given, with the results of scientific research, and the processes of historical investigation and criticism. But, unless they be matters of salvation, or important for "instruction in righteousness," he should be as slow to publish the processes or results of such research, as he should be to denounce them, or to discourage and embarrass the freest investigation. He who presumes to make himself the champion of truth by the dogmatic method some exhibit in fighting doubtful errors, will find that he has taken hold of a dangerous two-edged weapon, which may be hurled back against him with disastrous effect, and do irreparable harm to the cause of sound biblical learning.

LIBERTY OF THOUGHT AND ITS LIMITATIONS.

BY PROF. THEODORE W. HUNT, LITT. D., PRINCETON COLLEGE, NEW JERSEY

WE are living in the days of free discussion. From the time of Lactantius and Lucretius down to the present, men have insisted, with more or less earnestness, upon looking at the multiform questions of life from their own point of view and reaching conclusions in their own way. Whenever, for any reason or for any length of time, such freedom of debate has been denied, serious results have followed, taking the form at times of political and religious revolution. It was so in Europe after the repressive influences of the Middle Ages. It was so in the stirring days of the Protestant Reaction and Reformation. It was so in English politics, in the reign of King John; in the Revolution of 1640, and in that of 1688; as, also, in France and America, in the civil commotions of the eighteenth century. Such a history of English thought as that given us by Leslie Stephen or that by Dr. Draper, in his "Intellectual Development of Europe," is a signal confirmation of this spirit of agitation so germane to the nature of man and so essential to all true progress.

Hence, we notice, first of all, the right and duty of free inquiry. We may call it by various names—the right of private judgment, freedom of thought and speech, the claims of personal opinion. By whatever designation it is known, it is assumed to be an inalienable possession, involved in the nature of man as man, becoming more and more pronounced as the questions and interests with which it deals deepen in their significance. In theology, philosophy, literature and morals; in matters of social and economic import; in the multiplied topics that emerge from the daily evolution of individual and public life, intelligent men may think, and ought to think, for themselves just to the degree in which they are intelligent, and recognize their status as rational and accountable beings. The Biblical statement, that "every man must give account of himself to God," is not confined in its application to the day of final judgment, nor, indeed, to the special sphere of moral conduct in this life, but covers a scope as wide as the area of human relationships. Personal accountability applies to our intellectual as well as our ethical judgments. In this sense every man should be a Protestant, taking just exception to any code or class that seeks to seriously invade his personal privileges, and oblige him, at all hazards, to argue and conclude along the lines that others have laid down. So Milton reasoned in his "Areopagitica," with respect to freedom of speech and political theory, and in his "Christian Doctrine" with reference to religious truth. He had determined "to swear in the words of no master," however high in repute; never to follow blindly any course proposed just because it was proposed, and to carry his natural right of private judgment into every matter that came before him for investigation. So D'Aubigné and Chillingworth and Bishop Burnet contended in their defence of Reformation principles against the assumption of the Papacy, and so have all contended who either for themselves or their generation have revealed the fallacies of existing errors and opened out the way to sounder and safer beliefs. Upon such a freedom of thinking mental and moral vigor depends, as also national and personal self-respect. By such insistence of private right are men and nations saved from becoming the dupes and deputies of others, and place themselves in right relations to God and the world. Never has there been a time when, with all the boasted independence of scope and view, it has been easier to be led and misled than now, so that even while we deem ourselves the most fully free in thought and action, we may be the veriest servants of others. No man can afford to unman himself in the interests of others, be the interests what they may. The duty of assent or of dissent is as important as the right, and he is the likeliest to place a proper estimate upon that freedom of discussion and belief that belongs to others who sacredly guards it as a privilege belonging equally fully to himself. All this is true, but it is not the whole of the truth, and, in a sense, not the most significant. The prerogative of private judgment carries with it, when properly interpreted, its own conditions and restrictions, without the acknowledgment and enforcement of which such a liberty defeats its own ends and becomes the occasion of the direst results. It is just because we are living in an age of open discussion that it is essential to state and apply these conditions, and most especially within the domain of religious truth. Liberty of opinion is one thing, license or mental lawlessness is another ; scope for fair and full debate is one thing, unlimited range of means and methods is another ; to raise the question, What is truth ? every man has a right as a man ; in the final settlement of that question every contestant must admit the validity of certain well-established limitations under the governance of which he must conduct the controversy. Religious thought involves, in the very nature of the case, what Dr. Mansel has called the limits of religious thought. To some of these limitations or conditions we may briefly refer :

1. The Acceptance of Postulates as a basis of Argument.

We may call these axioms in morals, ethical and mental intuitions, first truths, fundamental ideas, or by other terms. They stand as logical postulates without which, or something like them, it is impossible to proceed with the discussion. Without them discussion is forestalled. A starting-point there must be; some things must be assumed. There is a sense in which all reasoning within the sphere of morals and religion, as in mathematics, must have an *a priori* element in it. What the earlier Scottish school called the common-sense philosophy is a philosophy and form of logic far older than the Scottish school and far wider in its range. If we are to begin discussion with the so-called creed of the agnostic with knowing nothing and believing nothing and accepting nothing till proved, and insist that the presumption is always against the possibility of truth and reality as at present existing—then the debate begins and ends at the same point, and freedom of thought is free to a fault and caught, at the outset, in its own meshes.

2. Defence to the History of Opinion.

There is such a thing as a consensus of view, a concurrent testimony, strong and vital because it is concurrent and so pronounced in its character that no discreet debatant can afford to ignore it. The right and duty of private judgment does not, at this point, stand by itself, and could not if it would. It must, unwillingly or perforce, concede the existence, at least, of public opinion and listen to what it says. It is so in all spheres—mental and moral; in all departments of inquiry, philosophic, linguistic and literary. Due account must be taken of what others have thought upon the same subjects; what conclusions they have reached and how they have reached them, while the individual inquirer, in the purest and fullest mental liberty, is bound to ask himself why he is called to depart from such conclusions already attained. Certain it is that, if there is such a departure on his side, he is bound logically to justify it and to show that he cannot be true to his own convictions and the accepted principles of reasoning and think as others have thought. This is not servility in any sense, nor does it call for a craven endorsement of what others say, but is an intelligent, conscientious and manly procedure, demanded alike of the claims of other thinkers and of the general interests of truth. It invites candor and unselfishness ; makes a ready surrender of prejudice and pride of opinion for the mere sake of opinion ; concedes the element of fallibility in the wisest of men, and lifts the entire discussion that may be pending to the plane of a dignified and earnest exercise of mind.

3. The Desire and Purpose to reach the Truth.

Just here is one of the crucial tests of ingenuous procedure. Argument for the sake of argument, or a discussion which does not even contemplate securing a definite issue, is disingenuous, when men are supposed to be contending for truth and right. Scholastic practice in the way of debate and as exemplified in the educational training of young men may justify itself on forensic grounds, in aiming at the practice itself as the final end of the exercise, but not so outside the preparatory drill work of the school-room, when the gravest questions are in hand for examination and settlement. It is thus that Carlyle speaks of "jesting Pilate, asking, What is truth?" and significantly adds, "Jesting Pilate had not the smallest chance to establish what was truth. He could not have known it had a god shown it to him." Precisely so, the Pharisees and scoffers of Christ's day could not reach the truth as declared by Him and embodied in Him simply because it was not their sincere and serious purpose to reach it. Hence, all nice distinctions of casuistry for the sake of the distinctions, all subterfuge, evasion, quibbling and twisting of the truth ; all intentional ambiguity and sophistry and double dealings in the use of mean and ends, is directly counter to the spirit of honest discussion, a gross abuse of that freedom of thought which is one of the highest privileges of man. Such freedom, properly interpreted, is a trust and a moral responsibility, making it incumbent on every one who possesses it to take heed how he uses it, lest he justly forfeit it.

Such are a few of those limitations or conditions which form a kind of guide-line around the inherited right of personal liberty of thought, lest that liberty trespass upon the rights of others, and thus transgress the very principle that characterizes it. No one can carefully observe the manner in which such a natural privilege is exercised without seeing the frequent violations of these conditions, and, most especially so, within the realm of religious truth. Long established postulates, which have been seen to be trustworthy, and are supposed to lie at the basis of all fair discussion, are either ignored, or, if accepted, accepted but in part. With such reasoners there is no such thing as a "faith once delivered"; no such thing as fundamental and known truth on which to rise to something higher, and, as yet, unknown. In the exercise of a supposed liberty devoid of all restraint, the only method, it is urged, is to begin with denying all; to bring what is called an absolutely unbiased mind to the discussion and to accept nothing save perforce. Moreover, a captious and suspicious spirit takes the place of honest investigation. Lessing's famous preference of the "search after truth" to the truth itself becomes the guiding impulse; questions historically settled and so accepted are reopened and revoked or modified without the presence of any new evidence to justify it, and, if so be any truth emerges outside the limits of the material and natural, it is thereby regarded as untrustworthy. As Prof. Mansel has tersely expressed it, all such reasoning is "speculative, not regulative," a lawless application of free thinking with no practical ultimatum in view, and the more vague and visionary the better. Hence, hypothesis takes the place of history, and imagination that of reason, and no progress is made in the discovery of truth. By such a false conception of what freedom of opinion is many have come, at length, in theological issues, to have no opinions at all. What Prof. Bryce has termed "an age of discontent" is thus induced, and not a few are pleased to have it so. Even the sea is, at times, at calm, but in the wild waters of agitation for the sake of agitation, there is no peace. An endless round of question and answer becomes the ideal condition. In the onward course of life there is no period or full stop, nothing but interrogation or exclamation or parenthesis or dash, and so this moral history repeats itself without cessation, bringing in the reign of rationalism and then of naturalism, and then of pessimism—each for himself and all for the worst. The Seekers and Levellers are not confined to the days of Cromwell, but are now busily at work, under the plea of freedom of thinking, undermining all ethical distinctions, all existing moral institutions. To explain truth is not the object, but rather to explain it away; not to reach it so as to diffuse it, but to uproot and destroy it and bid every man think as he pleases, despite all precedent, condition and possible result.

Personal liberty of thought under well-adjusted limitations is one of the urgent needs of the time, so as not to run athwart the laws of God and the rights of men and the interests of truth. The spirit of intellectual humility in the pursuit of truth is another need equally urgent, so as not, once again, to commit the personal sin of usurping God's place in the universe as the source of all wisdom and knowledge. Personal pride of opinion is at the basis of a large part of the religious scepticism of the day; the right of private judgment carried to so gross and revolting an extreme as to provoke the righteous wrath of God and all good men and ruin the souls of those who indulge it.

There are some things in the realm of thought and truth which even German specialists in theology do not know; some things too high even for the highest criticism; and the first thing for these modern wiseacres to do is to get down upon their knees in the dust with Job and confess that they were not personally present when God laid the foundations of the earth and outlined its moral order. The spirit of humility and discipleship is the spirit that we need in the world and in the Church. The theory that we know or can know everything is as false in philosophy and religion as that we know and can know nothing. It is an abuse of personal liberty. God alone is unconditionally free.

SHEOL.

By Professor Thomas Hill Rich, Cobb Divinity,
School, Lewiston, Me.

SHEOL is derived from the Hebrew *shaal*, " to dig," " to excavate," and then, figuratively, " to inquire," " to ask." From asking comes the thought of insatiableness. "There are three things never satisfied; four that never say, ' Enough ' " (Prov. xxx. 15, 16). Sheol is one of these four. From insatiableness comes the thought of a monster who without measure opens his mouth seeking to glut his greed (Is. v. 14; Hab. ii. 5); who is cruel (or hard) and inexorably holds his victim (see Song of Solomon viii. 6); and from whose grasp God only can release (Ps. xlix. 15).

From its primary meaning to "excavate," Sheol was conceived of as a deep cavern (Job xi. 8), having depths upon depths (Prov. ix. 18); as in the centre of the earth (Numb. xvi. 30; Deut. xxxii. 22); and as fastened with gates and bars (Is. xxxviii. 10; Job xvii. 16).

Forth from vigorous life, Dathan and Abiram went down to Sheol (Numb. xvi. 30); to Sheol all the wicked will have to retreat (Ps. ix. 17); sickness brought King David and King Hezekiah to its borders (Ps. xxx. 3; Is. xxxviii. 10); and Jacob expected to go down thither— mourning all the way for his son Joseph (Gen. xxxvii. 35). Sheol is the destination of all mankind (Eccles. ix. 10); and Job no doubt has reference to Sheol when he speaks of " the house appointed (the house of meeting; see orig.) for all the living" (Job xxx. 23), *i. e.*, the house where the living are to convene (compare " tabernacle of the congregation," Ex. xxix. 44, and elsewhere—for which the margin and the Revision give "tabernacle of meeting.")

By the Hebrew Rephaim, occurring in Job xxvi. 5 ; Is. xiv. 9 ; Is. xxvi; xiv. 19 ; Prov. xxi. 16; Ps. lxxxviii. 10, we are to understand not the dead, but that part of man that survives death. So in the margin of these passages the Revision has "the shades," which in common English usage corresponds to the Hebrew conception of Rephaim. In Is. xiv. 9, Sheol is said to be in commotion at the approach of the King of Babylon, who, if not unexpected, was not expected so soon. The Rephaim (the shades), especially the former leaders of the nations, are so amazed that they start up from their thrones, exclaiming : " Art thou also become weak as we ? Art thou made like to us ? " Though this is poetic language, as the prophet indicates in verse 4, yet we may conclude that it expresses the popular ideas of his time ; and that the Rephaim, the inhabitants of Sheol, were regarded as a reflection, a shadow of what they were on this side of the grave. So Homer in his famous "Nekyia" represents the lower world not so much as the place of retribution, as an image of this present life, a place where mortals still live on, retaining their former character and habits.

A like idea of future existence seems to have prevailed among simple peoples and among barbarians in every age, from the early inhabitants of the East to the aborigines of our Western wilderness, who, by burying with their dead, articles that they were wont to use here, declare a belief in a world beyond this. Accordingly the familiar Scripture phrase, "being gathered to his fathers," does not mean dying as they died, nor the being placed in the family sepulchre, but the coming to the assembly—to "the shades"—of one's fathers, in Sheol.

Sheol is never used of the individual grave, or sepulchre ; and so it is not said that Jacob set up a pillar on the Sheol of Rachel (Gen. xxxv. 20); nor was it at Abner's Sheol that King David and the people wept (II. Sam. iii. 32).

Another word, fitly translated "grave," was used by the Hebrews to denote the place where the mortal remains are laid away. But as our word "grave" can have a metaphorical sense, and signify the abode of the dead in general, it could likewise be used to translate Sheol, as was done in thirty-one passages of the authorized version. In the Hebrew, words meaning pit are synonyms of Sheol, and so in the authorized version "pit" is thrice its representative, owing to the fondness of King James' revisers for a varied translation of the same original. The word "hell" belongs to the Teutonic languages, and means "the hollow place." Curiously enough, it is one in etymology with the Latin *coelum* (Gr. *koilon*), heaven—the concave above; hell is the concave (Gr. *koilon*, allied to Ger. *hohl*, and English hollow) beneath As now used, the word hell has only an incidental relation to Sheol; but by its like etymology, and by its former use, being closely allied to Sheol, could once translate it; and so in the authorized version it does that service in the thirty-one remaining passages where Sheol occurs.

The Douay Bible, of nearly the like date with the authorized version, almost uniformly rendered Sheol by the word hell. The Douay represents Jacob as saying: "I will go down to my son into hell, mourning (Gen. xxxvii. 35).

The Apostles' Creed, which passed into the English Church in 1534, uses the word hell in the same sense.

These different translations of Sheol are perplexing to those who can study the Bible in English only. It would have greatly aided such in their investigations if Sheol had been everywhere left untranslated; as indeed it should have been, since it is a proper name.

Men naturally speak of "going down" to the grave; and men of olden times thought of the passage to the region beyond the grave, as likewise a descent, and accounted the inhabitants of such lower region dreamy shadows, since evidently divested of their former substance. Like Homer, the Old Testament writers draw a gloomy picture of this world of shades; and were, perhaps, inspired to utter their dim views upon future existence rather than to make revelations in respect to life and immortality—subjects thereafter, to be lighted up by the Gospel of Christ. Yet the pious Israelite, assured that it was well with the righteous (Is. iii. 10), and should forever be so, had hope in death (Prov. xiv. 32). Struggling to rise above the popular conception, he was enabled by the Spirit, sometimes at least, to say: ' God will not abandon me (orig. my soul) to Sheol ; nor suffer his servant to experience the pit" (Ps. xvi. 10). "God will redeem me from the power (lit. the hand) of Sheol, for he shall receive me "—snatch me away as he did Enoch and Elijah (so the original suggests).

Hades, according to the classics, "the under world," or, according to the common derivation, "the unseen world," as being the Greek word nearest Sheol, stands for it in the Septuagint. However, we must not at once infer that with this choice of Hades, all its Greek associations were likewise adopted.

We find this choice of the LXX. approved by the New Testament writers. Here Hades, like Sheol, is deep (Matt. xi. 23), and powerful; but its gates (in Oriental speech gates stand for power) shall not prevail against the congregation of the faithful (Matt. xvi. 18), *i.e.*, Christ's Church is inextinguishable; it shall not be blotted from the earth.

He to whom all is alike manifest teaches us that the rich man in Hades—"the unseen world"—being in torments, sees Lazarus there, but afar off, separated by an impassable chasm—in Abraham's bosom (*i.e.*, resting in bliss, according to Jewish view; see Luke xvi. 23).

Christ on the day of His crucifixion went into Hades, and

there on the same day the thief found with Him Paradise (Luke xxiii. 43). There, too, as it would seem, Christ's servants, after leaving the body, dwell amid His ever-manifested presence (see orig. II. Cor. v. 8).

But though, put to death as regarded His body, Christ entered Hades, still death could not hold Him there (Acts ii. 24); and made alive again, in His glorified body He ascended to the right hand of the Majesty on high. Henceforth He has the keys of Hades (Rev. xi. 18), and Hades shall not retain His people, nor have victory over them (I. Cor. xv. 55). They, like their Lord, shall thence come forth at the resurrection of life to perfection of bliss—in body and soul, in the eternal and everlasting glory!

The tongue is not set on fire by Hades, but by Gehenna (James iii. 6—Gehenna is fitly translated hell as the word is now used); and he who calls his brother a fool is in danger of the Gehenna of fire (Matt. v. 22).

While death comes to all and Hades follows death (Rev. vi. 8), yet Gehenna can be escaped—though it may be with sacrifice of a right hand or a right eye (Matt. v. 29, 30).

NOTES ON THE NEGATIVE CRITICISM.

BY PROFESSOR W. H. ROBERTS, D.D., LL.D., LANE
THEOLOGICAL SEMINARY.

(I) There is very evidently in Germany, and to a certain extent in England and America, a party who are bent upon establishing a doctrine of inspiration and a rule of faith, which shall admit as their basis the fact of proved errors in the Holy Scriptures. This party is composed in the main of the negative critics. The critics, *i.e.*, the biblical scholars, who are engaged in the critical study of the text, authorship, etc., of the books of the Bible, are usually divided into two classes, the lower and the higher. The lower critics are those who are engaged, in the main, in studies dealing with the text of Scripture in its original languages; the higher critics are chiefly concerned with what may be termed the literary criticism of the Bible. The critics may again be divided into positive and negative, in view of the motives which control their work. The negative critics are thus called because the things which they assert are ordinarily denials or negations. They always oppose what they term the "traditional" views as to the integrity, authenticity and inspiration of the Holy Scriptures. They deny, for instance, that Moses wrote the Pentateuch, that Ezra was the editor of Chronicles, that Daniel is a canonical book, that the evangelists are accurate historians, and some of them, that the Word of God is anywhere an infallible record. They accord, as a rule, the Scriptures scant credit, and are more ready to believe secular than sacred historians. Their actual purpose, whether intentional or unintentional, is to discredit the Bible. Those of the number who are found in the United States, while they rebuke many Christians for being Bibliolatrists, are themselves decided Teutolatrists, repeating verbatim the lessons set them by their German masters.

(2) That the school of the negative critics first became a power in the world of religious thought some sixty years ago, but in that period of time the changes of position by the leaders in the school have been as rapid and as numerous as those of a kaleidoscope. In a recent number of the *Methodist Review* the well equipped Methodist scholar, Dr. Mendenhall, gives the following statistics respecting the theories concerning the several books of the Bible promulgated by the negative critics during the past forty years. He writes: "The grand number of theories respecting the Old Testament books is 539. The number of theories applied to the New Testament books is 208. Adding 539 and 208 we have a total of 747 theories applied to the biblical books since 1850." And then Dr. Mendenhall adds: "Of the 747 theories 603 are defunct, and many of the remaining 144 are in the last stages of degeneracy and dissolution." And yet certain of the negative critics desire the Church to follow them and accept as a basis of doctrine certain theories of the critical school which within ten years may be simply objects of scholarly curiosity and amusement. The Protestant Churches have no desire to place their creed as exhibits in a historical museum.

(3) The tide seems to be turning against the negative school. One of the latest works in the Old Testament department issued in Germany is "Zahn's Deuteronomy," dedicated to the "eminent American apologete, Dr. Wm. Henry Green, in Princeton, with sincere esteem." This treatise is one of great ability, and resolutely maintains the traditional views of the Mosaic authorship, historical accuracy and inspiration of Deuteronomy. Again, in Eng-

land the present trend of thought is unfavorable to the
negative school. I have seen the statement that recently
Prof. Margoliouth, Arabic Professor in Oxford University,
England, has vindicated the integrity and authenticity of
Daniel, and has compelled the acquiescence in his views of
Profs. Driver and Cheyne, the foremost champions in Great
Britain of the negative criticism. If this be true, then, so
far as that prophetical book is concerned, Prof. Briggs'
inaugural is already a back number. Literary critics, who
reconstruct the Bible out of their inner consciousness, are
continually meeting the fate of those German critics who
flatly denied that Bering, the navigator, ever visited the
northwest coast of the American continent. The log-books
of Bering's voyages have recently been given to the public
by the Russian Government, whose employee he was, and
German criticism has met by the publication an overwhelm-
ing defeat. It is now proven incontestably that Bering
sailed over the waters which bear his name. As in geographical, so in biblical records, the German critics are at war
with facts. Dr. W. C. Prime, one of the most eminent of
Egyptologists, writes: "The great discoveries of antiquities
which have been made in Egypt have a much broader significance and importance than in their mere historical
character. They not only reveal interesting facts in regard
to the intercourse between Egypt and Asia thirty centuries
ago, but in making these revelations they annihilate a very
large part of the so-called 'Biblical Criticism' which, during
the past quarter century, has assumed to judge ancient historical books and tell us how far they are true and how far
they are false." To put this third main point concisely: For
fifty years the advocates of negation have brought charge
after charge against the integrity of biblical books and the
accuracy of biblical history, only to go down to defeat
before the advance of knowledge in ancient Oriental history, and in biblical philology. The past unites with the

present in evidencing that the Bible is an anvil which has worn out every hammer lifted upon it.

(4) The positive class of critics is the one which has done acceptable and profitable work for Anglo-Saxon Christendom. It is in the main this class of critics who, laboring together in England and America, have satisfied for the time being the demands of that supreme work which God and His Church have entrusted to critical scholars, the giving to Christians not a list of the errors to be found in the Scriptures, but a revised biblical text. The German negative critics, on the other hand, with their imitators, have been engaged in the main in the work of depreciation and destruction. Criticism with them means usually disparagement of opponents and overthrow of the historical accuracy of the Word of God by any means within their power. If I know anything of Anglo-Saxon Christendom, with its intense practicality; with its readiness to believe the best about men, not the worst; with its insistence that the Bible, like other books, is to be judged even in this matter of inerrancy, by its general character, not by the discrepancies which may here and there appear in its text; then I am certain that this issue now raised will be settled in a decisive manner.

(5) The inerrancy of the Scriptures, whatever allegations may have been made to the contrary, is a doctrine of the Westminster Confession of Faith, and was the received doctrine of the Presbyterian Church at reunion. There is no probability that Presbyterians will adopt any doctrine of inspiration which admits as its basis alleged errors in the Scriptures. They do not believe that the Bible in its first and only inspired form, any more than man at his creation, was imperfect. It is with the uninspired human connection that change and imperfection appear therein. The alleged proved errors in the Holy Scriptures are either discrepancies, owing to errors made by copyists, or seeming

errors arising from human ignorance, and which, as already indicated, God is removing gradually by the increase of our knowledge.

(6) The main principles which control the two schools of criticism are totally opposed. I quote here a part of Dr. Watts' (Belfast) crushing reply to Prof. Blaikie (Edinburgh) in this very matter of inspiration, and apply it to the negative school and its adherents. The quotation reads, "While the principle of your theory [*i.e.*, the negative critics] is a mere inference from apparent discrepancies not yet explained, the principle of the theory you oppose is the formally expressed utterance of prophets and apostles and of Christ Himself." Protestants must refuse to follow the negative critics in taking biblical errors as a basis for a doctrine of inspiration. They should take for that basis the affirmations of Scripture, and should refuse to minimize Scripture doctrine in order to excuse inability to explain Scripture difficulties.

(7) Thorough-going Protestants do not believe in the inspiration of the Scriptures merely on an *a priori* theory, or on the testimony of any man or Church. Protestants believe that the Holy Scriptures are inspired because the Scriptures themselves make the claim. Are the Scriptures credible or are they not when they assert that they are inspired? Believing that the "Old Testament in Hebrew and the New Testament in Greek, being immediately inspired by God, are authentical" (Westm. Conf. of Faith, Chap i., Sec. 8), *i.e.*, are to be believed, Presbyterians should resolutely maintain the plenary inspiration and the infallibility of the Word of God.

BIBLICAL ARCHÆOLOGY AND THE HIGHER CRITICISM.

BY A. H. SAYCE, LL.D., PROFESSOR OF ASSYRIOLOGY, OXFORD.

"TWO truths cannot be contradictory." So we are told, and in this abstract form the assertion is, doubtless, correct. But what is meant by a "truth" is generally the statement of what we believe to be the truth, and it will be easily seen that such statements may be either actually or apparently inconsistent with one another. We can never know all the facts connected with a given subject; indeed, the fact itself is but a generalization from a limited series of phenomena. Hence it is quite possible for two statements to be each of them quite true in its own sphere,—an accurate representation of the facts with which it deals, so far as they are known,—and yet at the same time to be apparently irreconcilable. A certain group of facts, for instance, leads us to conclude that space is boundless; but there are other psychological facts which oblige us just as imperatively to maintain that the universe is finite.

When modern astronomy first began to find adherents, and again when geology began to take rank as a science, various attempts were made to "reconcile," as it was termed, the records of the Bible with the new scientific teaching. Such attempts are even now made from time to time, though it has at last been recognized that the student of theology and the astronomer or geologist deal with different branches of research, with different sets of facts, and that consequently they must necessarily move in different spheres.

Not until we know all the facts connected with astronomy or geology on the one hand, and with theology on the other, will it be time to form a science which shall embrace all alike. Then and then only will it be possible to solve the seeming contradictions which exist between the conclusions of the two lines of inquiry, and to construct a "harmony" which shall be a harmony indeed.

The controversy carried on between the advocates of science and the advocates of the traditional interpretation of the Bible has in these latter years shifted its ground.

Theology has at last been content to leave science alone to work out its results in its own way and its own sphere; and science in its turn is ceasing to occupy itself with framing new theological systems. It is no longer the bearing of physical science upon the statements of Scripture that arouses the war-cry of the controversialist, but the character and authenticity of those statements themselves. The "higher criticism" claims to sit in judgment on the traditions or beliefs of preceding centuries, and by the application of a more rigorous method of investigation, and of the principles of modern scientific thought to reverse or modify them.

The term "higher criticism" is an unfortunate one. It has the appearance of pretentiousness, and it may be feared that in some cases it has led to the unconscious assumption of a tone of superiority on the part of its professors and their followers. But in reality the word "higher" is used only in order to distinguish the form of criticism to which it is applied from textual criticism. Textual or "lower" criticism is mainly mechanical; the "higher" criticism requires a power of sifting and weighing evidence, and of balancing probabilities one against the other.

Its sphere of work is twofold. On the one hand, it investigates the age and composition of the documents with which it deals; on the other hand, the historical credibility

of the narratives which these documents contain. In the
one case, its object is literary analysis ; in the other, historical criticism. But it is obvious that the two objects
are closely connected with each other ; the historical credibility of a narrative often depends largely on the age of the
documents in which it is found, or the character of their
authors ; while the results of literary analysis can be best
verified, in many instances, by an appeal to history. If, for
instance, it could be shown by the historical critic that there
are two inconsistent accounts of the geography of the Exodus, one placing the passage of the sea in the Gulf of
Akabah, and the other at the head of the Gulf of Suez,
and further that the lines of division between the two
accounts correspond with the lines of division in the composition of the Book of Exodus presupposed by the literary
analyst, we should have an important verification of the
accuracy of the literary analysis, at all events in this particular instance.

The general results of literary analysis have had much
to do with the judgment passed on the earlier narratives
of the Old Testament Scripture. As long as it was believed
that the Pentateuch was written by Moses, it followed that
the account of the Exodus and of the wanderings of the
Israelites in the desert could be accepted without question.
But the case is altered if we accept the conclusions of the
most recent school of criticism, and not only regard the
Hexateuch as a composite work, but also hold that it did not
assume its present form until after the Exile. During the
long centuries which intervened between the age of Moses
and that of Ezra, the earlier history of the Israelitish people
would have had time to be forgotten, and to be replaced by
legendary tradition or even conscious fiction. Deprived of
the support of contemporaneous testimony, the story of
the legislation in the Wilderness, and the subsequent conquest of Canaan, could offer little resistance to the assaults

of historical criticism. Criticism, consequently, had little difficulty in showing that it was improbable and self-contradictory, borrowing many of its details from a state of things that did not exist until the age of the Exile, and filled with that atmosphere of miracle which we find in the pre-literary traditions of most nations.

The conclusions of the "higher criticism" were supported by an assumption and a tendency. The assumption was that writing was unknown to the Israelites, or even to the Canaanites, in the age of the Exodus. At the most, it was believed, they could engrave inscriptions on wood or stone; books were the product of a later and more cultured time. The tendency was the extreme skepticism with which the early periods of secular history were regarded. The more exact method of investigating ancient history and demanding adequate evidence for its statements, which had been made popular by Niebuhr, had resulted in making Greek history a blank page before the epoch of Peisistratos, and in refusing credit to the history of Rome before its capture by the Gauls. In Sir George Cornewall Lewis this tendency reached its extreme point. For him the history of civilization, and therefore of accurately known facts, begins with Herodotos and Thukydidês, and the counter-evidence of the monuments of Egypt and Assyria was got rid of by maintaining that they neither had been nor could be deciphered.

But Sir George Cornewall Lewis was scarcely dead before the reaction began. What the higher critics had so successfully demolished was again built up by the spade of the excavator and the patient skill of the decipherer, Schliemann, strong in a belief which no amount of skilful dialectic could shake, dug up the ruins of Troy and Mykenæ and Tiryns, and demonstrated that the old tales about the splendor and culture of the Akhæan princes, and of their intercourse with the shores of Asia Minor, were, after all, not so very far from the truth. Undeterred by the *à priori* demonstrations of Sir George Cornewall Lewis and his reviewers, the decipherers pursued their labors among the inscriptions of Egypt and Assyria, and reconstructed the lost history of the ancient Oriental world. And, what was even more important, they proved that the reading and writing of books was centuries older than the classical age of Greece; that ages before the time of Moses, or even of Abraham, libraries existed where scribes and readers were constantly at work, while literary intercourse was carried on from the banks of the Euphrates to those of the Nile.

Schliemann has been followed by many rivals in the field of excavation, and the small band of Orientalists who ventured to explore the unknown regions of Egyptian and Assyrian research at the risk of being accused of charlatanism, or neglect of exact philology, have now become a goodly company. Discovery has crowded upon discovery, each more marvellous than the last, until the student has come to believe, that, as in physical science, so too in Oriental archæology, all things are possible.

Naturally, the "higher criticism" is disinclined to see its assumptions swept away along with the conclusions which are based upon them, and to sit humbly at the feet of the newer science. At first, the results of Egyptian or Assyrian research were ignored ; then they were reluctantly admitted, so far as they did not clash with the preconceived opinions of the "higher" critics. It was urged, unfortunately with too much justice, that the decipherers were not, as a rule, trained critics, and that in the enthusiasm of research they often announced discoveries which proved to be false or only partially correct. But it must be remembered, on the other side, that this charge applies with equal force to all progressive studies, not excluding the "higher criticism" itself.

The time is now come for confronting the conclusions

of the "higher criticism," so far as it applies to the books of the Old Testament, with the ascertained results of modern Oriental research. The amount of certain knowledge now possessed by the Egyptologist and Assyriologist would be surprising to those who are not specialists in their branches of study, while the discovery of the Tel-el-Amarna tablets has poured a flood of light upon the ancient world, which is at once startling and revolutionary. As in the case of Greek history, so too in that of Israelitish history, the period of critical demolition is at an end, and it is time for the archæologist to reconstruct the fallen edifice.

But the very word "reconstruct" implies that what is built again will not be exactly that which existed before. It implies that the work of the "higher criticism" has not been in vain; on the contrary, the work it has performed has been a very needful and important one, and in its own sphere has helped us to the discovery of the truth. Egyptian or Assyrian research has not corroborated every historical statement which we find in the Old Testament any more than classical archæology has corroborated every statement which we find in the Greek writers; what it has done has been to show that the extreme skepticism of modern criticism is not justified, that the materials on which the history of Israel has been based may, and probably do, go back to an early date, and that much which the "higher" critics have declared to be mythical and impossible was really possible and true. The justification of these assertions must be deferred to another article.

THE UNITY OF GENESIS I. AND II. CHAPTERS.

BY PROF. WILLIAM HENRY GREEN, D.D., PRINCETON
THEOLOGICAL SEMINARY.

ARE the first two chapters of Genesis the continuous production of one writer, or are they a compilation from two antecedent documents?
It is alleged that Genesis ii. cannot have been written by the author of Genesis i., because it is a second account of the creation, and is superfluous for that reason; its statements are irreconcilable with those of chapter i; and its diction and style are different. The critics are at fault here in two respects; and these, it may be said, characterize their general method of procedure, and are their chief instruments in sundering the Pentateuch into what they regard as distinct documents:

1. The arbitrary assumption that two different parts of a narrative relating to matters quite distinct are variant accounts of the same thing. It is very easy to make two narratives, or two parts of the same narrative, which have certain points in common, but which really describe different transactions, and lay them alongside of one another and point out the lack of correspondence between them. There is no significance in this further than that the writer has finished one part of his story and has proceeded to another; and of course he does not detail over again what he had just detailed before.

2. Creating discordance where none really exists. Every form of expression, which, if isolated, might admit of a sig-

nification at varience with statements elsewhere, is pressed to the utmost, and urged as a proof of diverse representations; when, if it be allowed to bear its natural sense in the connection in which it stands, all appearance of discrepancy will disappear.

Chapter ii. is not, and does not profess to be, another account of the creation. It claims to be, and it is, a sequel to the account given in chapter i.

The current division into chapters obscures to the ordinary reader the plan upon which the Book of Genesis is constructed. After the introductory section describing the creation of all things, i., 1–ii., 3, it proceeds with the history, which is distributed into ten sections, each of which is introduced by a title of uniform pattern—"These are the generations," etc., ii. 4; v. 1; vi. 9; x. 1, etc. The section entitled "The Generations of Adam," v. 1, traces the descendants of Adam. "The Generations of Noah," vi. 9, records the history of Noah's family. And so, uniformly, "the generations of" any one do not detail his ancestry or his origin, but give either the history of his immediate family or the continuous line of his descendants. It is thus contrary to uniform analogy and to the proper sense of the words to regard "The generations of the heaven and the earth," ii. 4*a*, as a subscription to the preceding section, summing up its contents as an account of the origin of the heaven and the earth. It can only be the title to the section which it introduces, whose subject it announces to be, not the formation, but the offspring of heaven and earth; that is to say, man, the child of both worlds, his body formed of dust, his soul inbreathed by God Himself.

And, in point of fact, ii. 4, sq , do not contain a fresh account of the creation. The opening words, "In the day that Jehovah God made the earth and the heavens," presuppose the act of making, and proceed to indicate what was then the state of things and what followed subsequently. No account is given of the formation of the earth or the dry land; none of the sea and its occupants; none of the firmament or of the sun, moon, and stars; none of covering the earth with its varied vegetations, but only of the garden of Eden and its trees, vs. 8, 9. To say with Dr. Dillmann that all this was originally in chapter ii., but was omitted because it is treated sufficiently in chapter i., is a confession that chapter ii. is not what it would have been if the writer had intended to give a narative of the creation, and that its omissions are with definite reference to the contents of chapter i. Chapter ii. is introductory to the narrative of the fall in chapter iii., and hence describes the two constituents of man's nature, vs. 7, comp. iii. 19; the garden as the scene of the temptation, vs. 8–17; the actors Adam and Eve, vs. 18–25. These details would have been out of place in the general account of the creation.

All comparisons or contrasts between chapter i. and chapter ii. on the assumption that they relate to the same subject are fallacious. One deals with the world at large and all that it contains; the other with the garden of Eden and the relations of the first human pair. When it is said that chapter i. is generic, treating of species and classes, and chapter ii. individual, this grows necessarily out of their respective themes. So, when it is claimed that chapter i. deals in stereotyped phrases and is verbose and repetitious, while the style of chapter ii. is free and flowing. In chapter i. the almighty fiat is issued; the result precisely corresponds and is noted in identical language. There is the regular recurrence of each creative day, of the word of omnipotence, of God's approval of his work which precisely matches the divine idea, the name given to indicate its character, the blessing bestowed to enable it to accomplish its end. To mark all this in the most emphatic manner, the identical phrases are repeated throughout. Such a style would be utterly unsuited to simple narrative like chapter ii. and accordingly does not reappear even in those narrative passages which are assigned by the critics to the same document with chapter i. It is said that chapter i. proceeds from the lower to the higher, ending with man, while chapter ii. begins with man and proceeds to the lower forms of life But as chapter ii. continues the history begun in chapter i., it naturally starts where chapter i. ends, with the creation of man, especially as the whole object of the chapter is to depict his primitive condition.

These and other similar contrasts between chapter i, and chapter ii. explain themselves at once from the diversity of theme, and require no assumption of separate documents to account for them.

While each chapter pursues its own proper aim, they have certain points of contact in which the second chapter supplements the first, but there is no discrepancy between them. In fact it would be inconsistent with the document hypothesis itself to suppose that there were here two divergent stories of the creation. The redactor does not offer them as alternatives, but as equally true and to be credited alike, so that he could not have thought them imcompatible.

The writer begins the second section by reminding his readers, in conformity with chapter i., that "in the day that Jehovah God made earth and heaven, no bush of the field was yet in the earth, and no herb of the field had yet sprung up." The reason given is twofold: there was no rain to moisten the earth, and no man to till the ground. There is no variance here with chapter i. The suggestion that rain could not be needed if the land had just emerged from the water, leaves out of view that the earth was "dry," i. 9, 10, before any plants appeared upon its surface. And there is no implication that man preceded vegetation, contrary to i. 12, 27. For (1) chapter ii. says nothing of the production of plants generally, but only of the trees of the garden verses 8, 9. (2) Man was a condition of the existence of food-bearing plants only as they were designed for his use and required his tillage. (3) The order of statement is plainly not that of time, but association in thought. Verse 7, man is formed; verse 8, the garden planted and man put in it; verse 9, trees are made to spring up there; verse 15, man is taken and put in it. Must we infer that man was made and kept in suspense until the garden was planted; that he was then put there before the trees that were to supply him with food had sprung up; and when the trees were in readiness he was put there a second time.

It has been proposed, however, to bring about a conflict in this matter between chapter ii. and chapter i. by a grammatical construction, putting ii. 5, 6 in a parenthesis and linking verse 7 with verse 4. The meaning then will be: In the day that God made earth and heaven, he formed man of the dust of the ground, while no bush or herb had yet sprung up. But so long a parenthesis is questionable in Hebrew generally, and is impossible here. Verse 5 states a twofold reason why there were no plants adopted to human use. The first condition is supplied in verse 6, the second in verse 7; verses 6 and 7 must accordingly stand in like relation to verse 5, so that verse 6 cannot be included in the parenthesis and verse 7 linked to verse 4.

It has been charged that chapter ii. puts the creation of man before that of the lower animals, contrary to chapter i. The allegation rests upon the assumption that the Hebrew tense in ii. 19, necessarily implies a sequence in the order of time. But Dr. Delitzsch in the last edition of his "Genesis" says that according to Hebrew style there is no discrepancy here; it is quite possible to understand that the beasts now brought to Adam had been made some time before. Dr. Dillmann admits that, so far as the tense is concerned, this might be the case, but insists that the animals were made in pursuance of the divine purpose, verse 18, to make a help meet for Adam, and must therefore have been formed after he was. But God's purpose was not to make man a companion of some sort, or such as he might be willing to have, but a help *meet;* that is, literally rendered, a help corresponding to him. The beasts were brought, not as the companion intended for him, but "to see what he would call them"; that is, to let them make their impression on him and thus awaken in his mind a sense of his need of companionship and of their unfitness for the purpose. When this had been done Eve was made.

To insist that the order of statement must be regarded as the order of time will create absurdities in many passages. It would imply in Genesis xxiv. 64, 65, that Rebekah alighted out of respect to her future husband before she knew that it was he; Exodus iv. 31, that the people believed the words of Aaron before they heard them; Joshua ii. 22, the pursuers returned from their unsuccessful search before their search was begun; Isaiah xxxvii. 2-5, Hezekiah messengers told Isaiah their message before they came to him; in I. Kings xiii. 12, "saw" is plainly equivalent to "had seen," and so the Authorized Version renders it. Unless a principle of interpretation which leads to these absurd results be insisted on in the case before us, there is not a shadow of contrariety between chapter i. and chapter ii. in respect to the order of creation.

The distribution of the matter between these sections implies pre-arrangement. The creation of the world at large is described in chapter i. and assumed in chapter ii.; the latter simply supplies details necessarily passed over in the plan of the former, which were essential to an understanding of the account of the fall. God gave names to day and night, heaven, earth and seas, i. 5, 8, 10, and to Adam, v. 1; Adam gave names to the inferior animals, ii. 20, and to Eve, ii. 23; nothing is duplicated and nothing omitted. So the emphatic repetition in chapter i.—God saw that it was good, or very good—prepares the way for the reverse that was to follow in chapter iii.

The alleged difference of diction in these chapters is fallacious. The characteristic words imputed to chapter i. recur in part in the account of the flood, which equally affected all orders of creatures, but nowhere else in the same document, as the critics divide them, in Genesis. The creation, the flood, genealogies, and ritual legislation, which make up the bulk of one document, have little in common with the transactions of individual life, which constitute the substance of the other. The diversity of diction between the two is just the natural result of a partition so conducted, not a ground upon which that partition can be based.

Elohim, as the general term for God in nature and the world at large, is appropriately used in i. 1; ii. 3. Jehovah is the God of revelation and redemption, and is hence appropriate, ii. 4; iv. 26, where God's loving care of man in his original estate, the primal promise of mercy, and the goodness mingled with severity which ordered his condition subsequently, are detailed. And to show that the God of creation and Jehovah the God of grace are one and the same, both names are used in chapters ii. and iii. Is this appropriate use of these terms merely a lucky accident resulting from the combination of two independent documents, in each of which the names of God are regulated, not by their suitableness to the subject matter, but by the unmeaning habit of different writers? Again, as Elohim and Jehovah represent the Most High under different aspects of his being, they must, when used correctly and with regard to their proper meaning, be associated with different conceptions of God. This does not argue a diversity of writers, but simply that the divine name has each time been selected in accordance with the idea to be expressed.

This paper only touches the edge of a vast subject. If it has accomplished its aim, it has shown that the critical attempt to establish separate documents in the first two chapters of Genesis is unsuccessful. I believe that the same thing can be shown in the rest of Genesis and the entire Pentateuch.

MODERN CRITICISM OF THE PENTATEUCH.

BY PROFESSOR MATTHEW LEITCH, D.D., PRESBY-
TERIAN COLLEGE, BELFAST, IRELAND.

THE school of biblical criticism which is most widely dominant at the present day asks from us a complete reconstruction of the history of Israel, based on a new critical analysis of the Pentateuch.

In this school are two classes of critics, which must be carefully distinguished from each other. To the first class belong those who regard Christianity and its sacred books as the naturally developed product of the religious instinct of the human race. As the Greeks developed art, and the Romans law and politics, so, they say, the Hebrews developed religion. With critics of this class it is a fundamental assumption that a miracle never happened, a real prophecy was never uttered, and God never supernaturally revealed Himself to man. But the Pentateuch is full of the miraculous. They must, therefore, construct such theories of its origin and structure as will account for the existence of its miraculous element without admitting the truth of its miracles, and will explain the rest of its history without admitting the interference of any higher power than that of the religious instincts and impulses of the race, developing themselves according to natural laws. This they attempt to do by cleverly splitting up the Book into several parts, arranging these parts according to what they conceive to be the natural progressive development of the people, and assigning the narratives of miraculous events to men of a late age who in more or less good faith recorded them of their remote ancestors.

The second class of this school of criticism embraces

those who themselves believe in the supernatural, but adopt the critical theories of those who don't. There always has been a well-meaning class of scholars, who, fearing that the Bible and the Church will fall behind the age, are ever ready to readjust their criticism and their creed, so as to adapt it to any theory of science or philosophy that happens to be dominant for the day and claims to represent the advanced thought of the age. They sincerely believe that every passing form of thought that the "spirit of the age" calls forth is permanent and final.

Critics of this class all believe in the great miracle of the Incarnation. Some of them even accept the Westminster Confession of Faith, and some go so far as to trust in mystical supernatural endowments of an external Church organization; and yet they all adopt theories which are avowedly based by their authors on the incredibility of the supernatural in the Bible. What the first class calls myths, legends, sagas, or inventions of a later age, they call "idealizations of history," and they consider that to invent fictitious narratives of events that never happened, to devise codes of laws that never were enacted, to compose speeches that were never uttered, and to describe in detail institutions that never had existence, and to give to these fictions currency and authority by solemnly attributing them to Moses and to God Himself, is not inconsistent with honesty, or truth, or religion.

The weakness of this class of critics seems to be that they adopt the theories of the anti-supernatural critics, while they repudiate the fundamental reasons on which their authors base them. They take over the elaborate structure which others have raised, but they remove the substantial pillars on which it rested, retaining only a few buttresses which the original builders added to embellish rather than sustain it.

With the first class of these critics, who are chiefly Continental scholars, we have little to do directly. We believe in the living God, and in the incarnate Son, and in the Holy Ghost ever present and ever working in His people. We have, therefore, but little common ground with those who deny or ignore these fundamental doctrines of Christianity. It is with the second class we have to deal directly. They are for the most part British scholars, who occupy themselves in adapting to Christian faith the naturalistic theories of the others, modifying them, popularizing them, and striving hard to show that they do not destroy Christian faith and morality, and are not inconsistent with the divine inspiration of the Bible or the Deity and perfect humanity of Jesus Christ.

Let me, in the first place, endeavor to state what the most generally accepted of these theories are. It would be impossible in a brief space to give even a summary of all the theories of the Pentateuch which have been advanced by critics ever since Astruc, a French physician, in the middle of last century, published a book in which he set forth as a conjecture that Moses in the compilation of Genesis used various documents, some eleven in all, but chiefly two main documents, distinguished from each other by their use of Elohim or Jehovah as the name of God. Since that time there have been almost as many theories as there have been critics; each critic either dividing the Book anew into pieces for himself, or forming, as he shakes the critical kaleidoscope, new combinations of the old pieces into which it had been before divided. Indeed the whole series of these theories of the Pentateuch affords an excellent example of natural development, in which each new form, while preserving the common type, modifies and advances some form that went before, while there is ever going on a process of natural selection, by which that theory survives which best fits itself into the environing spirit and temper of its age.

The theory of the Pentateuch which seems to have best

fitted itself to the fashion of thought of the present day is somewhat as follows : The prominent critics of this school, while not agreeing in details, are generally agreed on the main lines of the division of the Pentateuch. They find three well-marked codes of laws, which differ from each other in style and phraseology as well as in religious conception, and which represent and reflect three different periods of the history of Israel.

1. The first code is that collection of laws contained in Exodus from the twenty-third verse of the twentieth chapter to the end of chapter twenty-three, commonly called the Book of the Covenant.   2. The second code is contained in Deuteronomy, chapters xii.–xxvi.   3. The third code is made up of the laws found in the rest of Exodus and in Leviticus and Numbers.

We all admit the existence of these three codes and the well-marked differences that distinguish them.

1. The first code seems to be composed chiefly of laws which, no doubt, had been observed among the Israelites during the long period of their existence as a tribe governed by elders and judges. Just as the law of the Sabbath existed before it was sanctioned on Sinai in the Decalogue, so may these laws have been long established in Israel previous to their being summarized and sanctioned at the beginning of the nation's life in the wilderness. Moses speaking to his father-in-law before Israel had come to Sinai refers to the existence of a body of divine laws, when he says: "When the people have a matter, they come unto me, and I judge between one and another, and I do make them know the statutes of God and His laws." Israel, therefore, had "statutes and laws of God" before the promulgation of the Sinaitic code. It might well be called the Judges' Code. Critics generally call it the Prophetical Code.

2. So also we find in the middle books of the Pentateuch a series of laws which may fairly enough be called the

Priests' Code. It consists of laws which deal chiefly with the functions of the priests in the national worship of Jehovah.

3. The Deuteronomic Code is also clearly different from the others. It is contained in those popular addresses which Moses delivered to the whole body of the Israelites at the close of their forty years of wandering. There is naturally a development or modification of some of the laws after thirty-eight years of experience in the wilderness, and this popular re-statement of them keeps in view the altered conditions under which the people are now to live as the settled occupants of Canaan. While this legislation presupposes and often refers to what is contained in the preceding books, it does not give the details of priestly duties, but addresses itself to the people as the People's Code, in prospect of their settlement in Canaan.

This explanation of the three codes, which is that of the record itself, accounts simply and naturally for the differences between them. But it is much too obvious to satisfy our advanced critics. They say that the first code was not given at Sinai, nor through Moses at all; that few, if any, laws of Israel came from Moses; that this code was compiled and written down about the time of the early kings of Israel in the ninth or eighth century before Christ—say about six hundred years after Moses.

The Deuteronomic Code, though it may contain some laws of earlier date, was written in the reign of Manasseh or Josiah, say about eight centuries after the time of Moses. The Priests' Code they say was not completed till after the exile, or nearly a thousand years later than Moses. The critics, however, are not agreed as to the date of the Priests' Code, and its relation to that in Deuteronomy. Some of the leading critics in Germany, such as Dillmann and Riehm, put it before Deuteronomy, and assign it to the year 800 B.C. However, the criticism which is at the present most in vogue, and is being popularized in England and Scotland, makes it post exilic.

But our critics find in the Pentateuch not only different codes of laws but different strata of historical narrative. The narrative associated with the First Code is called the prophetical narrative, because it is thought to present the history of the times of the patriarchs and Moses, from the point of view of the prophets. It uses sometimes Jehovah and sometimes Elohim as the name of God, and so it must itself be a combination of two older narratives, one Jehovistic and the other Elohistic. It is therefore called J E, and there is of course a Redactor (R) who combined the two and pieced them together so skilfully that it defies the critics themselves to tell which parts belong to the Jehovist and which to the Elohist, and which are the Redactor's own.

The Priests' Code has also its historical setting called the Priestly Narrative, known commonly as P, and comprising a great part of the Pentateuchal history. But various hands wrought at this narrative. There is a second P and a third, and a Redactor, or Redactors, to combine them.

The Deuteronomist is styled D. Then we have all these codes and narratives put together some time later than the exile by a very cunning and skilful Redactor who adapted them, harmonized them, and dove-tailed them together so as to make one continuous work, the Pentateuch, as we now have it.

Let us now consider by what evidence these ingenious and intricate theories are supported. It cannot be too emphatically stated that the authors of these theories proceed tacitly or expressly on the assumption that the miracles and prophecies recorded in the Old Testament are incredible. It is true that many of those who adopt and popularize these theories, especially English and Scotch critics, do not deny the credibility of the supernatural, and even vehemently assert that their views are not inconsistent with the fullest belief in the divine inspiration of the Bible. Still it cannot be denied, and it ought to be emphasized, that the men who originated and worked out these theories, and whose learning and reputation have gained acceptance for them, assume all through their arguments that the miraculous is incredible. To be convinced of this, one has only to examine, looking up the Scripture passages referred to, a few of the arguments of Wellhausen, who may be taken as a fair representative of such critics in Germany, or of Kuenen in Holland, or of Rénan in France. They everywhere take for granted that the narratives of miraculous events are mere legends, often recorded for unworthy ends, and that Jehovah was a mere local deity of Israel, with no more real existence than Baal or Chemosh. These assumptions, which to us seem simply blasphemous, underlie this whole theory, and form its philosophical basis. And when it is said that men like Canons Driver and Cheyne, or Dr. RobertsonSmith, or Mr. Gore, or other men of smaller reputation, accept these same theories, and yet are believers in miracle and prophecy; that only means that these critics have adopted the theories without accepting the grounds on which their authors have based them. They adopt the theories, but deny the validity of the main arguments on which they rest. We are, therefore, constrained to believe that it is not so much that the arguments of men like Wellhausen have convinced them, as that the imposing authority of great names has overborne their judgment.

This argument from the authority of the great critical experts has more weight, perhaps, than any other with ordinary students of the Bible. Canon Driver, for instance, uses it forcibly when he is replying to Dr. Green's objections to the analysis of the Pentateuch, and it is the only reply to them which he makes. Canon Driver says: "If it [the analysis in its main features] had rested as Dr. Green supposes solely upon illusion, there would not have been a succession of acute Continental critics—who are ready enough to dispute and overthrow one another's conclusions, if able to do so—virtually following in the same lines, and merely correcting or modifying in details the conclusions of their predecessors" (*Cont. Rev.*, Feb., 1890).

This argument from authority would have more weight with us if we did not remember that Continental critics one after another, and all with the same air of lofty infallibility, have been for generations propounding and defending theories both of the Gospels and the Pentateuch, which for a while were widely accepted, and are now universally rejected. It is true that these German theories mostly came to England after they were dead at home, while now our relations with Continental thought are closer and communication is more rapid, so that, though they are still short-lived, we get them before there is time for the natural term of their life to be expired and their successors to have taken their place. Yet the remembrance of this long succession of these exploded theories lessens the weight of the authority of the great scholars who in our day are propounding new ones.

And in regard to these theories of the Pentateuch it is not difficult to explain why these "acute Continental critics do not overthrow one another's conclusions." They could not do so, without controverting the principle with which they start—the incredibility of the supernatural. The question that they have virtually before them is, How to account for the Bible without admitting the supernatural. And we no more accept their conclusions, because they in the main agree, than we should accept the conclusions of several Roman Catholic controversialists, who, "though ready enough to dispute and overthrow one another's conclusions if able to do so," are not able, because they all start with the assumption of the infallibility of the pope. So these Continental critics agree in the main in their conclusions,

MODERN CRITICISM OF THE PENTATEUCH. 291

because they agree in the assumption with which they start, and which dominates all their arguments. And, therefore, it has now became the fashion of the day among the learned —for there are fashions in learning as well as in dress—to advocate the theories that the most renowned scholars adopt. Even such a spiritually-minded man as the late Dr. Delitzsch, in what we cannot but believe to be the weakness of his old age, was unable to stand against the prevailing current of German scholarship and surrendered the position which he had held, no doubt with some inconsistencies, through the maturity and vigor of his manhood.

But if we ask on what other evidence, apart from this philosophical assumption and the authority of great names, does this theory of the composition of the Pentateuch rest, we are told that it is on the internal evidence of the work itself. There is no other evidence. Not one tittle of external historical testimony is alleged for the list of authors, Jehovists, Elohists, and Redactors, about whom the critics talk as familiarly as if they were personally acquainted with them. Whatever external evidence there is, in the frequent statements of the work itself, in the references of the subsequent literature, in the unbroken traditions of the nation, in the unvarying testimony of prophets, and apostles, and of our Lord Himself—it is all without exception in favor of the authorship of Moses. Whether you assign to it much value or little, it is all on one side. There is not a particle of external evidence in favor of any other authorship.

But internal evidence may be of such a nature that it is of itself convincing and sufficient. It is on internal evidence alone that we believe that Moses did not write the last portion of Deuteronomy, which gives an account of his own death and burial. There is no particular statement that he wrote it or did not write it; but it stands there like the rest of the books, and yet we infer, by internal evidence, that it was not written by Moses, but by some subsequent author or editor. Similarly, there might be internal evidence sufficient to satisfy us that other passages are not written by Moses.

Now let us look at the nature of the internal evidence that is alleged in favor of the various authors to whom the critics assign the different parts of the Pentateuch. There are, they say, palpable differences in style and in words and phrases, by which they can distinguish one part from another. There are discrepancies where statements taken from one document contradict those taken from another. There are also differences in religious conception, and in historical point of view, and all these differences combine with each other and repeat themselves often, and so form unmistakable criteria, according to which critics can assign each part to its own author.

Before presenting some objections to these theories I think it right to state what seems to me the right attitude to take in regard to them. The philosophical assumption of the incredibility of miracle with which one class of critics start, and on the lines of which their detailed arguments are worked out, we cannot, of course accept. If there was no miracle, there was no Divine Saviour, and if we reject Him, we may well reject the whole Bible, Old Testament and New.

On the other hand, it is not necessary to believe all the traditional opinions of the Church as to the date, authorship, and structure of each book of the Bible, nor as to the mode of its inspiration by the Holy Ghost. We hold no brief for scholastic or ecclesiastic traditions. They may be wrong, and if so, must be rejected. We cannot oppose scientific criticism, for it is only a systematic method of reaching clearer, fuller, and more definite knowledge of what the Bible is and what it contains. If criticism brings to light any new facts about the Bible, we welcome them. We may have to distinguish between the theory of the critic and the facts of the criticism; but we accept the facts, not in unwilling concession, but in confidence that every truth makes for true religion. Any theory of the origin and authorship and structure of the books which is not inconsistent with the substantial truthfulness of Scripture is lawful for us to hold, and may be examined without prejudice.

MODERN CRITICISM OF THE PENTATEUCH: OBJECTIONS TO IT.

BY PROFESSOR MATTHEW LEITCH, D.D., PRESBYTERIAN COLLEGE, BELFAST, IRELAND.

I. THE first objection we make to the theory of this school of criticism is founded on the impossibility of making with any certainty such an analysis of the Pentateuch as these theories require.

To divide a book into two or three parts and assign each to a separate author, judging solely by internal evidence, might in certain circumstances be possible, but it is very difficult. It requires the exercise of nice literary taste and trained powers of discrimination, and a long familiar acquaintance with various works of the authors thus judged. Shakespeare in some of his plays has worked up the writings of older dramatists, and it is very difficult to decide what is Shakespeare's own and what is taken from others. No one is able to do it with any certainty unless he has some external evidence to guide him. And no one would attempt it, judging merely by style and phraseology if he has only brief scraps and extracts of the writing used. He must have long and varied passages if he is to judge by style at all.

Yet here are critics who can judge of the style and phraseology of a single verse, or half verse, and assign it with confidence to an author of whom they know little or nothing. They can tell not only what parts of lost documents were adopted by the compiler, but what were passed over; and not only what these lost fragments contained, but what they omitted. They can split up a small book like the

Pentateuch into fragments, and assign them to above a dozen otherwise unknown authors. Wellhausen actually divides the Hexateuch (the first six books of the Bible) among twenty-two different authors and redactors, and Kuenen, among at least eighteen! It is not without reason that the critic adds to his authors till he reaches the incredible number of twenty-two or eighteen. It would be far more suitable to have only four or five. But he is obliged by the necessities of his theory to add on Elohist to Elohist and redactor to redactor. A passage, for instance, which by his usual criteria is assigned to the Elohist, is found to have imbedded in it the name Jehovah, and so he is obliged to bring in a Jehovist redactor for the word or the clause that contains it. Again, a passage which has the criteria of one redactor is suddenly found to have a word or clause that he has shown elsewhere cannot have been used by him, and so he has to bring in a second or third redactor. And so by the very necessities of his theory the critic is obliged, however much he dislikes it, to multiply his documents and editors. It will not, therefore, do for a student of the Bible to say, as most of our British adopters of these theories say, "I will accept Wellhausen's four or five authors, but not his twenty-two." You are obliged for the same reasons for which you accept his five to accept his twenty-two. He himself, who understands best what his own theory demands, sees that, carrying out the principles that are essential to his theory and judging by the criteria which have guided him all through his work, he is obliged to add document to document and redactor to redactor. The criteria which gave you five different authors must not be ungratefully cast away, when by continuing to use them with the same intelligence and honesty you will get twenty-two. You have no right to repudiate the fundamental principles of your theory only when they lead you into absurdities. And surely, gentlemen, there is absurdity enough to damn any theory in the supposition that a book like the Pentateuch, which has vindicated its literary unity and powerful individuality by winning its way through charm of style and matter to the hearts of young and old throughout a hundred generations, is the result of the artificial combination of heterogeneous documents from different centuries patched together by half a dozen unknown compilers! We can believe in miracles, but not in absurdities like this.

But lest I might be supposed to be exaggerating the pretensions of critics in making their analysis of the Pentateuch, let me give you some specimens of the results of their labors. Take any chapter, almost at random, say the account of the plague of turning the waters of the Nile into blood (Exodus, chap. vii., from verse 17 to the end). According to Wellhausen's analysis of this passage, verse 17a (first part) is by the Jehovist (J), 17b (second part) by the Elohist (E), 18 is by J, 19 and 20a are by the priestly narrator, verse 20b and 21a and b (first and second clauses) are by E, 21c and 22 and 23 are by the priestly narrator, 24 by E, and 25 by J.

Take again the 7th chapter of Genesis, according to still more recent German critics (Kautsch and Socin, 1888). The first eight verses are chiefly by the second Jehovist J2, ver. 9, "They went in two and two (2d Jehovist, J2), the male and the female (Redactor R), to Noah into the ark, as (J2) Elohim (R) had commanded Noah" (J2), ver. 10 (J2), ver. 11 (P), ver. 12 (J2), ver. 13 to 16a (P), ver. 16b, "And Jehovah shut him in" (J2), ver. 17, "And the flood was (P) forty days (R) upon the earth" (P), "And the waters increased and bare up the ark" (J2). And so on and so on. It is impossible to read such stuff without a feeling of amazement, or perhaps amusement, at the pretensions to infallibility which such an analysis involves on the part of those Germans who work at it, not unmingled with some feeling of contempt for our obsequious British critics who with open mouths take it all in, and swallow it down as the sure results of scientific criticism, reached by a succession of "acute Continental critics."

The allegation that it is a proof of the correctness of this analysis that the critics, while differing in some details, are agreed in the main lines of their divisions, should not have the slightest weight with us. They are agreed in the main results, because they are agreed in the presumptions with which they start. It does not require great learning and critical skill to assign a passage where the name of God is Jehovah to the Jehovist, and where it is Elohim to the Elohist; and it is no marvel that the critics agree in such divisions. It is, however, to be noted that again and again they find that this criterion does not otherwise suit their theory, and they have to say that the word Jehovah or Elohim or the clause containing it has been inserted or changed by a redactor.

I think that I could give a few rules on which they act in such a way as to show how critics who argued in their theories should be also agreed in the main lines of their divisions.

Rule I.—Where Jehovah occurs, assign the passage to a Jehovist (No. 1 or 2), where Elohim, to an Elohist. If in any case the result is inconvenient to your theory, bring in a redactor who has inserted Jehovah or Elohim, as either suits you. There is also a convenient division called JE, an unresolvable combination of Jehovist and Elohist, to which you may assign either kind of passage, as suits your theory.

Rule II.—If there are two passages which describe the same events from different points of view, make them contradict each other and assign them to different authors. This contradiction can mostly be secured by straining the interpretation of either or both passages, but if not, a word or words may be omitted or added in the text.

Rule III.—If a passage contain a prophecy, assign it to a writer who lived after tthe event prophesied ; if a miracle, bring it down to a date so long after the event that no credibility can be attached to the narrative.

Rule IV.—If any laws, which by intrinsic evidence are proved to be ancient, are found in a code or narrative which your theory makes recent, you need not change your theory but say that some pre-existent usage has got incorporated in the late work. If you are always ready to adopt this device, you can defy chronology.

Rule V.—In general, everything favorable to your theory, accept and accentuate and exaggerate; everything adverse, suspect, ignore, readjust or reject.

If these rules are carefully observed, and the various passages ingeniously manipulated by any number of acute critics, I will guarantee that those who start with the same theory will agree in the main divisions of their analysis quite as closely as our Continental critics now do.

Nothing could be more manifest than that the theory is not based on the analysis, but the analysis is made to suit the theory.

The truth is, such an analysis as our critics propose of the Pentateuch is an impossibility. Moses may have used many documents, Elohistic if you like. But he has wrought them into an original work, and so woven them inextricably into its texture that they cannot now be separated. He may even have used contemporary scribes to write out narratives or laws that he has embodied in his work, just as Bezaleel used carpenters and goldsmiths in the construction of the tabernacle. But if so, all the material used, and all the workmanship done, have been combined by the force of one great creative mind inspired to do this work, so that every attempt to separate them is in vain, and the completed work has come down to us fused together by the genius and stamped with the authority of Moses, the man of God.

The time at my disposal will allow me to do little more than barely state the other objections to these theories.

II. The objection to them founded on what is called the Egypticity of the Pentateuch. Modern Egyptologists declare that the writer of the Pentateuch shows a minute and accurate knowledge of the history, politics, literature, religion, and social manners and customs of Egypt, which could not have been possessed by anyone who was not a resident in the country and learned in the wisdom of Egypt. And the Egypt which is so accurately delineated is not the Egypt of the time of the exile or of the kings of Israel, but the Egypt of the date of Moses. If the Pentateuch was not written at this date, but written at the time of the exile by some priest or scribe of Israel, we must suppose that the writer devoted himself to the study of the history and archæology of Egypt of a thousand years before his day, and got up his work so accurately and projected himself so thoroughly into the spirit of the distant times in a foreign country, that when he came to write of them he moves among all the thousand details of ancient Egyptian life with easy and confident step, and never makes a stumble. If the writer has done this he must be a marvellous genius, such as has no equal in all the literature of the world. If more writers than one are supposed, the force of this objection is multiplied. I should like to know how the advocates of these theories get over this objection.

III. Another objection, somewhat similar to this, is founded on the accurate description of the topography of Egypt and the wilderness found in the Pentateuch. A writer in ancient times who had no personal knowledge of these countries would be sure to make wild mistakes if he touched on their topography. And yet recent researches in Egypt and scientific surveys of the countries through which the Israelites passed on their journey from Egypt to Canaan, prove that the author had an accurate and detailed knowledge of these countries such as could hardly have been possessed by one who had not both resided in Egypt and travelled long in the wilderness.

IV. A fourth objection may be drawn from literature. The monuments of Babylonia and Egypt show that literature flourished in these countries long before the time of Moses. It used to be an objection to the Mosaic authorship that writing was not known in the time of Moses. But now we know that not only was writing known and historical composition practised, but poetry and novel-writing were cultivated, and literature was reckoned one of the most honorable of professions centuries before the date of the Exodus. It is hardly possible that the nation of Israel, which was so intimately connected with both these countries, should have no literature during the most flourishing periods of its history, and that all those masterpieces of literature that have become the admiration and delight of the whole civilized world should have been produced at the period of Israel's national bondage and degradation, and of its spiritual degeneracy and decay.

V. A fifth objection may be made on the ground of history. The history of Israel as presented in the only monuments and records of it which we possess, demands some basis to rest upon, such as is afforded by Moses and the Pentateuch. Take away these, and the whole history of the nation, with its laws and institutions and traditions clinging to it, are left hanging in the air.

Again, history tells that the Samaritans accepted the Pentateuch as loyally as the Jews. It must, therefore, have been established as a sacred and authoritative book in Israel long before the Samaritan schism. Yet these theories suppose that it was completed either after the date of the Samaritan schism or only a short time before it.

VI. A sixth objection is founded on language. It has been very recently argued with great ability and learning by one of the most brilliant Semitic scholars of this age, Professor Margoliouth, of Oxford, from a study of the original language of the book of Ecclesiasticus, that the original language of this book of the Apocrypha, written about 200 B.C., which was then "the classical language of Jerusalem, and the medium for prayer and philosophical and religious instruction and speculation" is so different from that of the books of the Old Testament "in its philosophical and religious terms, in its logical phrases and legal expressions, in its idioms and particles as well as in its grammar and structure, that between the language of Ecclesiasticus and that of the books of the Old Testament there must lie centuries. Nay, there must lie, in most cases, the deep waters of the captivity, the grave of the Old Hebrew and the Old Israel, and the womb of the New Hebrew and the New Israel."

If this position is ultimately maintained, and its defender seems to have been able hitherto to maintain it against the vigorous attacks of Cheyne, Driver, Neubauer, and Noldeke, it not only demolishes the theory of the exilic origin of the Pentateuch, but we shall hear no more of a Babylonian Isaiah, or Maccabean Psalms, or a second century Daniel.

VII. But to many minds the most formidable objections to these theories are drawn from religion and morality.

If Deuteronomy was composed in the time of Josiah to help him in his conflict with idolatry and his reformation of religion, then its imposition on the people as the law given by God to Moses and spoken by him to Israel when entering the promised land, was no mere literary fiction, but a political manœuvre, which can be justified by no righteous code of morality.

Similarly, if the priesthood in the time of the exile promulgated laws and invented untruthful narratives attributing these laws to Moses and to God for the purpose of securing prestige for their order and divine sanction for their ceremonies, then such a transaction was in the highest degree immoral.

Besides, if the history narrated in the Pentateuch has not substantial truthfulness, if its writers have not genuine veracity, then no euphemism of "idealization" will convince Christian men that it can be inspired of God. The conscience of Christendom refuses to attribute the inspiration of God to history that has not truth, and writers that have not veracity. Men who hold that a book is inspired of God, and yet historically untrue, cannot long maintain that position.

VIII. The objection founded on religion is that this theory makes it very difficult to believe in the divinity or perfect humanity of Jesus Christ, and thus it saps the foundation of the Christian faith.

It is not a mere question of the *kenosis* theory, though that is important nor is it a question of the limitation of our Lord's knowledge in matters of criticism to that of the time and circumstances in which He lived. The theory involves the ignorance and error of Jesus in that special sphere of religious truth in which we must trust Him if we trust Him at all.

If Jesus bases religious teaching on facts recorded in the Pentateuch, which turn out to be no facts at all, if He claims acceptance for Himself on the ground that Moses wrote of Him and it is proved that Moses never wrote at all, and if He everywhere treats these books of Moses with the reverence and submission due to the words of His Father, and teaches their supreme authority in morals and religion, and even regards them as the source and basis of His own religious teaching, and if these books are shown by this theory to be largely the words of some unknown and unauthorized priest of the exile, who wrote narratives that were historically untrue and falsely attributed his work to

Moses—then I do not see how we could trust Jesus to be the revealer of the Father and the witness to the Truth which we know He is.

I am not here to judge other men who in their life take Jesus as their Divine Saviour, and in their creed accept "the Holy Scripture as the Word of God written," and yet teach that Jesus was in ignorance and error on this essentially religious question, and that the Scripture is not historically truthful, but consists largely of narratives of events that never happened, and contains descriptions of institutions (such as the tabernacle and its utensils and its sacrifices) which never existed. These men do not see the inconsistency of their own position, and we are not judging them. But I think we have a right to demand from them that they declare in plain unambiguous language what their position is. They must not hide their belief in the historical untruthfulness of the Old Testament under vague and misleading terms, such as "idealization" and "systematization of history." They have no right under false colors to surreptitiously introduce their theories into the Church to get them accepted by the young and unwary. Let them call truth truth, and falsehood a lie, and then plain men will understand what is meant by the acceptance of these theories. If they are presented in their naked truth I have little doubt they will be ultimately rejected. For a while the spirit of the age and the temper of the times may lead to their adoption, but the fashion of the time is ever changing, while the Word of God abideth forever.

In conclusion I may say that any of these objections worked out in detail (as no doubt they will be by competent scholars) would be sufficient to overturn this theory of the Pentateuch. But the strength of the argument lies in the accumulated force of all the objections together. When this has been clearly exhibited and candidly weighed it will be seen that this theory, which is the fashion of the day, is as unscientific, as untrue to the facts of the Bible, the facts of history, and the facts of human nature as any of the hundred other theories now exploded and forgotten which originated in the ponderous learning, the ill-balanced judgment, and the aggressive infidelity of Continental scholars.

THE ORIGIN AND RELIGIOUS CONTENTS OF THE PSALTER.*

COLLATED BY REV. JAMES D. STEELE, B.D., LECTURER IN HEBREW, COLUMBIA COLLEGE, NEW YORK CITY.

DR. C. A. BRIGGS gives his verdict upon this book of Canon Cheyne in *The North American Review* for January as being the most important theological work of the year. "The author," he says, "is somewhat cramped by the form of the lecture, but he has managed by numerous notes and appendices to give the freshest, richest and most fruitful piece of criticism that has appeared for many a year; showing an amount of original research and a wealth of knowledge that can hardly be surpassed by any Biblical scholar now living." Hebrew scholars generally will doubtless concur in this verdict so far as respects the scholarship of the learned Oxford professor, but many will at once and with great propriety take issue with the conclusions at which the lecturer arrives. Time honored views will not readily be surrendered and humble and pious Christians will refuse to regard David's Psalm-book as being only the expression of the religious experience of Israel in the Persian, Greek, and Maccabean periods. Indeed, a careful reading of these Bampton lectures for 1889 but emphasizes more and more the truth that much of the higher criticism is mere guess work, is based on insufficient premises, and owes its surroundings largely to the imagination. Cautious students

---

* The Origin and Religious Contents of the Psalter in the Light of Old Testament Criticism and the History of Religions. Bampton Lectures for 1889. By T. K. Cheyne, D.D.

need not be very particular about affirming or denying its various positions so long as confirmation is lacking.

But now let us notice the results of the writer's patient and learned researches. These will surely be startling to many. He holds that the Psalter is "a monument of the best religious ideas of the great post Exile Jewish Church." He will not allow David the authorship of a single Psalm, nor does he believe that one was written before the Exile, unless it be Psalm xviii., and this, he rather unwillingly allows, may have been written about the time of Josiah. The evidence of II. Samuel xxii. to the authorship of Psalm xviii., which will be conclusive to most Bible students, according to Canon Cheyne, "only proves that the poem was conjecturally ascribed to the idealized David not long before the Exile." A few Psalms, about twenty-five in number, are assigned to the period of the Maccabees, Simon the Maccabee being understood to have edited the Books IV. and V. of the Psalter. The great majority of the Psalms were, however, according to the writer, written during the Persian period, especially its later portion. Canon Cheyne's view is that authors of the late Persian period "think themselves back into the soul of David"; if early phrases and forms of expression are used, he says that later writers "archaized," or that they employed "affectations of archaic roughness." The method adopted in these lectures leads to some strange results. Things truly are not what they seem. Psalms xlv. and lxxii. refer to Ptolemy Philadelphus! Even Psalm cxxxvii. cannot be allowed the place during or immediately after the Exile which its language seems to imply. Canon Cheyne says, "Let us group it with Psalms cxxxv. and cxxxvi. and place it in the time of Simon the Maccabee. It is in the fullest sense a 'dramatic lyric.' Just as the author of Psalm xviii. thinks himself into the soul of David, so a later temple-singer identifies himself by sympathy with his exiled predecessors in Babylon." Psalm cx. is described as Maccabean. "It sets before us Simon as a 'king of righteousness,' and as sitting at Jehovah's right hand on Mount Zion."

The pious Christian and Bible reader who refuses to allow the spirit of free criticism to make shipwreck of his faith will have little difficulty in deciding between the opinion of Christ and His Apostles as to the Davidic authorship of certain Psalms and that of Dr. Cheyne, notwithstanding his undoubted learning, for "great men are not always wise." Nor will lovers of the Psalms generally agree with the statement that the apologist of Christianity has nothing to lose, but everything to gain, if the Psalter, as a whole, can be shown to be of post-Exilic growth. Ptolemy Philadelphus in Psalm lxxii. is a poor substitute for Solomon as a type of the coming Messiah, and few will make Psalm cx. centre around Simon the Maccabee, an apocryphal character, in opposition to the plain teaching of our Divine Master.

Even on critical grounds, however, there are serious objections to the chronology of the Psalms adopted by the Bampton lecturer. Before passing to these, however, it may be remarked that the later lectures (VI.–VIII.) describe with some fulness the religious ideas of the Psalter, and trace out their development as the author conceives it to have taken place. He does not assert that those ideas, including "an intenser monotheism," a freer universalism, and a belief in immortality and resurrection to judgment, were borrowed from surrounding nations, but he does hold that the influence of those nations was needed to cause the germ of the truth latent in earlier Judaism to spring forth, so that, in his own words, "from Jeremiah onwards there has been a continuous development through the co-operation of some of the noblest non-Jewish races and the unerring guidance of the adorable Spirit of truth, in the direction which leads to Christ." The professor's theory is that the ideas of immortality and resurrection to judgment are native Hebrew ideas, which, however, owe their development and popularization to the fostering influence of Zoroastrianism, the religion of their over-lords and neighbors the Persians.

The real ground for assigning so late a date to the Psalter is not found in the use of certain names such as *Shaddai* and *El 'Elyon* for God, but the necessity comes from the consistent maintenance of the ideas of religious development in Israel, as held by Wellhausen and his school. If these views, which now, to some extent, rule the critical world, are taken as proved, then there is supplied the tacit premise which alone gives force to Canon Cheyne's otherwise arbitrary assumptions and unwarrantable conclusions. True, he does not in so many words assume, say, the post-Exilic date of the priestly code, but all his arguments concerning Davidic Psalms virtually rest upon the improbability that "the versatile condottiere, chieftain, and king" composed such spiritual songs as those attributed to him, and the much greater likelihood that the Moses, the Elijah, the David of whom we read in the Old Testament, are not historical figures, but idealizations of a later day. The real significance, therefore, of Canon Cheyne's position is in this volume thrown into the background. His reasoning is full of assumptions, esteemed, many of them, as matter of course by himself and those of his school, but strenuously repudiated by those who hold different views of revelation. These lectures may be considered as an answer to the question, How can the Psalter be harmonized with the prevailing critical view of Old Testament history?

And now, briefly, as to some objections which may be urged against Canon Cheyne's theory. Four criteria are laid down by him for determining Maccabean Psalms. They imply that there should be (1) some fairly distinct allusions to Maccabean circumstances; (2) a uniquely strong Church feeling; (3) an intensity of monotheistic faith; and (4) in the later Psalms "an ardor of gratitude for some unexampled stepping forth of the one Lord Jehovah into history." The first is a good test, but not easily applied, because the allusions in most cases are not distinct, but general, and very few indeed can be said to be decisive. The last criterion is equally faulty, for Jewish history contains more than one " stepping forth of Jehovah " on behalf of His people. The second we are not ready to admit, because Canon Cheyne's views on the collective " I " of the Psalms, though interesting, are by no means established ; and the third rests upon a basis of assumption concerning the history of the idea of God among the Jews, which requires, to say the least, careful examination before we can grant that the presence of "intense monotheism " marks a Psalm as Maccabean.

Throughout the books such external evidence as is forthcoming receives very slight attention. While external evidence may be scanty, the indirect importance of certain facts in the Septuagint version and some of the Apocryphal books is considerable. True, we do not know at what date the completed Psalter was translated into Greek, but if the Pentateuch of the LXX. dates from about 250 B.C., a Greek Psalter of some sort—for is it not a commonplace that "the Psalter contains the answer of the worshipping community to the demands made upon it in the law"?—could not long have been delayed. The ignorance displayed by the Greek translators of the meaning of so many of the titles to the Psalms, which are admittedly much older than the Maccabean period, seems to argue for a greater antiquity than Canon Cheyne allows. With regard to two Psalms in particular, the LXX. imperatively forbids the acceptance of his views. One of the least successful of Dr. Cheyne's chronologies is that of Psalms xlv. and lxxii. in the reign of Ptolemy Philadelphus, the former being a panegyric from the pen of a Jewish admirer (whose name is given) on the occasion of this prince's marriage with Arsinoe, the daughter of Lysimachus ! It is admitted that such poems could not have gained admission into the canonical Psalter till the history of their origin had been forgotten and they had acquired another and higher interpretation. But even if such an accident were possible at Jerusalem, it must surely have been impossible at Alexandria, the capital of the Ptolemies. This is altogether apart from the difficulties of interpretation, not to mention other difficulties which such an assignment involves.

Dr. Cheyne admits that there is no external evidence for the existence of Maccabean Psalms, but thinks there is great *a priori* probability that such were written. Is it wise and sound criticism to lay the foundation of an investigation of this kind in a mere hypothesis such as the following: "What more natural than that Simon should follow the example of David, his prototype, as described in Chronicles, and make fresh regulations for the liturgical services of the sanctuary?" Nothing is said of any reconstruction of temple psalmody in I. Maccabees, though there is a notice of the attention paid by Simon to the sanctuary and the vessels of the temple. Prof. Cheyne argues, "Is it likely that he beautified the exterior and took no thought for the greatest of the spiritual glories of the temple?" The argument from silence here may fairly be urged the other way. At all events, sober criticism should hardly pass by with a sneer (p. 458) the external evidence as to date supplied by the titles to the Psalms in the LXX. version, in order to clear the way, not for some testimony of cardinal importance, but for a guess that it is "natural" that something should take place of which we have no record or hint in history, and the probability of which has been questioned by nearly all critics, German and English, with two or three exceptions. Ewald, as is well known, held that no Maccabean Psalms are included in the canon, but Prof. Cheyne has left his former teacher far behind.

Decided objection must be taken to the extreme views

urged concerning pre-Exilic Psalms. To adopt the author's own method of reasoning. Is it "likely" that no such Psalms were composed, that David's fame as a Psalm-writer rests on no foundation? or if, as the Bampton lecturer appears to admit, David did write some Psalms, and many temple songs were written and sung before the Exile is it likely that all these were lost in the course of a few generations among a people well qualified and heartily disposed to preserve such sacred strains? The nationalistic interpretation of the Psalms, a theory on which much stress is laid in these lectures, assumes that the authors of the Hebrew Psalms, almost without exception, speak and write "not as individuals, but in the name of the Church nation. In the Psalmists, as such, the individual consciousness was all but lost in the corporate. They had their private joys and sorrows, but they did not make these the theme of song" (p. 265). The consistent application of this theory leads to the whole Psalter being relegated to post-Exilic times, when the "remnant" of the Hebrew nation had become the Jewish Church. The Church of pre-Exilic days, we are told again and again, was "too germinal" to appropriate the advanced religious ideas of this or that Psalm, and therefore the latter must be the post-Exilic. Surely it is far more probable that choice spirits of the days of the Monarchy may have seen visions of divine things to which the mass, even of the godly in Israel, were blind, just as the mountain-peaks catch the first rays of the rising sun, while the valleys below are still in darkness.

Throughout the book is characterized by conjectures and assumptions, and a bold and ingenious theorizing not justified at all by the arguments actually adduced. However, the work is marked, it is needless to say, by great learning; it contains abundant suggestion for the exegete, and must be full of stimulus to the earnest student of the Old Testament, whatever be his personal opinions.

THE BIBLICAL CRITICISM OF OUR DAY.

BY REV. PROF. GEORGE H. SCHODDE, PH.D., COLUMBUS, OHIO.

BIBLICAL criticism is no new science. From the days of the earliest literary opponents of Christianity in the first and second centuries down to our own times, the claims of Holy Writ to be the revelation of God, given by inspiration to man, have provoked investigation, although probably never before has the doctrine of the sacred Scriptures been the burning question within the circle of Christian scholarship, as this is the case at present and is becoming more and more to be the case with the steady progress of modern biblical research. This is not at all an accidental affair. The present status of Bible study is the natural result and outcome of causes which have been operative for years in the English-speaking theological world and for decades in Germany and elsewhere on the Continent. Our age is characterized by the special prominence it gives to the human side of the Scriptures, both in their origin, contents and history. Without necessarily in principle or degree depriving the divine factor in the Word of its full rights and powers, the conviction has compelled recognition also in conservative circles that the Scriptures, without being any the less divine, are also human, given to man through man; that both the process of religious development which forms the burden and substance of their contents, as well as the record of this process are in close touch and tone with human history and thought ; and that, as a consequence, the historic principle of interpretation, which aims to reproduce with the exactness of science the very thoughts and ideas originally put into their writings by the sacred scribes, as these thoughts and ideas appear when viewed in the light of the entire historical background and surroundings of the original composition, is the correct and only legitimate method and manner of scriptural exposition. In this way the literary, historical, archæological and allied problems in connection with the study of the Scriptures came to the front as they never did before. Scholars began to look upon the sacred books as a literature with a record and history of their own. This new departure in the principles and methods of biblical investigation, which, when correctly and carefully applied, would only be hailed as a valuable aid to the elucidation of the scriptural ideas in their whole length, breadth and depth, leads to the recognition of facts in connection with the several books of the Bible, notably as far as their literary history was concerned, which could not be made to harmonize with some current and traditional views as to how these books became to be such as they are. The discussion of such detail investigation as the Pentateucha question, the Deutero-Isaiah, the Synoptic problem, the Fourth Gospel riddle implied principles and standpoints which, of a necessity, lead to re-examination of the doctrine of the Scriptures, as such. The controversy on the extent of inspiration, on the absolute inerrancy of Scriptures in each and every particular is the natural result of the special investigations which have been going on for years and still are going on. Modern biblical criticism, both as to matter and manner, is neither a spasmodic nor an illogical phenomenon. It needed neither a prophet nor a prophet's son, but only an intelligent understanding of its currents and tendencies, to see that consistently its course and final shape could be none other than these are at present.

The legitimate existence of this science no genuine scholar nor true lover of God's Word will deny. If the Scriptures cannot stand the test of lawful investigation and legitimate criticism they do not deserve to be regarded as of divine origin and of authoritative character. The Scriptures themselves not only challenge, but require investigation of their merits. It would be deplorable if they could not bear this, and the Christian could give no why and wherefore for his confidence in them and their teachings. Accordingly, neither those who in days gone by have devoted acumen, art and learning to the problem of the origin and history and character of the biblical books, nor those who in the present times are pursuing the same tasks are for that reason to be regarded with the suspicion of being tainted with the leprosy of heterodoxy or rationalism. Such a policy is suicidal to Christian theology and a *testimonium paupertatis*, or confession of weakness, on the part of the Church that professes to base its all on the written Word; nor is the fact that criticism does not always end in a confirmation of the traditional views of the Church in reference to the authorship, date, purpose or teachings of a book in itself a cause for condemnation. It is a historical right of Christians and of Protestants to search all things, and to adhere to that which is good. This right no one exercised with more determination than did the Fathers of the Reformation. Their rejection of the Apocrypha in the Greek Canon of the Old Testament after their acceptance by the Church in general for nearly fifteen hundred years, was a masterstroke of biblical criticism, and that too of "Higher" Criticism. To investigate and study the Scriptures independently but reverently is the unalienable birthright of Protestantism. The fact that modern biblical criticism has produced not only gold and silver, but also hay and stubble, is no impeachment of its right to existence in the family of theological sciences. The abuse of it does not do away with its use ; and it requires but a superficial knowledge of the history of recent Bible criticism to see that its blessings have been many and manifold, far outweighing the incidental and accidental harms it may have done. Among the various special problems that are in the forefront of the biblical criticism of the day, the Pentateuchal undoubtedly takes the lead. To this rank it is entitled not only on account of the interest naturally centering in the discussions dealing with the oldest books in the Bible, but still more because of the new departures, and even radical changes in the current views, not only of the Pentateuch, but of the whole course of Old Testament history and religious development, made necessary by an acceptance of the critical views of the hour in reference to the Five Books of Moses. For the documentary theory which parcels out to various authors of different dates, either from Moses or from the early days of the Kings down to post-exilic period, the parts and portions that are claimed to enter into the present composition of the Pentateuch, is more than a chronological change in the date of the books. It signifies an entire reconstruction in the origin, character and history of Old Testament revelation, of the factors and forces and course of this development, and thus involves a more or less new conception of the Bible religion as such. The mere literary change involved in the theory, as also the theory in itself and divorced of the conclusions drawn from it, may be even improvements of the traditional views. It should never be forgotten that the documentary theory or analysis of the Pentateuch was not originally a device invented to break down traditional views, but was first put forth for the purpose of defending the Mosaic authorship. Astruc, the French Roman Catholic physician, who, in his Memoirs more than a century ago, proposed the dissection of the Pentateuch into a number of documents, added as a subtitle to his volume the words: "Of the documents which Moses seems to have used in the composition of the Pentateuch." Even when the Germans first took up and developed the idea, it was done in the interests of the old view. Notably was this the case with Eichhorn, who was the first among the Germans to utilize the idea. Only later, when a consistent and rigid application of the method seemed to necessitate a post-Mosaic period for at least certain portions of these books, did the current views obtain hold and ground among scholars. Astruc's position was perfectly i. telligible and natural. Even accepting that Moses did write the whole or the bulk of Five Books, it is almost absolutely necessary in the interests of the reliability of his writings that for those portions which antedate his age he must have had documents of various kinds from which he drew his information. No theory of inspiration is so mechanical that would assign to the Holy Spirit the function of giving Moses the historical data he employs in Genesis or early part of Exodus. That he doubtless learned in the ordinary way, and the use of documents and earlier writings is much more plausible and certainly much more confidence-inspiring than if he had drawn them entirely from the unwritten traditions of the people, even if the agency of the inspiring Spirit was directing his heart and mind against errors or faults.

No; the danger and harm of the Pentateuchal analysis does not lie in it as a merely literary problem. And, indeed, this is not the heart and soul of the problem at all; this is but the preliminary phase, the means to the end. This end is the reconstruction of Israel's religious development. A comparison of the actual commands and prohibitions of the Pentateuch, with the events of history in Israel, reveals the not at all surprising fact that the conduct of the people was never up to the ideals of their law book, and, in fact, was often a grave violation of this book. But to conclude from this the non-existence of this book, is an abuse of the *argumentum ex silentio* that cannot be justified. With the same right we could conclude, from this universal acceptance of the anti-scriptural doctrine of justification by works before the days of Luther and the Reformation, that the Bible, with its clear enunciation of the doctrine of grace and free pardon, did not exist in the Church; and from the existence and antagonism of the various denominations of Christianity, we could with an equal right conclude that the New Testament, the common authority of them all, contains no behest that Christians should be one.

Still less justifiable is the reconstruction of the Old Testament history based upon this literary reconstruction. The law is made the outcome and final development of Israel's religious development, not its fountain-head and source, and it, as a rule, brings with it a naturalizing and naturalistic conception of their entire religion and its history. Kuenen, one of the most radical and most honest of the new school, frankly states that he and his followers start out from the standpoint that the religion of Israel was one of the greatest of the world's religions, nothing less, but also nothing more. In other words, while the religion of Israel was developed to an extent unheard of among other nations, this superior development was nevertheless the natural outgrowth of the genius of the people, just as the superiority of the Greeks in philosophical thought and of the Romans in administration grew out of the natural talents and trends of these nations. The reduction to as small a limit as possible, or even the entire elimination of the special divine element in Israel's religion is tacitly or openly the accepted ideal of the more advanced school, although not at all shared by the many conservative scholars who cannot accept the Mosaic authorship of the Pentateuch, and are ready to adopt some new views on the Old Testament and its contents in general. In other words, to use the words of the late lamented Delitzsch, the idea of advanced criticism is to develop a "religion of the era of Darwin." The idea of development has certainly been one of the most potent factors and forces in the history of modern sciences; but when applied to the Old or to the New Testament in order to explain the religion there taught as to origin and character is to force these on the Procrustean bed of a preconceived idea of religious development in general, as these hypotheses are concocted by that Pandora box of mischief—the modern science of Comparative Religion—this is to all intent and purpose a most flagrant *petitio principii*, and anything but exact science. The arrogant claim that the advanced or radical biblical criticism of the day is " scientific " is entirely without ground or basis : on the contrary, in more than one particular, it grossly violates the cardinal principle of scientific research. For instance, to mention no other point, the literary canon that the Old Testament books or parts of books are the results of the development which their contents describe and in no way the sources and causes of such a development, is entirely a gratuitous assumption and admits of no plausible demonstration, being also a direct contradiction of what is observed in other literatures.

The principles, practices, methods and manners employed in the Pentateuchal discussion are typical and representative of those carried on in other lines also. The new school, with others, is ever ready to criticise and correct the theologians of other and earlier generations for permitting their systems to be developed under the spell of the philosophical schemes of a Kant or Hegel. The protagonists of the new school in our own day and date do not practise what they preach, and fundamentally to a greater or less extent are under the spell of naturalistic ideas and ideals. Without doubt or debate the discussions of the last years have contributed not a little toward the elucidation particularly of the origin, history and development of the biblical books and the biblical religion ; that, however, the last word has been spoken, or that the radical critics of the day shall speak that word in biblical science, no unprejudiced scholar will dream of asserting. When the final settlement comes, it is quite possible that some of the old views will not be able to hold their own; but fundamentally the truth will stand that the Scriptures are a Supernatural Revelation and the history of this Revelation. Naturalism, or a criticism based upon naturalistic ideas, will never be able satisfactorily to explain the phenomena of the Scriptures. This can be done only by faith in them as God's Word, but God's Word given throughout to man and given amid human surroundings.

THE UNITY OF THE SCRIPTURES.

BY REV. PROF. GEORGE H. SCHODDE, PH.D., CAPITAL UNIVERSITY, COLUMBUS, O.

THE writings composing the Sacred Scriptures of the Old and the New Testaments are more than a collection of the literary remains of a most interesting Oriental people. Differing from the religious literatures of other nations, which consist of works more or less accidentally preserved, whose value and worth and mission lie only in their individual character, the Hebrew and Christian Scriptures, because they are the official documents of the development of one grand religious scheme, are internally most intimately connected, and therefore constitute one body of writings. To recall to mind this feature of the unique character of the Scriptures is a timely task, and by no means a work of supererrogation. The general trend and tendency of the advanced Biblical criticism of the day is to minimize the distinctive individuality of the Bible and its contents, especially from their divine sides, to develop, as Delitzsch says, "a religion of the era of Darwin." The naturalizing ideals and methods are very pronounced and potent, and the views of scholars on the Scriptures, as a literature, have been seriously influenced by this factor. While the unique character of the biblical books, as also of the historical process which forms the burden of their contents, are not denied, but even made especially prominent, yet this uniqueness is regarded rather as the result of historical, social and national environments, and not of agencies other than those operative elsewhere also. Israel's religious development is, by common consent, regarded as having far surpassed that of any other people ; but this superiority is declared the result of a natural endowment in this direction, just as the Greeks were the leaders among the ancients in philosophical thought, and the Romans in legal and administrative. As a further result, then, the literatures of the Biblical religion is regarded as not, in origin and kind, essentially differing from that of other people. The idea that they constitute a canon, a collection of books in which each is one member of the whole, is dropped ; the inner unity of these writings is discarded.

Such views, however, come into serious conflict with the position of Christ, the Apostles, and the entire New Testament over against the Old. For the New Testament the Old, both as a literature and as the unfolding of great religious principles, is an organic whole, separate and distinct in kind and character from every other literary collection or historical process. The direct citations show that for the New Testament speakers and writers the Old Testament was practically one sacred book. Compare, *e. g.*, Luke xxiv. 44; Matt. xxii. 29; Acts xviii. 24; Romans i. 2; II. Tim. iii. 15; John xix. 36; II. Pet. i. 20, for representative and typical formulas of citations. Recent research has shown that the earlier theories concerning the adoption of an Old Testament canon in the Ezra-Nehemiah period, or by the great Synagogue, indeed requires modification, and that this canon formation in pre-Christian Judaism was a gradual process extending over decades, as did the similar process in regard to the New Testament in the early Church; yet it also appears, with equal certainty, that this process had reached a definite conclusion before the advent of Christ, and that the great Teacher fully approved of the result, as does the entire New Testament literature.

This is shown to be the case still more clearly by the internal connection between the two Testaments than by the quotations mentioned. The entire New Testament consciously and *ex professo* stands upon the basis of the Old, of which it is the continuation and completion. The words in Luke xxiv. 44 are fundamental on this point, and find but another expression in the dictum of St. Augustine: *In Veteri Testamento Novum latet, in Novo Vetus patet* (Quest. in Exod. lxxiii.) And when the new thus refers to the Old, it is solely and alone to the canonical writings of the latter, to the Palestinian collection of Hebrew sacred books. It is a singular and most significant fact that neither directly nor indirectly have any other writings of that day and generation exerted a material influence upon the contents of the New Testament. That a formal influence was exerted from this source is not only undeniable, but the discovery and appreciation of this factor has been one of the most valuable of new tools employed by modern interpretation. The forms and moulds of thought which the New Testament writers have employed are all in direct touch and tone with the intellectual, moral and religious world of their day. The writers and speakers of the New Testament addressed themselves first and foremost to the audiences of their own times. There can be no doubt that the current ideas of mediatorship between God and man influenced the form in which St. John clothes his grand revelation of the Word having become flesh. It is equally certain that the figures and pictures that crowded the popular apocalyptic literature of Israel did their work in shaping the panorama of the future of the Church in revelation ; as also that Paul's familiarity with the dialectic methods of the Rabbinical schools gave shape and form at least in a measure to the elucidation of his central thesis of Christian doctrine, the justification by faith alone. And yet there is not a single indication of a non-canonical book having been quoted or having in the substance of the New Testament books influenced the writers or the speakers. The appeal, direct and indirect, is always to the canonical books of the Old as the sole authority and source of knowledge. While the New Testament does not thetically pronounce this proposition it does so by implication in a most emphatic manner; and the exclusion of all other sources is more than an *argumentum ex silentio*. It is true that there are echoes from non-canonical sources in the New Testament: but that is practically all. This is the case with what seems a free citation from the Book of Enoch found in Jude xiv., as also the references in v. 9 of the same Epistle to a statement not indeed found in what is now left of the *Assumptio Mosis*, but according to Origen, *De Principiis* iii. 2, 1. was contained in that book. In Heb. xi. 35, sq., here is an echo of II. Macc. 6 f. The reference in Heb. xi. 37, and II. Tim. iii. 8, are more than doubtful; while several to Ecclesiasticus, *e.g.*, cf. James i. 19, with Eccles. v. 11, are clear. Other passages are sometimes quoted in this connection, such as Luke xi. 49; James v. 5, 6; John vii. 38; Matt. xxvii. 9; but all of these are of a very uncertain character. Data like these show in a rather remarkable manner that the New Testament literature, which by no means is hermetically sealed to other writings, as is seen from its use of Septuagint, its citations of Greek poets, its moving and living in the atmosphere of its age, in the establishment of its principles and doctrines, builds upon and appeals solely and alone to the canonical writings of the Old Testament, and to these alone, because they and they alone are the inspired Revelation of the God to man. For the New Testament the unity of the Old is a fixed and fundamental fact.

And this is in full agreement with the character of the biblical books. They are the record of a gradual unfolding of God's plans for the redemption of man, and, in fact, this is the golden chord that connects them all and makes them one. The sacred literature of no other people can lay claim to this unique feature. While it may be difficult at present to assign to each and every book its peculiar position and necessary rôle in the development, yet it must not be forgotton that some of the books are as yet imperfectly understood. Who can affirm that we have with a certainty the key to unlock the mysteries of Ecclesiastes or the Apocalypse of St. John? When these riddles are answered, then, too, we will doubtless better see and appreciate than now what links these somewhat enigmatical writings constitute in the chain of Scriptural literature. But this is known, that these books, as far as clearly understood, represent the different stages in one process, the development of principles from germ to full fruit. In this process these books, one and all, have some portion or part to record; and it would be difficult to show that even the smallest could be omitted without in one or the other material point injuring our understanding of the unfolding of God's kingdom on earth; and, on the other hand, there is no material stage in this process on which the canonical writings are silent Internally they constitute a oneness; their unity is undeniable.

Again, it must not be forgotten that even according to the readjustment and reconstruction hypotheses of the modern school, the fact of this unity as a unique character of Scripture stands. The modern views do indeed seriously modify the old, in fact, revolutionize them; yet the result is that these books, far from being merely individual writings without inner agreement or connection, are, on the contrary, when correctly or chronologically arranged, the expression and exponents of a religious process, and solely that. Comparative religious science can claim no phenomenon of this kind for any other nation. Even when under the scalpel of modern criticism, the truth that the Scriptures practically constitute one volume, consisting of parts mutually complementary and supplementary, remains.

DOES THE CHRISTIAN MINISTRY MEET THE EDUCATIONAL REQUIREMENTS OF THE AGE?

BY PRESIDENT E. BENJ. ANDREWS, D.D., LL.D., BROWN
UNIVERSITY, PROVIDENCE, R. I.

THE average education of ministers is probably better than that of lawyers, physicians or journalists. A larger proportion of ministers than of the others begin with liberal training, and ministers' occupation keeps them more familiar than the majority of other professional men with general and elevated thought. It is, in fact, one of the chief attractions of the ministry as a profession, that it summons, urges, almost forces its devotees to read noble and broadening books. The Bible is by itself at once a literature and a history. To study it thoroughly is to educate one's self in these branches as well as in a vast number besides. Other of the great practical callings may drill and discipline the mind: none of them can feed or enrich the mind as does faithful ministerial work. There is no other profession where you find so large an array of men well informed upon intellectual questions at large. Lawyers have more knowledge of a strictly practical kind; physicians more that is related to science; but neither class equals ministers in all-around, high mental equipment. Nor can any other set of men whatever vie with ministers as felicitous and effective public speakers.

For all this, one must admit that the educational outfit of the average minister is very inadequate to the demands of these times This is true not only of ministers as a class, but also of such as have enjoyed the advantages of college and seminary life. The fault lies partly in the men who study for the ministry, partly in the methods employed in educating them.

The ministry loses much intellectual power in that many able young men now take up law, medicine, or journalism who would enter the ministry but for the present prevalence of more or less reasonable doubts touching matters of faith. Every one conversant with students in college has known many who have been turned from the path by this consideration. Not always, to be sure, but often, if not usually, they are youths of special mark and promise. Determined to think freely and to act as they believe, they fear to begin the study of theology lest this, and the sacred work to which it naturally leads, shall require them, if they will succeed, to stifle certain convictions. They commonly magnify the danger, but the danger has not always been imaginary. It were fatal, of course, to fill our pulpits with convictionless men. Conservatism the most senseless and extreme is not now doing the Church more harm than the influence of a few callow preachers who regard no truth as settled, and seek each Sunday to edify the people of God with the doubts that their giddy brains have suggested during the week. Still, the quality of our ministry suffers from a too rigid exaction, at ordination, of assent to dogmas. An evangelical spirit and purpose should excuse much theological misconception, for, mark it well, the main aim of the Gospel is not correct doctrine but holy living.

Fortunately, no small number of excellent young men study for the ministry after all; but, owing in part to the matter which is taught them and in part to the methods whereby this is done, their education is far less valuable than it ought to be. Hardly one of our theological institutions is well endowed. The courses offered in them are few. Pupils are forced mostly to pursue the same lines of study, whether they prefer them or not. Certain parts of the theological curriculum, as Homiletics and the outlines of Dogmatics, are indeed needful for all students. These should be insisted on. But the theological curriculum would with the best results admit the elective principle far more broadly than has yet been anywhere done—more broadly than were proper in schools of law or of medicine. The ideally organized theological seminary would present, in each great branch, one very general course of instruction, and a large number of special courses. None of the special courses would be required, and only the indispensable ones among the general. Though immensely desirable, it is still not absolutely indispensable to success in the ministry that a candidate should be able to read Greek or Hebrew, or that he should have spent a solid year upon Systematic Divinity. Let some spend their time mainly in general Church history, others in the history of doctrine, others in Biblical history, others in Biblical introduction, and so on. Personal preference in study would thus be gratified, with the consequence that new zeal and a vastly larger fruitage of attainments would attend the pursuit of theology.

Such a reformation would offer to students who desired it—as the best would certainly do—time and place for a much more ample canvass than is at present possible of several disciplines now much neglected, which I conceive to be indescribably important in a minister's outfit. Logic is one of these. How few preachers, even when they do their best, work out a truly methodical sermon! How few habitually grasp the exact meaning of words! How few recognize with any clearness the difference between a valid inference and a fallacy! How few argue logically or fairly, or appreciate the multitudinous and subtle sources of mental error! Every thoughtful church-goer knows that sermons very often fail of effect solely because the matter in them is not properly marshalled. Sometimes intrinsically heterogeneous materials are piled together, each piece proper and rich enough in itself, but powerless in such an *ensemble*. More often what is offered is susceptible of unitary treatment, but the artist has placed cart before horse. I once listened to a sermon which might have been a thunderbolt had the preacher done a little work of definition at the outset. As it was, his thought went "flying all abroad," since no hearer could possibly divine what any of his main conceptions meant. Unity may be present but no progress mark the thought—another grievous fault. Many sermons are very interesting on other accounts, though extremely illogical. Let no preacher whose work is of this character flatter himself that the study of method in speech is of no account for him. By it he might double or treble the effect of his utterances.

A worse defect—leaving, now, the form of thought and coming to its matter—lies in the fact that even our ablest ministers have so little knowledge of Practical Ethics. Every reflecting man must feel how painful society at present needs ethical instruction. Much of the conduct which shocks us in our fellow-men is due to nothing else but ignorance of what is right. Many people are keenly aware of their lack in this regard, and would rejoice to be enlightened. Whence is the light to come unless from our religious teachers? The Church is the only institution recognized as charged with the important duty of training human beings in morals, and ministers are its spokesmen. So far as the writer is aware, schools for ministerial education in America, one or two alone excepted, have no appliances worthy the name for teaching concrete ethics. Students are at best put off with a few more or less edifying lessons upon the family, society, the state, and the more obvious duties arising from these. If any of the difficult moral problems of modern society are broached, none of them are fathomed. Marriage and Divorce, for instance, Prison Legislation,

Copyright and Bankrupt Laws, Hours of Labor for Women and Children, Socialism and Communism, the Land Question, Taxation, Honest Money, Stock Gambling, Strikes, the Care of the Poor, the Aged and the Insane, Monoply, Our Indian Policy—these and many more are essentially ethical problems, of pressing and vital importance ; but scarcely a school of sacred learning deems them worthy of more than the most superficial treatment at its hands. No doubt many of these subjects are too delicate to be formally handled from the pulpit, yet who will deny that ministers should know about them? Clergymen are incessantly consulted in a private way respecting such matters, and this would occur far oftener if people found it of avail. The mere opinion of an intelligent and honest man upon any important topic carries great weight, and will become known throughout his community whether publicly proclaimed or not. At present, alas, ministers too often have no opinions touching most questions of this sort, and the few who espouse one side or the other of any of them commonly do it with so little information as neither to carry conviction nor to win respect. These problems are deep and intricate. They need long, careful and unprejudiced exposition. The preacher who enters upon his work without training in them can hardly expect to master the ground by subsequent effort. The study ought to be carried on under competent teachers defore ordination.

Adequate ethical instruction for intending clergymen would also include a course in casuistry, covering those numerous difficult cases of conscience which arise in ordinary conduct. Many of these might be treated directly in sermons, giving offence to none, light and relief to many. What pastor has not found good people distressed over queries like the following : Whether a Christian has a right to be rich ; whether the spirit of Christ fully possessing one would not lead him to share his all with the first beggar he met ; whether intentional deception is in any case justifiable; whether a debtor whom bankrupt law has absolved from payment ought still to pay if ever able; whether it is right to take an oath, and many more.

Most Christians, like most other people, conceive wealth, whether in any one community or in the world, as a given, fixed sum, so that if one man gains, another must necessarily lose. It is, of course, entirely an error, yet I once heard this precise doctrine from a very able preacher in King's Chapel, Boston. It is, he said, the property only of immaterial goods to grow by use: in material wealth your gain means my loss, and *vice versa*.

How rarely preachers discriminate as they should between vice and virtue or between vice and vice. We are perhaps duly careful not to call evil good, but do we not continually denounce certain forms of good as evil? Things merely reprehensible are continually classed with those to which blackest guilt attaches, no distinction or gradation in evil quality being attempted. I have heard of a church which excluded a young lady from its membership for dancing, but retained in good standing a deacon who had been guilty of murder.

It is a complaint as just as it is common that ministers have so little of that education which comes from close and rough contact with men. They do not know enough of human nature. This is the more a pity from the fact that means of instruction in this kind are so ready to hand. Men are all about us: the poor, the rich, high and low, good and bad, believers and unbelievers, fortunate and unfortunate, optimists and pessimists. The great laboratory of an anthropology is open. Whosoever will, may enter and pursue the study according to the most approved demonstrative methods. Some culture in this way the minister may, to be sure, if he will, obtain after he has begun his life-work. But it is then much harder. He is now "the minister," and men will not behave normally before him. He sees for the most part only the good side of good people and the evil side of bad people. An earlier schooling in actual life would enable him to allow for these artificial appearances in both directions, so, giving to his preaching and to his entire influence a healthier tone.

Probably few preachers, when, in their sermons, they refer to the affairs of Wall Street, have any idea how their hearers who are familiar with that region inwardly smile. Many pastors of congregations not the wealthiest, habitually, next Sunday after returning from vacation, preach upon vacation experiences. I never hear such a sermon without pain having had occasion to be sure that they are always a source of pain to the large class of hearers who, alas! are forbidden to know from personal experience what a holiday or an outing means. Sermons of this order serve but to remind the poor how poor they are. This ministerial habit is an illustrative fact. My observation is to the effect that the proportion of clergymen who have much more than a theoretical sympathy with the very poor is small; fewer still have the slighest notion of the peculiar trials which beset the rich, but this imperfection is from the nature.of the case more excusable.

Longer tuition in the school of real life would enable ministers to sympathize, as too many of them do not now, with the terrible moral struggles and questioning which are peculiar to this age. We need to know what our parishoners are thinking about, what it is that tries them, what phases of their life are most fruitful of temptation, and, looking out over society at large, precisely where given evils have their root. The common diagnosis of intemperance, for instance, is extremely shallow. Men drink, it is said, because of a liquor habit. Yes; but whence this habit? The habit itself is an effect and not a cause only. The ultimate causes of intemperance need to be investigated. They are mainly two, unbelief and poverty. To a good extent the unbelief may be further traced to the poverty, and this to vicious social and economic arrangements.

Who can doubt that a deeper grasp by our ministers upon these great affairs of humanity's actual life would give added power to their preaching? People are wont, if religious teachers are obviously in error or ill advised rgarding important secular matters, to infer their exceeding fallibility in relation to those of a spiritual nature. We cannot prevent this. But most of the social interests so much discussed nowadays are not wholly or mainly secular. They have their moral and religious aspects, which in many of them are very pronounced. So long as the clergy ignore these mighty interests, dawdle with them, treat them as having no relation to the Church's mission and duty, as topics to be studied by eccentric, leisurely, or worldly-minded clergymen alone, so long shall we wait in vain to see the effect of preaching what it once was, what it ought to be to-day.

OPPORTUNITIES AND OBLIGATIONS OF COLLEGE EDUCATION.*

By Professor George P. Fisher, D.D., LL.D., Yale College, Conn.

"I HAVE to confess that, when I accepted the invitation to be here to night, my idea of the purpose of the meeting was somewhat vague. But one thing was clear; that the meeting was to be composed of college men, graduates and undergraduates. I judged, therefore, that a few words bearing on college education, and the opportunities and obligations resulting from it, would not be out of place. The course of study in our colleges has been a good deal modified during the last twenty or thirty years. The increased importance of the modern languages, and of the literatures that belong to them, and, still more, perhaps, the astonishing growth of the natural and physical sciences, have obliged the colleges to make room for other branches, which were loudly knocking at the door and demanding admission.

"One result of the diversifying of study has been the introduction of elective courses. The bill of fare had become too long for the time at the student's command, and for the digestion of any single individual. But the general aims of a college education are not essentially altered There is still the same end in view—the development and culture of the mental powers. For the college aims, or ought to aim, at something more than the equipment of specialists. Behind the specialist there must be the man,

* Delivered to college alumni, Brooklyn, December 29th, 1891. Published by request, from copy furnished by the author.

who has been taught to look out in more than one direction ; with powers and tastes, if I may so say, of a catholic variety and range. No doubt, discipline is a prime object to be kept in view ; and discipline, if compared with the amassing of knowledge, is the more important of the two. But then the term ' discipline' must be interpreted in a broad way. Cardinal Newman said that the aim of education is accuracy.

"He is educated who has learned to distinguish between things that differ, and to see things just as they really are. There is a great deal of truth, and yet only a part of the truth, in this proposition. Here is, indeed, a criterion, serving to divide men by a clearly defined line into two classes. But the ideal of college training is more comprehensive. There is a realm of beauty, as well as of truth. The imagination and sentiments have their rights. Without enlarging on this point—for which there is not the time— there is one thing at least that college ought to do for a man ; one good thing that he ought to gain. The college should awaken within him the intellectual life. It should unseal his vision, enabling him to discern 'the things of the spirit,' and to find delight in them. The student's turn may be for science, in the strict sense of the term. But he must rejoice in the perception of scientific truths for its own sake, as well as for its utility.

"When the old philosopher was asked, ' What is the use of philosophy ?' he answered, ' It is too good to be useful'; by which he meant that it is an end in itself, and not merely a means to something else. But how is the man of science enriched by an added appreciation of the treasures of literature and art ! The intellectual life, defined in any proper way, is a priceless possession. How does the student bless the teacher, or the book, that first opened his eyes, first touched the hidden spring within him, first refreshed his spirit with glimpses of a world not before seen !

" How shall the intellectual life, enkindled in college, be

kept up afterwards, in the busy occupations that follow graduation? This is one problem. Only one or two hints towards the solution of it can be given. One obvious answer is by reading, by communion with the authors best fitted to minister to the life within.

"Here we have to meet the difficulty arising from the want of time. Practical pursuits in this age and in this land are engrossing. It is a help to remember that it is not necessary to read many writers, however desirable it might be if one had the leisure for it. In fact, nowadays it is necessary to sift the literature of the day, to search for the grains of wheat in the heaps of chaff. For in this department there is an immense over-production. Look for a moment at the periodical literature of the time, the daily, semi-weekly, weekly, monthly, yearly journals. What a vast extent of space has to be covered by writing of some sort; the space being measured out for the types beforehand, and the contracts all made to fill it. The blocks of blank paper which have to be thus covered daily would make a pile as broad and as high as the largest pyramid that looks down on the Nile. There is much good writing in the current periodical literature. One who would be in contact with his time cannot neglect it. But a busy man, who is concerned in the way I have indicated for 'the things of the spirit,' must be sparing of his time. Suppose him to give his leisure hours to a few authors. Let him select six—we will say, Homer, Sophocles, Plato, Virgil, Dante, Shakespeare. Let him read these authors themselves, and not the thousand and one books written about them. It might almost be said of the works of any one of these master-spirits, that a thorough, thoughtful study of him is itself a liberal education. And if one chooses to follow out the suggestions, historical and literary, which the perusal of these authors brings before one, inviting and extensive fields of investigation and reading, fields of indefinite extent, yet capable of being gradually traversed, are opened. Besides reading, for the nourishment of the intellectual life, the society of kindred spirits is needful. The stimulus flowing from the interchange of ideas, from the play of sympathy, is very helpful. Some minds need, in their intellectual progress, the aid of the social element more than others. But there are comparatively few who can very well spare it.

"And now, in connection with the social intercourse which one needs for his own intellectual advantage, we may connect the duty which every educated man should perform, of being, in a sense, a missionary of culture. In this time of material prosperity, when material enjoyments are so eagerly sought for and prized, it surely behooves men who have received a college training, to do all that they can, in combination as well as separately, to lift up society to a higher level, to hold up worthy ideas, to inspire the community with a becoming regard for the supreme value of 'the things of the spirit.'

"Societies which have for their end the diffusion of culture, by bringing together educated men, and by placing them in contact with aspiring youth who lack the advantages of a college training, are deserving of honor and support. May the association within whose walls we meet to night, with other good work, do its part in the discharge of this noble and beneficent duty!

"I will take leave to add that the intellectual life, and the influence emanating from it, should be leavened with the spirit of religion. The religion of the men of the class whom I have in mind should be thoughtful. It should have its root in intelligent convictions. One should be able to give a reason for the faith that is in him. It should be, also, virile. I should include in it a sound, robust morality, with a healthy abhorrence of all forms of so-called piety that lack this quality. And it should be practical, no 'cloistered virtue,' but going forth to do good—to help the needy, and to infuse new strength and hope into those who have fallen in the race."

BROTHERHOOD IN HIGHEST SERVICE.*

BY PRESIDENT MERRILL E. GATES, LL.D., AMHERST COLLEGE, MASS.

IN our general harmony of purpose, each institution is asked to sound here its own distinctive key-note in the higher education. I may speak freely of the ideals of Amherst, for they were formed and were known the world over before I came into those close relations with the college which give me the right to speak for Amherst. We seek to train clear, strong thinkers ; to make manly men; to send into social and political life men who will *make* their environment more nearly what it should be,—not men who seek the most agreeable or profitable environment, or yield to and are moulded by the environment in which they may find themselves.

To this end, Amherst believes in thorough and severe scholarship, sound morality, and a living, manly Christianity. This training, reinforced by the systematic development of each man's physical powers, we believe sends out into the world each year a powerful body of young alumni, who, accustomed to something of self-government, and students of our political institutions and our social needs, prove themselves staunch patriots and useful Christian citizens.

At this centre of American life, if we name Henry Ward Beecher and Roswell P. Hitchcock and Charles H. Parkhurst and Richard Salter Storrs, we feel that Amherst has spoken to you in the lives of her sons. If the goodly colony of Amherst men who teach at Columbia College may declare

* Address delivered to college alumni at Brooklyn, Dec. 29th, 1891. Published by request, from copy furnished by the author.

to you something of Amherst's ideals in higher education, and if the treasurer and the superintendent of that noble educational work, the Pratt Institute, may interpret to you certain Amherst ideals of practical philanthropy held and practised by our younger men, we will refrain from mentioning many other honored sons of Amherst whom we might well name.

But we recognize with deep joy, on an occasion like this, the fact that the aims and ideals which are precious to us and in these great twin cities, our metropolis, find wide expression in the lives of a host of men trained at our sister colleges.

The uplifting thought in my heart, as I face this assemblage, is, "How superbly strong for enlightened leadership and ennobling service of their age and their native land, is such a body of the alumni of our American colleges!" By the logic of events we are called to be leaders in the great work of diffusing ideas among our fellow-men—in bringing life, social, industrial and political, into harmony with the best ideas.

For this work your college training has especially fitted you. There is a sense in which all men are "self-made" men. No man is fully made a man, be he college-bred or not, unless he makes himself! He must be king of his own activity; ruling with imperial will, in the light of conscience! But whatever may be the strength or the virtues of the man who is commonly called "self-made"—of the man who forms his character outside the schools—it holds as the pre-eminent characteristic of college-bred men, that they have learned to deal with ideas as well as with facts. While business-life and active professional duties make of college-bred men the most intensely practical citizens—men who can "bring things to pass"—yet the man with a college diploma, if he has fairly earned it, is all his life long a citizen of the Republic of Ideas. He is open to reason,

He knows the power of thought. He has seen that "ideas after all rule the world."

It was this openness to ideas which marks the educated man, that led Aristotle to say, "He who has received an education differs from him who has not, as the living does from the dead." If thought is *the life of the soul*, the habit of answering quickly to ideas is the mark of the man who is truly alive. It is because we know that *some* theory is essential to all practice, and that the practical man is a "bungler" in life unless he has a true theory—it is for this reason that we do not fear the name of theorists. The theorist is by etymology the one who *sees* what he is attempting to do. The word means a *seer* of verities. He who despises all theories, merely argues for the awkward and foolish process known as "going it blind." The true theorist, the true man of ideas, takes all the facts into account in framing his theory, and has a clear aim in view in choosing the means to carry out his theory, to embody his ideas.

To fit for such work in life, the college course sought ought to call forth in us all the mental energy at our command. It sought to make our thinking clear, accurate, intense, and to make the love of truth our strongest motive. In so far as this has been done, we are "men of light and leading," among our fellow-men.

Each man of you, in the community in which he lives, we trust, is such a man "whose part is taken—who does not wait for society in anything," but acts fearlessly on his own convictions. How greatly the world needs such men! They are needed to break the foolish bonds of unworthy custom, to keep society above the level of the unthinking who dread a new idea, to whom a new idea is a positive pain simply *because they never had it before*—a terror to be fled from, if it comes at them as if it meant to influence their daily living; or, if they cannot escape its grasp, then an enemy to be closed with and if possible throttled, that all things may be as they were before.

This is the type of man of whom Crabbe writes:

> "His habits are his only test of truth:
> It must be right, I've done it since my youth."

So many men shrink from any and every act that would show intelligent self-direction and individuality! So intensely do most men fear to break over customs, however foolish and hurtful!

For the love of humanity, we are to be fellow-workers with all good men everywhere in diffusing the light of the truth and intelligence. Many who see the truth will not obey it. But if they do not see it certainly they cannot obey it! And "Of all plagues, ignorance is the most pernicious." Wherever your work, then, and as long as you live, as college bred men you are bound to be dispellers of ignorance, bearers of light and help to men.

To do this we must live strong lives ourselves.

It is not because scholars *have ideas*, that self-styled "practical men" now and then venture to sneer at scholars as "visionaries." It is because scholars do not *live by these ideas!* We must hold to ideas and enforce them in our own living if we would win respect both for the truth and for ourselves!

The world looks to us to *live by* those ideas which are *the life of the soul!*

Let us live up to the level of our own best thinking, in our social and political relations as well as in our private life. Since our conviction is clear that there is no reason why public office should be regarded as "the spoils" of a successful campaign, let us *stand* for civil-service reform. Let us speak out clearly on all occasions, in favor of clean, honest administrations of city and state government, and against jobbery and trickery of all kinds in elections and in administration. Let us not allow our standard of morality to become lower in political affairs than in business affairs. Since we know well that buying a vote is a sin and a disgrace, a wrong to the manhood of both buyer and seller, and the gravest danger that threatens our free government, let us *speak out* against it, whoever does it! Whatever the social position, the wealth or the influence of the man who is guilty of buying votes or attempting to gerrymander a district, whether he belongs to your party or not, let him know, and let the community know, that you hold him criminally guilty! The quiet toleration of what we know to be immoral will undermine our own principles and relax our own moral tone.

Let our ends be fair and just, and the means by which we seek to attain them honorable.

" Him, only him, the shield of Jove defends,
Whose means are fair and spotless as his ends."

That we may live fully and strongly in all our nature, physical, intellectual and moral, and so living may give new life and fresh impulse to all with whom we come in contact— this is our wish and hope for the college-bred men of America.

To do this we must be leaders and masters of men in the highest and best sense. We must lead by first climbing the hard places ourselves that we may help others up. We must do more work and better work than other men. We must study more assiduously to be useful, for all men who succeed in life are life-long students of that in which they succeed! We must put into our life more of self-sacrifice; for it is only by serving others that we can truly be leaders. Our highest wish is that each man of us may attain to what Ruskin has well called "the one pure kingship, that which consists in a stronger moral state and a truer thoughtful state than that of others, enabling you therefore to guide them and to raise them toward a better life."

How can we attain to this state, and by noble service keep ourselves "true kings of men"?

Be helpful! Communicate ideas! Give out moral energy! Let the light we have *shine!* We do not *lose* moral or intellectual power by giving an impulse to our neighbor. Here is the difference between mechanical forces, and intellectual, moral, social forces. If you give your neighbor a "cut off" with half the electric current that lights your house or runs your factory, your own house must go half-lighted, your own factory can do but half its work. But when you give him your best thought and your heartiest, friendliest sympathy, there is more light, more warmth, more power for you both. By giving, *you gain.* Your own thought becomes clearer. Your own conviction is more intense. Your own power of right feeling and right willing is strengthened. By such unselfish efforts for others we keep the horizon broader and the heart fresher.

To do such service we shall need a steady fire of love in the heart. To overcome inertia in ourselves and in others, not to be overawed and silenced by the numbers of the dull, the timid and the vicious who oppose all changes for the better; to make our way up steep grades of moral progress; to *draw our load* steadily, every day, and with our own burdens to bear also the burdens of others less strong than we—this calls for an impelling power constantly renewed and unfailing.

The early invented locomotives all failed of practical usefulness, because they could not generate a sufficient power of steam. Then came the Stephensons, and by their invention of the steam blast took the very breath of heaven into league with the fires within the engine. The steam that did the first few pounds of work was used to make a vacuum by which the pure air of heaven was hungrily sucked in, to feed the fires and make more heat. Thus was given to the world the secret of the power of all our modern locomotives.

In this feeding of the fires within by the very winds of heaven, the great possibilities of our modern civilizing force stood revealed.

To enable us to do the heavy, up-grade work of helpers of the weak and ignorant, to uplift society and raise our fellow-men to higher planes of thought and action, we shall need to have a breath from Heaven itself feed the fires of love and life in our hearts.

"'Tis life whereof our nerves are scant,
More life and fuller, that we want."

Such life and power as we need in our life-work comes only from God, who feeds our souls with thoughts of Himself, with His Truth, which is Life.

We believe, then, that there is an especial fitness in our meeting a body of college alumni, in the Hall of the Young Men's Christian Association. As men come to understand the solidarity of interest that binds the entire race, everywhere, the world round, there goes up a yearning cry for that true brotherhood among men which is possible only as men understand the Fatherhood of God. And if college-men are to undertake, with deeper earnestness each year, the duties and responsibilities that belong to " men of light and leading," dispellers of gloom, how can they more hopefully and happily do this than by putting themselves under the leadership of Him whom we know as the Eternal God, Giver of Light and Wisdom, and whose glorious, inspiring power for service the Greeks dimly discerned when they spoke of their Sun-God, Apollo, as the radiant one, " Whose bright eye lends brightness and never yet saw a shadow "?

ESSENTIALS OF THE CURRICULUM.*

BY PRESIDENT B. P. RAYMOND, WESLEYAN UNIVERSITY, MIDDLETOWN, CONN.

WITH such a theme and in such a presence, one can but wish for the opportunities of a volume rather than that of fifteen minutes. We congratulate ourselves, however, on this advantage at least, we can address ourselves to the theme immediately. You need no introduction to the subject. Moreover, we can count on you to supply many missing logical links, which must be presupposed at the outset and implied in the development of the theme.

Like the navigator, the educator must have clearly determined the port whence he sails, and the harbor in which he proposes to furl sail and drop anchor. The educator starts from the cradle. His subject, be it observed, is an it, an it, sensitive to every ripple of sound, to every ray of light, to the gentlest touch of the breast upon which its head is pillowed; potentially responsive to every thought of the race, potentially accessible to motives that would blacken the fame of a Nero, accessible to the high ideals that would grace and crown an archangel. But an it.

The educator receives this helpless giant from the embrace of his mother's love, and by the wise use of educative agencies must transmute this impersonal subject into a man. Personality is the goal; personality, rich and regnant.

It is easy to determine thus the starting point and the

* Address delivered to College Alumni, at Brooklyn, December 29th, 1891. Published by request, from copy furnished by the author.

goal, easy to read up the pedagogical theories of the ages with their wealth of details, rich in suggestive errors and pitiful failures; but the question is still on our hands under new conditions, complex enough to confuse and perplex the wisest, and with possibilities that might well stir the soul of the most indifferent. It is the how and the why that put to the test all our theories. Upon questions of method, who dare dogmatize? Here the problems multiply. There ought to be a rationale of our curricula, and of our pedagogical appliances. Dr. Hermann Lotze affirms that there is only one complete personality, one being alone, who, conscious of all His resources, is perfectly self-directive in the use of all, and that is God. Be it so. The goal of our work is the completest personality possible for man.

Assuming that the cry from this cradle, a cry which voices a hunger for all the universe has to give, has been progressively met and that the subject is no longer in it, that the boy under favorable conditions has been prepared for college, how shall the years of college life carry forward this work to maturity?

How shall the college man be met and treated? I answer first of all, and emphatically, as a man; as a man who must think and act for himself. All growth is from instinct and impulse toward personality, and growing personality means the self-directed life in the light of reason. Hence, the college man should be met with the fewest authoritative restrictions possible, and with the most intense, intellectual, moral and religious inspirations possible.

The curriculum has its rationale.

We do not need to argue the study of mathematics. They have held their place for more than 2,000 years.

And shall we study languages? Most assuredly. And unless the boy starts too late, both ancient and modern. The latter will hold its place because we live in an age intensely practical and in a country intensely utilitarian.

This has grown out of our circumstances. We are still pioneers, and the pioneer, with his axe, is driven by exigencies which demand that every blow shall count for something that can be transmuted immediately into service. But if that were all, it is very questionable whether the translation is not cheaper far than to translate. But that is not all. To master a language is to acquire a new sense. The sense of hearing gives the melody and harmony of the world's voices, and makes accessible its oratorios; the sense of sight brings the rapt vision of morning and evening's glow, the radiant bush of autumn which burns and is not consumed, and the revelations of art, heroic as the tramp of armies, or sacred with the forms of saints and madonnas. What power could describe the glory of the setting sun? Or what language communicate the hallelujah chorus? The soul of either would be lost by the translation. To read into the literature of any great language is to feel the heart throb of the spirit of another age in its best utterance; to master a language is not only the power to translate an author. We might well ask who can do that? Who can translate Luther's battle hymn, "Eine feste Burg ist unser Gott"? It is to acquire capacity to see and feel. And to master this classic Greek, which, with its philosophy, has dominated the thought of twenty three centuries, has furnished permanent ideals for the sculptor and architect, is to add to that new sense microscopic accuracy and telescopic vision. The thing we have to fear is lest in the swing of the pendulum from the false dominance of classics we may by virtue of the momentum of practical considerations lose our hold upon that ideal and esthetic side of life without which life itself would be emptied of its contents.

And shall we study science? Emphatically, I answer, Yes. And that, too, not chiefly because it can be used, but because of its power to develop capacity. Let every man be required to study science. Not every man can become a specialist, but every man can master the fundamental elements of some department, and thus relate himself to the world with its fundamental all-comprehensive principle of mechanism. For, as Leibnitz taught, every monad reflects the universe. Conjure with the word evolution, and measure the response in the mind of Mr. Spencer. Contrast it with the mental reaction of the man who has simply learned the definition of the term. Spencer is an intellectual millionnaire, and the boor a candidate for the poorhouse.

To this must be added the study of philosophy, both as a discipline and as a counterpoise to science, which always works with purely mechanical notions. Philosophy, however, finds itself compelled, in the study of society, government or history, to work with ethical notions as its necessary presuppositions. The several disciplines indicated may be considered as fairly comprehensive of the essential notions which quicken the human intellect and stir the human heart. These are the disciplines which in a liberal education must not be left out.

But the college curriculum, could we detail it never so perfectly, would give but the most barren account of the inspiring and constructive forces which operate to build the man. These agencies work almost exclusively upon the intellect. The scientist cries out against the atrophy of the powers, which results in an irremediable inaptitude for scientific notions. In the man of best training and most perfectly developed personality there must be no atrophy of powers. Nature does not stop with the intellect. She follows the boy up through his boyhood, with questions which start from every empty bird's nest, interrogation marks on every speckled egg, in every crystal of the snow, in every phase of nature. They follow him into manhood. They rise up out of the earth to meet him. The markings of the glacial period, the tiled strata, the tracks of the birds which stalked over the Connecticut sand-stone startle him with their how and their why. The falling apple, the phases of the interior planets, the returning comet—yea, every green leaf and gorgeous maple, the gentlest note of spring and the reverberating thunder of August speak to this boy, make him uneasy with questions which he can neither answer nor leave unanswered, determined to call out the intellect in all of its power. But nature does not stop here. Nature sets this boy in relations with others like himself. He must recognize the rights of others, and demand like recognition for his own rights. He must love, and have love. And in that hour when the conscience comes to birth, when the boy says "I ought," and "I ought not," he hears a note that rings the harmony of the spheres, the keynote of the highest and holiest in the universe. The weird yet charming music in that note is the voice of God from the throne eternal. He has not sounded all the diapasons of that voice, but he knows that all degradation and despair are to be measured by their departure from the law there announced, and that obedience thereto is the bliss of heaven. Nature's plan is to act upon the child by powers from without and awaken the response of the powers within. I wish to add another salient factor ; nature's method is to act with powers from without upon all the powers of the boy, and call them all out into energetic, harmonious and adequate response. She seeks for the most perfect type of man. With her, indeed, the fittest alone survive.

Taking his clue from nature, the educator dare not rest with brilliant intellectual achievements. Intellect alone does not constitute the fulness of the personal life. He must summon the moral and religious life into being. The most difficult and delicate task of all, and the most important. This left undone, and there is atrophy of powers at the very summit of being. For success in this task, he must count on plenty of work, from the highest motives;

on the high character of the men that teach; and, finally, on the grace of God.

What characteristics in his personality stand for the influence of these years in the college-bred man? If a compound photograph of 1,000 college-bred men could set forth the mental habitude, the comprehensiveness of grasp, the scope of vision, and the ideals of life, would that photograph not differentiate these men from every other 1,000 men of given training that could be found? A recent number of *The College Man* affirms that "the college men of the United States are but a small fraction of one per cent. of the voters; yet they hold 58 per cent. of the highest offices." Another writer affirms that a free common school education adds 50 per cent. to the productive power of the laborer; an academical education, 100 per cent., and an average collegiate, or university, education, 200 to 300 per cent.

Liberally educated men, with a comprehensive knowledge of facts, a firm grasp of principles, and almost prophetic scope of vision, men of truest purpose, who dare welcome light from every source, even though it come from heaven itself, of generous and tolerant spirit, of lofty ideals, are always more needed than gold or silver, armies or navies, guns or forts. And, although the number of such men can never be proportionately large, they are the men, who, first made masters of themselves, become masters of the world. The Great Teacher, as one writer has pointed out, spent much time on twelve men. We shall make no mistake if we spend our millions upon even the comparatively few men who seek the most liberal training. These men must lead the thought of the age, and put forth for society a kind of vicarious volition along the line of action where all others must and will follow.

THE MORAL AND RELIGIOUS VALUE OF HIGHER EDUCATION.*

BY PRESIDENT E. BENJAMIN ANDREWS, LL.D., BROWN UNIVERSITY, PROVIDENCE, R. I.

LEARNING for its own sake, in the strict sense of this phrase, meaning that we learn without any reference whatever to any good, either to ourselves or to others to be had thereby, is a contradiction. If such a course were conceivable or possible, it would still be irrational. But let us be convinced that we are vital members of human society; that our mental cultivation will count in furtherance of human progress, that our fellow-men are to be made happier and better through the training which we are giving and receiving ; we then see it to be reasonable and good to exert ourselves to the utmost. Only under the stimulus of such a view, I believe, can a thoughtful man permanently do his best. Now, I profoundly believe that such an intimate relation between the higher learning and the weal of all actually exists.

We see it, first, on the ordinary level of material welfare. Civilization as to its material basis, as to those aspects of it that fill men's minds, alas, mostly to the exclusion of the higher phases—civilization in its practical efficiency, is in the last analysis totally dependent on the work done at the centres of learning. Nearly all the great advances in industry which make goods cheaper and life happier involve principles which have been carefully wrought out in the study or the laboratory. Edison could do little but for the science of physics, which less practical men elaborated and made

* Address delivered before College Alumni, Brooklyn, N. Y., Dec. 29th, 1891.

ready for his use. Physics, in turn, depends at every step upon the higher mathematics. Bichloride of mercury, which has given to recent surgery its glorious successes and which, in medicine, has taken its main terrors from that once awful disease, diphtheria, is a chemical invention. And the power of research in these high realms pays. Witness the case of Germany, which manufactures 83 per cent. of the chemicals used on the continent of Europe, because of the chemical discoveries made and the knowledge of chemistry diffused among her people through the agency of her universities. It is for lack of chemical knowledge of clays that America as yet makes no such porcelain as Germany or Austria, and the same lack wastes for us every year millions of dollars' worth of materials and labor in such third or fourth class pottery as we do make. In the effort of America to compete industrially with European nations, no one thing is more important than the promotion among us of scientific training in its higher forms.

No tongue can tell the debt which the practical, everyday science on which the world now lives owes to the great masters and law-givers of science in the departments of mathematics and physics, and every one of them was the offspring of some institution for high learning. Nearest to an exception is Descartes, whose pupilage ended early, and who is distinguished among historic thinkers for having wrought out some of the most recondite philosophical and mathematical truths known to man in a soldier's hut and by a soldier's camp fire. But Descartes could certainly never have done this had it not been for his eight years at the excellent school of La Fleche, founded by Henry of Navarre.

The same, if not a closer, relation exists between good schools and practical science in the department of sociology. One section in the broad field of social science, people nearly always forget when speaking of human progress, though it is most closely related thereto, I refer to law. In discussions upon the rise and evolution of culture among the Romans, we always make great note of Roman law, but it seems to be taken for granted that elsewhere culture has been built up nearly or quite independently of legal institutions and reforms. So far is this from being the case that one may well doubt whether the tie between legal systems and the progress of civilization was ever so close as in modern times. Few men in the last hundred years have done more for human advancement than Savigny, Bentham, John Austin and Sir Henry Maine. All of these were lawyers, and all were also university graduates, whose influence, but for their special training, the world would, in all probability, never have felt. If possible, even more than theology, law derives its progress and power from professional study and teaching. Of course, learned institutions cannot claim all the credit for the beneficial influence exerted by those whom they educate. Schools cannot create genius, but they do what is quite as important, they call it out and train it.

The same high utility attaches to learning in the domain of culture. This is in fact an aspect of the good of education which peculiarly exalts it. It is more vitally important than aught else, save character, to the perfection of civilization. Mere material resources do not constitute or create fine civilization. Wealth, unaccompanied by what is higher, breeds Philistinism, which can be naught but degrading to a nation's character. Things can never take the place of men. Trade, commerce, business, industry—these are important factors in human culture, but by themselves they have in no case yet made a nation great. The exaltation of a nation's rank has never come alone or mainly through the operation of commercial motives. It requires a certain elevation of spirit, a devotion to ideals, a philosophic composure, to which the atmosphere of the market is a deadly foe. Now, while it cannot be said that the school of learning is the sole nursery of the sublime temper necessary to splendor of civilization, it is certainly a most important, even an indispensable, one. Very much of this higher life of the spirit connects itself with literature and religion, and every observer of men or reader of history knows that both these are almost absolutely dependent on schools. Very few literary celebrities are there who are not children of the schools, and the rest are, at least, grand-children.

There is a still more important field where it can be seen that learning enriches the higher life of humanity not out of its intellectual funds alone. Ethical principle and practice are stiffened by influences from the same source. Instance the love of right for right's sake, the idea of simple truth, irrespective of consequences, which has come into being almost solely from the inculcation of exact science. This is a result for which those who love righteousness should be grateful to the Positive Philosophy. In this respect, the positivists have, without thinking of it, become powerful ethical teachers. They have insisted, as had never been done before, upon the importance of laying aside prejudice and interest, and getting at simple, unalloyed fact. There has been called into existence thus a new, distinct and most beautiful form of the love for truth. This noble phase of virtue is emphasized and nourished to-day in every scientific laboratory and class-room throughout the world. It has come to possess even theology and will yet revolutionize that science. It has gone over into the study of the past and founded the science of historical investigation. Many false but time honored judgments touching the men and things of former times are changing in consequence of the truer historical apprehension engendered from this cause. It results that national and ecclesiastical animosities are becoming less intense, opening the way for larger peace and good-will among men.

To this ascription of a positive ethical value to training

in science some demur. Moral character, they rightly say, ultimately depends upon religious belief, and this, they further declare, science undermines and dispels. There is an idea, as prevalent as it is baseless and mischievous, that the doctrine of evolution, in particular, so far as it is accepted, renders all theistic or properly religious belief unnecessary and stupid. Nothing could be more untrue. The logical necessity of theistic belief evolution does not so much as touch. One may admit all that Darwin himself ever asserted and yet remain orthodox as Athanasius. Logicians never had clumsier fallacies to laugh at than those by which sciolists have inferred a Godless cosmology entire from a scientist's proof—itself far from irrefragable—of one single point, the origin of species. Darwin made no pretense of having explained the beginning of life. And further, as has been said, the survival of the fittest does nothing to explain the arrival of the fittest. In other words, those peculiarities from those variations of type that occur "ever and anon," as novelists say, and play so famous a part in zoölogical evolution by getting themselves transmitted, these are as deep a mystery as life itself. Darwin knew enough to know that he did not know enough to explain them.

One important thing the great man did suppose that he had made clear, viz.: the rise of our moral consciousness But he was mistaken. This is the sovereign mystery of all, and it is a commonplace of ethical study to-day that, deftly as Darwin and Herbert Spencer have shown something else to be derivative, Kant was correct in taking man's sense of right as an immediate, underived piece of human nature.

Not only does the great generalization by Darwin offer no necessary offense to faith, but it opens the way for an apprehension of the Divine Being, and His modes of procedure, far more rational, helpful and uplifting than the old view. Natural theology will have to be recast, but its new form will add indefinitely to its impressiveness. We shall find it no loss to have relinquished the untenable distributive teleology of Paley, when in its stead is installed that grander thought of a perfect cosmic unity reached through the clash of forces energizing apparently without aim. Science is destined to prove at this point an immense missionary power.

Nor here alone. There is another realm where theological propositions stand up much more boldly in consequence of what science has done. The central citadel of all conviction and assurance, which ancient philosophy evacuated as hopelessly breached and forever untenable, modern science has put in repair and rendered impregnable. Radical skepticism, which is the bane of Greek philosophy, can never come back. One who reads in the Theætetus the logic whereby Plato pulverizes Protagoras and his doctrine of the subjectivity of knowledge, wonders how that pestilential error could ever have reappeared. Yet it did. It flourished, even, and by what a skeptic, could he have done so consistently with his theory, would have called a just retribution, it became the distinguishing characteristic of the new academy, of the very thinkers who hailed Plato as their philosophic head.

The skeptic's mind, like a weak stomach, could keep nothing down. Pyrrho could not admit that anything is true or certain. "Say not," he bade, "'This is so,'" but only, "This seems to me to be so," "It is possible," "It may be," and the like. The new academy, with a keener insight than Pyrrho's, seeing that this very suspension of judgment was a sort of affirmation, laid it down that a man can know nothing save that he knows nothing, and that this is not proper knowledge, but feeling. The utter impossibility of knowledge, and the fatuity of all pretense thereto—these were the invariable tenets of skepticism as it flourished of old.

Well, science has made these tenets impossible now. Thinkers of all stripes read of them to-day with a smile. The ten "tropoi," for instance, of which ancient skepticism made so much, meant to provide that we cannot know, are rendered ludicrous by the demonstrated data of physics and psychology. They all reduce to a few logical puzzles and certain errors in sense-perception. In the merely logical part of this triumph metaphysics has had some share, but its physical and psychological part is purely and distinctly the work of that modern science which has been so reviled as the foe of faith.

If asked, then, why I love academic life and work, I reply: Because in it we have the privilege of delightfully exercising our minds in the pursuit of truth, a joy doubly rich in that the work can be carried on by many of us in common; that our activity is useful as well as agreeable, not only aiding the race to live, but refining and carrying forward civilization, widening the skirts of light and forwarding all the high interests of humankind, being vital to the advance of the material and of the social sciences alike; and, lastly, that it is a pronounced and positive force in a strictly moral and religious way, establishing, not weakening, rectitude in conduct, promoting, not withstanding, faith in a spiritual world and a living God.

www.ingramcontent.com/pod-product-compliance
Lightning Source LLC
Chambersburg PA
CBHW031427230426
43668CB00007B/472